CARE AND TEACHERS IN THE INDUCTION YEARS

This edited volume focuses on understandings and enactments of care in teacher induction in a landscape reshaped by the recent pandemic, ongoing societal issues, and increased expectations of teachers. Building on the editors' book *Reconstructing Care in Teacher Education after COVID-19: Caring Enough to Change*, this volume extends reconsiderations of care and teacher development into K-12 schools, aiming to explore how care is, should, and can be operationalized in teacher induction now.

Each chapter draws on research, practice, and reflection to provide recommendations to move teacher induction forward in responsive and caring ways. Authors include teacher educators, practicing teachers, and administrators representing different subject areas and educational levels. The operationalization of care also takes many forms, from mentorship and professional learning communities to support in navigating burnout and staff shortages. Chapters offer specific examples from contributors' own teaching experiences and conclude with suggestions for adapting the model or practice for readers' own programs and students.

Ideal for faculty working with preservice educators and administrators supporting newly hired teachers, this book can also serve as recommended or supplementary reading in undergraduate or graduate teacher education, curriculum and instruction, leadership, and educational administration courses as well as within professional development opportunities.

Angela W. Webb is an associate professor of science education in the College of Education at James Madison University, USA.

Melanie Shoffner is a professor of English education in the College of Education at James Madison University, USA.

CARE AND TEACHERS IN THE INDUCTION YEARS

Supporting Early Career Educators in Today's Teaching Landscape

Edited by Angela W. Webb and Melanie Shoffner

Designed cover image: © Getty Images

First published 2025
by Routledge
605 Third Avenue, New York, NY 10158

and by Routledge
4 Park Square, Milton Park, Abingdon, Oxon, OX14 4RN

Routledge is an imprint of the Taylor & Francis Group, an informa business

© 2025 selection and editorial matter, Angela W. Webb and Melanie Shoffner; individual chapters, the contributors

The right of Angela W. Webb and Melanie Shoffner to be identified as the authors of the editorial material, and of the authors for their individual chapters, has been asserted in accordance with sections 77 and 78 of the Copyright, Designs and Patents Act 1988.

All rights reserved. No part of this book may be reprinted or reproduced or utilised in any form or by any electronic, mechanical, or other means, now known or hereafter invented, including photocopying and recording, or in any information storage or retrieval system, without permission in writing from the publishers.

Trademark notice: Product or corporate names may be trademarks or registered trademarks, and are used only for identification and explanation without intent to infringe.

ISBN: 978-1-032-70745-7 (hbk)
ISBN: 978-1-032-67891-7 (pbk)
ISBN: 978-1-032-70747-1 (ebk)

DOI: 10.4324/9781032707471

Typeset in Galliard
by MPS Limited, Dehradun

To the first-year teachers, the beginning teachers, the new teachers, the induction teachers:

Thank you

for entering a profession that will never care as much as you do.

We see you

and we are so lucky to work with you.

CONTENTS

About the Editors	*x*
List of Contributors	*xi*
Foreword by Barbara B. Levin	*xvii*
Acknowledgements	*xix*

Considerations of Care in Teacher Induction: Caring for Those
Newest to the Profession   1
Angela W. Webb and Melanie Shoffner

PART I
Navigating Care as Beginning Teachers   **9**

1 Self-Care Needs and Practices in Newly Hired Science Teachers   11
*Shannon L. Navy, Lisa Borgerding, Adepeju Prince,
Elizabeth Ayano, and Julie A. Luft*

2 How Novice Teachers View Their Teacher Preparation Experiences
Related to Care in the Classroom   22
*Catherine Scott, Richard H. Costner, Heather Hagan,
Jamia Richmond, and Kristal Curry*

3 "I Wasn't Planning on Yelling": Beginning English Teachers and
Pandemic-Inflected SEL Curriculum   34
Katie Nagrotsky

viii Contents

4 Reshaping Teacher Induction through Care and Community 43
Allison Wynhoff Olsen

5 Encouraging and Uplifting New Teachers by Demonstrating Care and
Fostering Growth Mindset to Build Resilience 53
Amanda Steiner, Julie Bell, and Chris Wilcoxen

PART II
Care through Mentorship and Formal Induction 63

6 New Beginnings: Making Connections and Navigating Transitions for
Enacting Care in Secondary Mathematics Classrooms 65
Jennifer A. Wolfe and Elaine Saunders

7 Extinguishing the Flame of Burnout: Mentorship and Care to Support
Teacher Induction 76
Crystal L. Beach and Leigh Anne Turner

8 The Need for Care: An Australian Perspective on Teacher Induction
Post-COVID 86
Ceridwen Owen

9 Protocols as a Mechanism of Care: Helping Novice Science Educators 96
Elizabeth W. Edmondson

10 "I am terrified of being one of my students' bad memories": Stories of
Teacher Induction through a Lens of Care 106
John Weaver, Shelbie Witte, and Nicole Skeen

PART III
Partnerships and Community as Sites of Care 117

11 Understanding and Responding to the New Teacher Experience:
One TEP's Commitment to Connections of Care 119
*Megan Guise, Sarah Hegg, Jesse Sanford, Tanya Flushman, and
Nancy Stauch*

12 "I am lucky to be surrounded by so much talent": Growing a
Professional Learning Community for Early Career Teacher Mentors 130
*Jessica Murdter-Atkinson, Elizabeth Colquitt Ries, Beth Maloch,
LeAnne Hernandez, Kerry Alexander, Audrey Stein Wright, and
Melissa Mosley Wetzel*

Contents **ix**

13 Reflections on Caring for Early Career Teachers in Times of Challenge   141
Angela W. Webb, Robbie Higdon, and Jennifer Gibson

14 Writing as Healing: Reflections from Veteran Teachers as a Way to
Understand Needs for Teacher Induction   153
Kristen Hawley Turner and Kara B. Douma

Invitations for Caring Induction   164
Angela W. Webb and Melanie Shoffner

Index   *168*

ABOUT THE EDITORS

Angela W. Webb, Ph.D., is an associate professor of science education in the College of Education at James Madison University (Virginia, USA), where she teaches courses in general methods, science methods, and curriculum theory. Her scholarship centers primarily on the preparation and early career development of science teachers, with specific attention to science teacher identity. Her work on teacher education and induction has been published in *Theory Into Practice*, *Journal of Educational Research and Practice*, *Teacher Education and Practice*, as well as the edited book *Newly Hired Teachers of Science: A Better Beginning* (Luft & Dubois, Eds.), among others. Her previous edited book with Routledge is *Reconstructing Care in Teacher Education after COVID-19: Caring Enough to Change* (2022).

Melanie Shoffner, Ph.D., is a professor of English education at James Madison University (Virginia, USA). She is the current editor of *English Education* and a former Fulbright Scholar to Romania. Her scholarship examines issues of ELA teacher preparation, preservice teacher development, and reflective practice. Her work has been published in *Pedagogies: An International Journal*, *The Teacher Educator*, and *Teachers and Teaching: Theory and Practice*, among others. Her most recent book is the co-edited *Reconstructing Care in Teacher Education after COVID-19: Caring Enough to Change* (Routledge).

CONTRIBUTORS

Kerry Alexander is an assistant professor of literacy education at the University of Maryland at College Park (USA). She is an artist, writer, university instructor, and literacy researcher dedicated to community-centered inquiry and responsive pedagogical design in elementary literacy classrooms.

Elizabeth I. Ayano is a doctoral student at the University of Georgia (USA). She earned her master's degree in science education from the University of the Western Cape South Africa. Her research focuses on teacher education, specifically how newly hired science teachers can be equipped and retained in their teaching careers.

Crystal L. Beach has served in a variety of teaching and leadership roles with school districts and is a part-time assistant professor in the Department of Language and Literacy Education at the University of Georgia (USA). Her scholarship explores the intersections between literacy, multimodality, teacher education, rural education, and classroom practices with digital tools.

Julie Bell is an associate professor of teacher education and secondary literacy at the University of Nebraska at Omaha (USA) where she also serves as the secondary education graduate Chair. Her research focuses on English education and the mentoring of preservice and in-service teachers. A former high school English, speech, and theatre teacher, Dr. Bell currently teaches undergraduate and graduate courses in literacy and the secondary education graduate capstone course.

Lisa Borgerding is in her sixteenth year as a professor of science education at Kent State University (USA). She coordinates the secondary science teacher education program for undergraduates and masters students and teaches courses in science methods, science education, and mixed methods research. Her research interests include science teacher

xii Contributors

education with a special focus on the teaching of controversial issues including evolution and climate change.

Richard H. Costner is a professor of elementary education in the Spadoni College of Education and Social Sciences at Coastal Carolina University (USA). He researches teacher behavior and student performance. His work was recently published in *Teacher Educators' Journal* and *Journal of Research in Education*.

Kristal Curry is a professor for the MAT and Ph.D. programs and a department chair in the Spadoni College of Education and Social Sciences at Coastal Carolina University (USA). She researches social studies education and responsive education practices. Her work was recently published in *The Councilor: A Journal of the Social Studies* and *Democracy & Education*.

Kara Douma is a supervisor of English language arts in the Morris School District in New Jersey (USA) and a teacher consultant for the Drew Writing Project and Digital Literacies Collaborative.

Elizabeth W. Edmondson is a research associate professor in the Department of Teaching and Learning in the School of Education at Virginia Commonwealth University (USA). Her research interests include student engagement in classroom dialogue, culturally relevant practices in science classrooms, teachers as researchers, and teacher retention and induction models.

Tanya Flushman is a professor of education and coordinator of the MA Curriculum & Instruction program at California Polytechnic State University, San Luis Obispo (USA). She also serves as the co-director of the CSU Center for the Advancement of Reading and Writing. Her recent work has been published in *Teacher Education Quarterly* and *The California Reader*.

Jennifer Gibson is a lecturer of mathematics education in the College of Science and Mathematics at James Madison University (USA). Her research centers on the development and continued support of fraction content knowledge of prospective PreK-8 teachers as well as on prospective teachers' mathematical mindsets and dispositions.

Megan Guise is a professor of education and coordinator of the English education program at California Polytechnic State University, San Luis Obispo (USA). Her research interests include teacher induction, coteaching in the clinical experience, and feedback on instructional practice. Her recent work has been published in *Teaching and Teacher Education*, *The New Educator*, *Journal of Teacher Education*, and *Teacher Education Quarterly*.

Heather N. Hagan is an associate professor of elementary education in the Spadoni College of Education and Social Sciences at Coastal Carolina University (USA). She researches elementary social studies methods including inquiry and integration with other subject areas. She recently published *Integrating Inquiry in Social Studies Classrooms.*

Sarah Hegg is a program manager working with the School of Education and Center for Engineering, Science and Mathematics Education (CESAME) at California Polytechnic State University, San Luis Obispo (USA). Her recent work has been published in *The New Educator*, *Journal of Teacher Education*, and *Teacher Education Quarterly.*

LeAnne Hernandez is the director of Texas Education START (USA). She served in Texas public schools for 24 years prior to joining the University of Texas. Her academic interests include improving mentoring and induction programs to build self-efficacy and equitable teaching practices in early career teachers.

Robbie Higdon teaches general instructional methods and supervises field experiences in grades 6-12 at James Madison University (USA). Her research focus includes preservice teacher identity development and the recruitment and retention of science educators in grades 6-12. She also mentors pre-service teachers in the development and implementation of STEM outreach activities within local schools and community agencies.

Julie A. Luft is Distinguished Research Professor, Athletic Association Professor of Science and Mathematics Education, and an adjunct professor in biochemistry and molecular biology at the University of Georgia (USA). Her most significant publication involves editing the *Handbook of Research of Science Teacher Education.* Her current research is focused on the learning, persistence, and resilience of early career science teachers.

Beth Maloch is a professor of language and literacy studies at the University of Texas at Austin (USA). She currently serves as the Senior Associate Dean for the College of Education and as the PI for the Texas Education START research project.

Jessica Murdter-Atkinson is an assistant professor of literacy education at the University of North Texas (USA). Her research focuses on the intersections of culturally sustaining pedagogies, coaching/mentoring, and literacy teacher preparation.

Katie Nagrotsky is an assistant clinical professor at the University of Connecticut (USA) and supports a cohort of new teachers at the Stamford regional campus. Her research is at the intersection of writing studies and teacher education, driven by her experiences as a writing teacher at the secondary and community college level and a desire to make schools more equitable spaces.

Shannon L. Navy is an associate professor of science education at Kent State University (USA). Her research investigates the use of resources and the development of resilience in newly hired science teachers, and the quality of educational curriculum resources from online teaching repositories for science teachers. Her research is currently funded by the National Science Foundation.

Ceridwen Owen is an academic at Deakin University, Melbourne (Australia). Her research interests are in teacher development, initial teacher education, and becoming, and the transition of preservice teachers to the teaching profession.

Adepeju Prince is a Ph.D. student and graduate research assistant in science education at Kent State University (USA). She received a Bachelor of Science Education in Physics Education from Adeyemi College of Education, Ondo, Nigeria. She obtained a Master of Science Education from the University of Ibadan, Ibadan, Nigeria. She taught middle school Mathematics and Physics in Nigeria before refocusing her career goal on science teachers' development and retention. Her current research focuses on the relationship between resources accessed by newly hired science teachers and resilience displayed during science teaching.

Jamia Thomas Richmond is a professor of special education and interim dean of the Spadoni College of Education and Social Sciences at Coastal Carolina University (USA). Her work was recently published in *Teacher Education Journal of South Carolina* and *The Ethics of Cultural Competence in Higher Education* (Apple Academic Press).

Elizabeth Colquitt Ries is an assistant professor of instruction at the University of Texas at Austin (USA). Her research focuses on critical and equity-oriented pedagogies and literacy teacher preparation.

Jesse Sanford is a research assistant and part-time lecturer at California Polytechnic State University, San Luis Obispo (USA). He also works as a new teacher mentor for a local school district and has served as both a cooperating teacher and university supervisor for teacher candidates. His research interests include culturally responsive teaching practices, pre-service teacher education, and ongoing teacher development and learning.

Elaine Saunders is a full-time first-year secondary mathematics teacher at Sahuarita High School in Arizona (USA). Her class focuses on process over answers and is guided by the goal of creating a classroom environment where students feel safe, seen, and heard.

Catherine Scott is a professor of elementary education and associate dean in the Spadoni College of Education and Social Sciences at Coastal Carolina University (USA). Her work was recently published in the *Handbook of Research on Building STEM Skills through Environmental Education* and *Journal of College Science Teaching*.

Nicole Skeen served as a middle school teacher, instructional coach, induction coordinator, professional development leader, and adjunct instructor at the University of South Carolina (USA) before joining the College of Education faculty full-time in 2017. Skeen is the founding director of the Carolina Teacher Induction Program.

Nancy Stauch is a lecturer in the Liberal Studies Department at California Polytechnic State University, San Luis Obispo (USA). Her research interests include enhancing the implementation of coteaching during the clinical experience and ongoing new teacher support. Her recent work has been published in *Teacher Education Quarterly* and *The Handbook of Research on Teacher Education and Professional Development.*

Amanda Steiner is an associate professor of elementary education at the University of Nebraska at Omaha (USA) where she also serves as the elementary education graduate chair. Her research includes examining the role of the instructional coach and best practices in coaching to support teachers in growing in their self-efficacy.

Kristen Hawley Turner (@teachkht) is a professor and director of teacher education at Drew University in New Jersey (USA). Her research focuses on the intersections between technology and literacy. She is the co-author of *Connected Reading: Teaching Adolescent Readers in a Digital World* and *Argument in the Real World: Teaching Students to Read and Write Digital Texts* as well as editor of *The ethics of digital literacy: Developing knowledge and skills across grade levels.*

Leigh Anne Turner is a teacher in Georgia (USA). She endeavors daily to challenge herself as an early career learning professional and high school coach.

John Weaver is a teaching assistant professor in mathematics and science education at Oklahoma State University (USA) and the founding director of The Retention of Innovative Educators (OK-Thrive), a university-based teacher induction program that supports early career educators.

Melissa Mosley Wetzel is a professor of language and literacy studies at the University of Texas at Austin (USA) and the chair of the Department of Curriculum and Instruction. Her scholarship focuses on the preparation of teachers in literacy for equity-focused practices and the development of justice-focused coaching and mentoring in preservice and in-service settings.

Chris Wilcoxen is the teacher education graduate chair, director of the CADRE Project, and assistant professor at the University of Nebraska at Omaha (USA). Her research focuses on teacher development, induction, mentoring, coaching, instructional leadership, clinical practice, field-based preparation, and assessment.

Shelbie Witte is the Watson Endowed Chair and Senior Director of Teacher Education at Oklahoma State University (USA), where she leads the School of Teaching, Learning and Educational Sciences. She is the site director emeritus of the OSU Writing Project and the founding director of the Initiative for Literacy in a Digital Age. Witte has published extensively in the area of digital literacies and 21st-century literacies.

Jennifer A. Wolfe is an associate professor of mathematics education at The University of Arizona (USA). She was recently awarded an Innovation in Teaching Award for her efforts to effectively implement equitable teaching practices for engaging students in mathematics collaborative groupwork.

Audrey Stein Wright is a doctoral student in learning technologies at the University of Texas at Austin (USA). Her research explores the potential of digital platforms as mediums for trauma-informed communication between school leaders and teachers.

Allison Wynhoff Olsen is an associate professor of English education at Montana State University (USA) and director of the Yellowstone Writing Project. Her research aims to better understand how teachers and students co-construct knowledge and to affect change when it comes to the teaching and learning of English and literacies across a range of contexts.

FOREWORD

Barbara B. Levin

Professor Emeritus, School of Education, University of North Carolina at Greensboro

My entire career in higher education was focused on helping prepare new teachers for the reality of classroom life. My research focused on how teachers develop their pedagogical knowledge and beliefs about how children develop, behave, and learn, and what it means to teach. I also studied how teachers' beliefs change over time. Longitudinal case studies revealed several factors that influence teachers' development: their personal beliefs about teaching and learning, and about children's behavior and development; their vision for what their classroom and teaching experience could be; their sense of belonging in their workplace and the profession; and their identity, especially how their identities change and are influenced by the context in which they live and work.

So, when I was asked to write a foreword to this edited book of 14 carefully curated chapters about the role of care in supporting teachers during their induction years, I was very excited because I know empirically that caring support is a key factor that influences teachers to remain in the profession and continue to grow and develop into master teachers. Without caring support, I learned in my research that teachers wither and die, leaving the profession before they can share and develop their expertise, enact their beliefs, or enact care for their students. Authentic caring influences the development of teachers' identities, their resilience, sense of belonging, and ability to enact their beliefs.

In addition, knowing that Angela Webb has continued studying and supporting new teachers during their induction years since I was on her dissertation committee, and that her co-author, Melanie Shoffner, has similar expertise, these scholars are especially well-suited to build on their previous research and writing to curate, edit, and organize the chapters in this, their second, book about care and teacher induction.

Among the highlights of this book are the variety of contexts, disciplines, and content areas that ground the settings for the induction programs described in these chapters. Based on both research studies and practical experiences, the ideas shared in the chapters are numerous, authentic, and worthwhile considering by anyone interested in infusing care into the induction process. Furthermore, the rationale for this book about the need for authentic care in supporting teachers because of the lingering effects of the recent pandemic, public discontent with the value of education and questioning of teachers' expertise, and increasing political and social turmoil, rings true for anyone working in schools today. At the very least teaching well is a difficult undertaking these days, so those new to the profession deserve both formal and informal support based on an ethic of care. When Nell Noddings (2019) wrote that choice, continuity, and connection are key concepts in the application of care theory to education, she would have been thrilled to see how these concepts are prominent in the examples of induction support described in the chapters of this book.

For all these reasons, I strongly recommend this book to teacher educators, teacher leaders, mentor teachers, coaches, and school and district leaders in the position to assist teachers during the induction years as they design activities and create programs that infuse an ethic of care—not just to keep developing teachers in the profession but to help them become the best teachers for our diverse student population they possibly can. The time and effort expended reading about the experiences and ideas shared in these chapters, and finding ways to enact them in your specific context, will be well worth it.

Reference

Noddings, N. (2019). Concepts of care in teacher education. In J. Lampert (Ed.), *The Oxford encyclopedia of global perspectives on teacher education* (pp. 139–159). Oxford University Press. 10. 1093/acrefore/9780190264093.013.371

ACKNOWLEDGEMENTS

This book developed from the recognition that our K-12 and teacher education classrooms are forever changed—and the ways we care for those entering these spaces should be, too.

****

Our thanks to Julia Dolinger and Sophie Ganesh at Routledge for their interest in the book and guidance toward its completion. We also thank the anonymous reviewers for their time with and pertinent feedback on our initial proposal.

****

Many thanks to the people in our professional lives who motivated us to create this book: our colleagues, our students, and our cheerleaders.

CONSIDERATIONS OF CARE IN TEACHER INDUCTION

Caring for Those Newest to the Profession

Angela W. Webb and Melanie Shoffner

It takes little imagination to see that today's educational landscape is vastly different from the ones either of us entered decades ago as newly minted teachers. Teaching has been aggravated and reshaped by events we couldn't have fathomed during our own induction into the profession. The COVID-19 pandemic, social and political unrest, and distrust in teachers and schooling, among other factors, have remade—and are still remaking—the classrooms, schools, and communities those newest to the profession are stepping into. If we are to champion teachers and the teaching profession, those who work with teachers must reexamine understandings and enactments of care across teachers' career trajectories.

In our previous book (Shoffner & Webb, 2022), we argue that the disruption of COVID-19 to K-12 and higher education requires a reconsideration and reconceptualization of care in teacher education. Preservice teachers experienced emergency pivots to online instruction in their university courses as well as the K-12 classrooms in which they were completing practicum or student teaching. Those who persisted to graduation and certification are now early career teachers, inducted into a profession still recovering from the pandemic's disruptions. While many might make assumptions about these early career teachers' preparedness and induction needs—often wrongly (see Darling-Hammond & Hyler, 2020)—we agree with those who claim that previous ways of inducting, supporting, and retaining those newest to the teaching profession no longer suffice. The prevailing models of teacher induction are based largely in contexts, from perspectives, on understandings that no longer exist in today's classrooms and schools. Rather than continue unproblematically with previous enactments of and views toward teacher induction, we believe there should be an intentional reconsideration, one that positions induction for those entering our changed, and still-changing, profession through the lens of care.

The Intricacy of Teacher Induction

Many think they know what it takes to teach by virtue of being students themselves and seeing what teachers do (Lortie, 1975). They are wrong. Teaching is a complex endeavor, requiring

DOI: 10.4324/9781032707471-1

an understanding of and responsiveness to constantly changing subject matter, content standards, state and local directives, societal issues, and sociopolitical factors in order to teach students who are equally complex and delightfully diverse human beings (e.g., Noel & Shoffner, 2019; Sleeter & Carmona, 2017; Talley-Matthews & Wiggan, 2018; Venet, 2021).

While formal learning about curriculum and pedagogy begins in teacher education programs, teachers' learning does not stop with graduation and certification. Regardless of how well positioned they are by their teacher education programs, early career teachers still have much to learn on the job (Bartell, 2005; Feiman-Nemser, 2001). Once in the classroom, those newest to the profession embark on an essential time of transition and continued learning: the induction phase of their careers.

Teachers are generally considered in the induction phase of the profession for their first three to five years of teaching. These early career phases in a teacher's professional life are characterized by career entry (years 1–3) and stabilization (years 4–6) (Blonder & Vescio, 2022; Huberman, 1989). Career entry is marked by "a process of survival and discovery … during which the gulf between [teachers'] professional ideals and daily classroom life is exposed, and the self-doubts and initial enthusiasm are entwined" (Blonder & Vescio, 2022, p. 302). Stabilization is marked by a decisive commitment (or not) to the profession. Should they stay, "the teacher has already mastered the profession, has pedagogical stability, and can more easily navigate complex situations in class; [the teacher] feels comfortable in class and experiences joy and stability" (Blonder & Vescio, 2022, p. 302).

That teachers will stay through the stabilization phase into their mid-career years, however, is not a given. Approximately 40–50% of those who entered teaching from 1987 to 2018 left the profession within five years (Ingersoll et al., 2022), leading to a great deal of attention on teacher induction (see Ingersoll & Strong, 2011; Strong, 2009)—a focus that continues now as much of the United States faces teacher shortages (Jones, 2023). Yet, *induction* is not a single, obvious thing to be fixed in order to improve teacher retention. Rather, *teacher induction* has multiple, interconnected meanings across research and practice (Feiman-Nemser, 2010).

One meaning of induction refers to a distinctive phase in learning to teach (Feiman-Nemser, 2010). This understanding of induction recognizes that "new teachers have two jobs—they have to teach and they have to learn to teach" (Feiman-Nemser, 2001, p. 1026). During their initial years in the classroom, new teachers are deepening and fine-tuning the understandings and abilities learned as students in teacher education—yet these early career teachers are expected to demonstrate the same knowledge, skills, and dispositions and fulfill the same responsibilities as their more experienced colleagues. This reality crafts a distinctive learning agenda for induction, one that focuses on knowing students, curriculum, and school contexts; designing responsive curriculum and instruction; enacting meaningful practices; creating a classroom learning community; reflecting on practice; and developing a professional identity (Feiman-Nemser, 2001).

Another meaning of induction refers to a process of socialization (Feiman-Nemser, 2010). Like all of us, early career teachers learn in and through social practices and, in the process, are inducted into a group's culture (Lave & Wenger, 1991; Wenger, 1998). As they learn and take up "the dominant language, values, norms, and knowledge" (Feiman-Nemser, 2010, p. 19) of their field (e.g., science education, English education, special education) and community (i.e., department, school, or school division), early career teachers learn, explicitly and implicitly, what it means to be a valued and successful teacher in that context.

To this end, "The primary mechanism of induction as socialization is everyday experience. By doing the work of teaching and interacting with colleagues, new teachers learn what is expected of them" (Feiman-Nemser, 2010, p. 20).

The final meaning of induction is likely the most popularly used: induction as a formal program (Feiman-Nemser, 2010). Despite the specificity of defining induction as a formal program (as opposed to a phase or a process), there is a wide variety in the components, duration, and quality of induction programs (Feiman-Nemser, 2010; Villani, 2009), with "what counts as an induction program rang[ing] from a statewide system of support and assessment to a district-sponsored orientation for new teachers" (Feiman-Nemser, 2010, p. 16). Generally, "'comprehensive induction' is defined as a package of support, development, and standards-based assessments provided to beginning teachers during at least their first two years of full-time professional teaching" (Alliance for Excellent Education, 2004, p. 11). Such a comprehensive induction package tends to involve high-quality mentoring, common planning and collaboration time with colleagues, ongoing and developmentally appropriate professional development, participation in an external network of teachers, and standards-based teacher evaluation (Alliance for Excellent Education, 2004; Ingersoll, 2012). Whereas comprehensive induction may lead to reductions in teacher attrition and improved teacher quality and student achievement (Alliance for Excellent Education, 2004), associating these specific outcomes with formal induction programs poses significant challenges for both research (Strong, 2009) and practice (Feiman-Nemser, 2010).

Although educational researchers and those who support early career teachers (e.g., mentors, coaches, administrators, university-based teacher educators) may consider these distinct conceptions of teacher induction in their work, these are not disparate for early career teachers themselves; these meanings of induction are always-already intertwined in their lived experiences. Inherent in this, then, is the recognition that induction is always-already happening, formally and informally, intentionally and unintentionally. The complexities of teacher induction—both its meaning and its enactment—require us to address a specific concern: Induction for whose agenda? Whose needs are being served by a formal induction program? How are new teachers being socialized and to what end? We argue that induction must always foreground the expressed needs—not our assumptions of those needs (Noddings, 2012, 2019)—of early career teachers; in short, induction must be grounded in authentic care.

The Complexity of Caring for Early Career Teachers

Giving early career teachers what *they* most need from induction necessitates caring about and for them (Gay, 2018; Noddings, 1999). While many may claim to care about early career teachers—often through expressions of concern and hope they persist in the profession—comparatively few seem to actively engage in caring for early career teachers.

Caring *for* others "encompasses a combination of concern, compassion, commitment, responsibility, and action" (Gay, 2018, p. 58). Caring interactions are grounded in love and focused on well-being (Love, 2019), supporting "authentic relationships [that] are reciprocal and foster growth and change for [all] those involved" (Trout, 2018, p. 44). The complex and multifaceted nature of care, however, means the actual practice of care lacks codification:

Caring is one of those things that most educators agree is important in working effectively with students, but they are hard-pressed to characterize it in actual practice, or to put a functional face on it that goes beyond feelings of empathy and emotional attachment. (Gay, 2018, pp. 57–58)

Difficult to reify, perhaps, but care is always relational in its implementation:

Both carer and cared-for contribute to this relation. If, for whatever reason, the cared-for denies that she or he is cared for, there is no caring relation. When that happens, it is not necessarily the fault of the carer; it may be that the cared-for is stubborn, insensitive, or just plain difficult … [or] … the situation in which the carer and cared-for meet may make it difficult to establish caring relations. (Noddings, 2005, p. xv)

As Noddings (2005) establishes, if the cared-for does not understand the carer's actions as such, care does not exist—and this applies to the ways in which we support early career teachers. For instance, however comprehensive an induction program may be, it is not a *caring* induction program unless the early career teachers engaged in it receive and perceive it as such. An informal network, however, can be an immense source of care and support if the early career teacher deems it to be. When it comes to the induction of early career teachers, then, support cannot simply equate to more demands on their time (e.g., for meetings or mentoring sessions) or additional duties (e.g., submitted paperwork) unless they perceive meaningful care in the pro-offered support.

To understand what early career teachers need during induction—to survive as well as thrive in the profession—we cannot treat them as passive recipients of generalized supportive acts. Induction for early career teachers must be grounded in care. Caring induction occurs in reciprocal relationships, includes authentic listening, and responds to expressed needs (Noddings, 2012, 2019). Caring induction acknowledges and responds to teachers as people—not automatons or cogs in the educational wheel or replaceable employees. Caring induction expresses "concern for [teachers'] psychoemotional well-being and academic success, personal morality and social actions, obligations and celebrations, communality and individuality, and unique cultural connections and universal human bonds" (Gay, 2018, p. 59).

If we expect early career teachers to engage in caring, reciprocal relationships with their students, then we—whether mentors, coaches, administrators, or university-based teacher educators—must do the same with early career teachers. As a profession, as educators, as individuals, we cannot claim to care for K-12 students if we do not also care for their teachers.

Examining Care

Over three decades ago, Noddings (1992) noted that "the need for care in our present culture is acute" (p. xi). The observation still rings true today—across all aspects of society, broadly speaking, and particularly for those stepping into today's classrooms as early career teachers. Recognizing this need for care and championing better beginnings in the profession sparked the idea for this book. Those being inducted into teaching deserve responsive and supportive care in order to thrive in the profession they chose. The educators who authored chapters in this book share our belief in the need for caring teacher induction and, importantly, they have ideas for developing and facilitating such care.

Part I: Navigating Care as Beginning Teachers includes five chapters that foreground the voices and experiences of those to whom this book is dedicated: the early career teachers who enter today's classrooms undeterred. Three chapters detail beginning teachers' navigation of care, for their students or for themselves. In the opening chapter, Shannon L. Navy, Lisa Borgerding, Adepeju Prince, Elizabeth Ayano, and Julie A. Luft consider the self-care needs and practices of newly hired secondary science teachers, highlighting the importance of including self-care strategies and supports in teacher education and induction programs. In Chapter 2, Catherine Scott, Richard H. Costner, Heather Hagan, Jamia Richmond, and Kristal Curry examine first-year teachers' reflections on their preparedness to establish caring, supportive environments for their K-12 students. Similarly, Katie Nagrotsky chronicles the experiences of two first-year secondary English teachers and their use of antiracist social and emotional learning curriculum to exhibit care in Chapter 3. The remaining chapters in Part One feature teacher educators and support providers exploring the ways in which early career teachers navigate the support provided to them. In Chapter 4, Allison Wynhoff Olsen reflects on opportunities for dialogue and care within a community established during teacher education and continued during induction. Amanda Steiner, Julie Bell, and Chris Wilcoxen reflect on coaches' and early career teachers' experiences in a 25-year-old induction program focused on building teacher resilience through care in Chapter 5.

Part II: Care through Mentorship and Formal Induction includes five chapters that explore mentoring relationships, induction policy, and induction programs. Jennifer A. Wolfe and Elaine Saunders in Chapter 6 explore a transformative mentoring relationship in mathematics teaching. Similarly, in Chapter 7, Crystal Beach and Leigh Anne Turner reflect on an English teaching mentoring relationship that privileges care over outcomes. The mentoring relationships in both of these chapters started formally in teacher education and continued informally into the induction years. In Chapter 8, Ceridwen Owen considers the shortcomings of current induction policies in Victoria, Australia before proposing a care approach to teacher induction that better meets the needs of new teachers. The remaining chapters in Part Two discuss how specific induction programs care for early career teachers. In Chapter 9, Elizabeth W. Edmondson reflects on the use of protocols within a caring network of early career science teachers while, in Chapter 10, John Weaver, Shelbie Witte, and Nicole Skeen examine the three care-related principles that frame two university-based induction programs.

Part III: Partnerships and Community as Sites of Care includes four chapters that recognize that showing meaningful care to early career teachers is not a solo endeavor; a caring community is essential. In Chapter 11, Megan Guise, Sarah Hegg, Jesse Sanford, Tanya Flushman, and Nancy Stauch explore one teacher education program's partnership with a local school division to provide wrap-around support to new teachers. Unsurprisingly, early career teachers aren't the only ones to benefit from community support. In Chapter 12, Jessica Murdter-Atkinson, Elizabeth Colquitt Ries, Beth Maloch, LeAnne Hernandez, Kerry Alexander, Audrey Stein Wright, and Melissa Mosley Wetzel discuss the value of a robust, care-centered professional learning community that supports mentors caring for early career teachers. In Chapter 13, Angela W. Webb, Robbie Higdon, and Jennifer Gibson reflect on their experiences facilitating a professional learning community that supports early career science and mathematics teachers, drawing attention to the need to listen and respond to the expressed needs of early career teachers. Kristen Hawley Turner and Kara B. Douma bring the book's consideration of care for those newest to the profession to a close with reflections from experienced teachers. In Chapter 14, they describe the ways in which they and other veteran teachers drew on a writing community to process past and recent traumas related to their work, emphasizing the promise of such a reflective activity for early career teachers in processing both the stressful and mundane aspects of their induction experiences.

References

Alliance for Excellent Education. (2004). *Tapping the potential: Retaining and developing high-quality new teachers*. Author.

Bartell, A. C. (2005). *Cultivating high-quality teaching through induction and mentoring*. Corwin Press.

Blonder, R., & Vescio, V. (2022). Professional learning communities across science teachers' careers: The importance of differentiating learning. In J. A. Luft & M. G. Jones (Eds.), *Handbook of research on science teacher education* (pp. 300–312). Routledge.

Darling-Hammond, L., & Hyler, M. E. (2020). Preparing educators for the time of COVID ... and beyond. *European Journal of Teacher Education*, *43*(4), 457–465. 10.1080/02619768.2020. 1816961

Feiman-Nemser, S. (2001). From preparation to practice: Designing a continuum to strengthen and sustain teaching. *Teachers College Record*, *103*, 1013–1055.

Feiman-Nemser, S. (2010). Multiple meanings of new teacher induction. In J. Wang, S. J. Odell, & R. T. Clift (Eds.), *Past, present, and future research on teacher induction: An anthology for researchers, policy makers, and practitioners* (pp. 15–30). Rowman & Littlefield Publishers Inc.

Gay, G. (2018). *Culturally responsive teaching: Theory, research, and practice* (3rd ed.). Teachers College Press.

Huberman, M. (1989). On teachers' careers: Once over lightly, with a broad brush. *International Journal of Educational Research*, *13*(4), 347–362. 10.1016/0883-0355(89)90033-5

Ingersoll, R. (2012). Beginning teacher induction: What the data tell us. *Phi Delta Kappan*, *93*(8), 47–52.

Ingersoll, R. M., & Strong, M. (2011). The impact of induction and mentoring programs for beginning teachers: A critical review of the research. *Review of Educational Research*, *81*(2), 201–233. 10.3102/0034654311403323

Ingersoll, R. M., Merrill, E., Stuckey, D., Collins, G., & Harrison, B. (2022). Five trends shaping the teaching force. *State Education Standard*, *22*(3), 6.

Jones, A., II. (2023, February 11). Most of the US is dealing with a teaching shortage, but the data isn't so simple. ABC News. https://abcnews.go.com/US/map-shows-us-states-dealing-teaching-shortage-data/story?id=96752632

Lave J., & Wenger, E. (1991). *Situated learning: Legitimate peripheral participation*. Cambridge University Press.

Lortie, D. C. (1975). *Schoolteacher: A sociological study*. University of Chicago Press.

Love, B. L. (2019). *We want to do more than survive: Abolitionist teaching and the pursuit of educational freedom*. Beacon Press.

Noddings, N. (1992). *The challenge to care in schools: An alternative approach to education*. Teachers College Press.

Noddings, N. (1999). Response: Two concepts of caring. *Philosophy of Education Archive*, 36–39.

Noddings, N. (2005). *The challenge to care in schools* (2nd ed.). Teachers College Press.

Noddings, N. (2012). The caring relation in teaching. *Oxford Review of Education*, *38*(6), 771–781. 10.1080/03054985.2012.745047

Noddings, N. (2019). Concepts of care in teacher education. In J. Lampert (Ed.), *The Oxford encyclopedia of global perspectives on teacher education* (pp. 139–150). Oxford University Press. 10.1093/acrefore/9780190264093.013.371

Noel, T. K., & Shoffner, M. (2019). From preservice to practice: Expectations of/in the secondary ELA classroom. *World Journal of Education*, *9*(6), 35–44.

Shoffner, M., & Webb, A. W. (Eds.). (2022). *Reconstructing care in teacher education after COVID-19: Caring enough to change*. Routledge.

Sleeter, C. E., & Carmona, J. F. (2017). *Un-standardizing curriculum: Multicultural teaching in the standards-based classroom* (2nd ed.). Teachers College Press.

Strong, M. (2009). *Effective teacher induction and mentoring: Assessing the evidence*. Teachers College Press.

Talley-Matthews, S., & Wiggan, G. (2018). Culturally sustaining pedagogy: How teachers can teach the new majority in public schools. *Black History Bulletin, 81*(2), 24–27.

Trout, M. (2018). Embodying care: Igniting a critical turn in a teacher educator's relational practice. *Studying Teaching Education, 14*(1), 39–55.

Venet, A. S. (2021). *Equity-centered trauma-informed education*. W.W. Norton & Company.

Villani, S. (2009). *Comprehensive mentoring programs for new teachers: Models of induction and support* (2nd ed.). Corwin.

Wenger, E. (1998). *Communities of practice: Learning, meaning, and identity*. Cambridge University Press.

PART I

NAVIGATING CARE AS BEGINNING TEACHERS

1

SELF-CARE NEEDS AND PRACTICES IN NEWLY HIRED SCIENCE TEACHERS

Shannon L. Navy, Lisa Borgerding, Adepeju Prince, Elizabeth Ayano, and Julie A. Luft

Learning to teach science is especially challenging for newly hired science teachers (NHSTs). For instance, new science teachers are faced with learning about the myriad of instructional approaches and monitoring for student learning (e.g., Davis et al., 2006; Luft et al., 2015; Navy et al., 2022). Less discussed is the emotional side of teaching faced by NHSTs (Bellocchi & Amat, 2021).

More recently, emergency remote learning environments created additional stress for teachers (Marshall et al., 2020). Finding materials, working with colleagues, and conceptualizing lessons became more difficult because many teachers had not taught online previously. Furthermore, teachers were asked to attend to the emotions of students in their classroom (National Education Association, 2020), yet they were not provided with adequate support to ensure their own well-being or self-care (Gillani et al., 2022).

The well-being of teachers is linked to their ability to engage in self-care (Murphy et al., 2020). By managing their stress and practicing self-care, teachers can work more effectively with students in challenging settings, reduce their feelings of burnout, and improve their experience as new teachers (Baker, 2020; Miller & Flint-Stipp, 2019). Unfortunately, little is known about how new science teachers engage in self-care. Therefore, two questions guided this study:

1 To what extent do newly hired science teachers express the need for self-care?
2 How do newly hired science teachers characterize self-care practices for themselves as teachers?

Framing

Self-care has been defined in various ways: as practices, abilities, or activities to maintain, improve, and protect overall health, well-being, and happiness (Baker, 2020; Grise-Owens & Miller, 2018; Murphy et al., 2020; Ray et al., 2020). Park et al. (2020) considered self-care through the lens of maintaining a balance between life and work, which is essential to taking

DOI: 10.4324/9781032707471-3

care of others. For teachers, specifically, self-care helps keep teachers stable amidst various barriers (Baumgartner et al., 2009; Baumgartner et al., 2021).

Caring for self is one important dimension in Noddings' (2005) relational view of care, in which she acknowledged that "in one sense, everything we care about is somehow caught up in concerns about self" (p. 74). To elucidate the ways in which self-care can exist, Noddings' (2005) proposed six categories. *Physical self-care* includes caring for the physical self in ways such as exercise, rest, nutrition, and hygiene. *Spiritual self-care* relates to spirituality, religion, meditation, and prayer. *Occupational self-care* connects to a person's work setting and includes learning from working, engaging fully in one's work, and maintaining a work-life balance. *Recreational self-care* centers on one's hobbies, for example, gardening, doing puzzles, or reading a book. *Emotional self-care* involves caring for oneself emotionally by engaging in actions such as focusing on the positive, being self-compassionate, balancing stress, and managing emotions. *Intellectual self-care* connects to engaging in something new that stimulates the mind. Overall, these categories depict the ways the teachers in this study cared for themselves alongside caring for students.

Related Literature

Classroom teachers experience stress in their jobs and they attribute this stress to many factors: overwhelming workload, student behavior, parental involvement, school climate, personal factors, lack of resources, changes in the education system, personal problems, classroom management, limited agency, and pressure to account for students' success (Baker, 2020; Murphy et al., 2020). Additionally, many teachers experience secondary trauma as they contend with students' stories of primary trauma from violence, racism, and/or hunger (Miller & Flint-Stipp, 2019).

Teachers use self-care and coping strategies to alleviate their occupational stress. Greater self-care practices have been associated with less anxiety and stress as well as more problem-focused coping abilities (Ciuhan et al., 2022; Cleofas & Mijares, 2022). Herman et al. (2020) postulated that teacher stress and coping abilities are influenced by coping strategies, teacher competence, and the school context, highlighting the importance of teacher-level factors (i.e., coping strategies and competence) and school/system-level factors (i.e., school context). Importantly, teacher stress and coping impact students. When Herman et al. (2018) compared student outcomes to teacher stress, coping, efficacy, and burnout, they found that student outcomes were lowest for teachers in the high-stress/low-coping/high-burnout profile.

Teachers use a variety of self-care practices to manage their occupational stress. Individual-level self-care practices include exercising, getting sufficient sleep, eating healthy, engaging in hobbies, spending time with family and friends, having a positive attitude, taking breaks, practicing meditation, having supportive colleagues, and seeking professional help (Baker, 2020; Glazzard & Rose, 2020; Murphy et al., 2020). At a higher organizational stratum, schools support teachers in coping with stress by offering flexible working environments (Glazzard & Rose, 2020), excused days off, or access to social support services. While teachers often recognize the need for self-care, they do not regularly engage in these practices (Miller & Flint-Stipp, 2019).

TABLE 1.1 Teacher Demographics

Pseudonym	Gender	Race	Years of Teaching	Grade Level	School Classification	US Geographic Region
Christopher	male	white	4	high school	suburban	Midwest
Erica	female	white	1	high school	rural	Southeast
Henry	male	white	1	high school	rural	Northwest
Natalie	female	white	1	high school	suburban	Northwest
Sydney	female	white	3	middle school	urban	Midwest

Methods

This multiple case study explored the self-care of five NHSTs in high-need schools in the United States (US). The teachers ranged in experience from one to four years of teaching, taught in three different regions of the US, and were scholars of the National Science Foundation's Robert Noyce Teacher Scholarship Program (see Table 1.1).

Data were gathered during the 2021–22 school year when teachers were back to school after the COVID-19 disruption. Four sources of data guided this study. First, a pre-interview (Pre) obtained a sense of the teachers' school contexts and self-care practices. Second, two post-observation interviews (Post-Obs) had teachers reflect on their successes, challenges, and responses during observed lessons. The third data source was written reflections (Ref) in which the teachers described teaching successes and challenges associated with their instruction. The final data source was an end-of-year (EOY) interview about the teachers' overall thoughts on the year.

Data were coded by four researchers using both a priori and inductive approaches (Miles et al., 2014). First, the researchers read through all the data looking for each teacher's self-care needs and practices. Each identified segment of data was coded using Noddings' (2005) six categories of self-care (i.e., physical, spiritual, occupational, emotional, recreational, and intellectual). The four researchers met and coded one case together. During this discussion, some categories of self-care emerged that did not fit within Noddings' (2005) a priori categories. In these instances, new codes were created: *avoiding and setting relational boundaries* and *care from others*. The final additional code that was created by the research team was *needing self-care*, which reflected instances when the teachers expressed stress, frustrations, or negative emotions.

After coding the first case together, the four researchers split into two teams with each team coding two of the remaining cases. The small research teams met and came to a consensus on the proposed codes. The entire group met to discuss the overall codes for each teacher and the cross-case analysis discussion. The team also looked at the overall quantity of self-care needs and practices for each teacher and determined where the teachers' self-care needs and practices fell on a continuum from low to high.

Findings

The findings are presented by each case, followed by a cross-case analysis discussion. The heading for each case portrays the extent of self-care need (from low to high) and engagement in self-care practices (from low to high) for that participant.

14 Shannon L. Navy et al.

Sydney: High Need, Low Practices

Sydney was a middle school science teacher in her third year of teaching. She worked in an environment that demanded a lot of her energy; as she explained,

> There's a lot of trauma within my student population, where they need a lot of extra support. It's a very, very big district and it's a lot to manage … I want the west side [of the city] to be serviced more than it is. I really put my heart and soul into it. (Pre)

As a result, many of the codes for Sydney reflected a high need for self-care. In addition to the overarching desire to serve an underserved community, she had "tense relationships" with other teachers in her team making her grow "into [her] own, more independently" and wishing she had "more support" (Pre). This continued into the end of the year when she reflected on everyday behaviors in the school: "The end of the year is getting to me, the horseplay in the hallways is getting really frustrating to handle" (Ref). This was coupled with the need for more time to accomplish teaching responsibilities which led to "stress … too much to do, and simply not enough time" to "attack … a million to-do lists" (EOY).

Sydney acknowledged her struggles and how she needed someone to help her emotionally. She reflected, "I feel like the resources that I'm struggling with are … emotional resources … I feel like I definitely need a therapist to talk to, hopefully … somebody in teaching or has been close with somebody and teaching" (EOY). Sydney believed that her commitment to teaching was not sustainable: "Emotionally, I don't believe that the way I am going is sustainable. And I will stand by that statement, 100%. If I am still going the way I am, in five more years, I'm probably going to quit" (EOY).

While Sydney stated she is "lacking [in] … investing in [her] own self" (EOY), she did engage in some self-care practices. Some were emotional self-care practices such as staying positive and remaining calm. For example, she tried to not "let [things] get [her] down" and "take things less personally" (Pre). She also practiced setting relational and work boundaries. For instance, she "actively avoided the teacher next door" (EOY) and sometimes she avoided her family as a self-care strategy. Her work-life boundaries included leaving work at work and being less of a perfectionist:

> I've been really trying to leave my work computer at work. It's just too much to be working at home and at school all the time … that's something that I'm doing to cope is just sequestering, it should just be there. The work will still be there for me tomorrow … And so it's just kind of being realistic. And being less of a perfectionist, just kind of get it done. (Pre)

Erica: High Need, High Practices

Erica, a first-year teacher, taught math and science in a small high school in a small rural community where most of her students were involved in agricultural programs. Although she viewed the school administration and community positively, Erica was frustrated with several aspects of her position. She felt like she had inadequate time to do her work: "I just wish I'd had more time. I just wish I had more time dedicated to planning - time that I was getting paid for" (EOY). Another demand on her time resulted from a substitute teacher shortage at her school. Erica said, "usually at least once a week during my planning … I have to go cover another class" (Pre). She resented the unfairness inherent to this situation because she "never [saw] any of the other teachers with the same planning period as me having to go cover [these classes]" and she did not receive additional compensation for this work (Pre). Erica was also frustrated by student apathy. After a class observation, she described how a student was not "trying in class, but then wants me to spend my extra time where I don't get paid to reteach all of it to her" (Post-Obs). By the end of the year, she reflected, "I'm so over this" because she felt that "these kids … they do not care" (EOY).

Erica actively used occupational, emotional, and physical self-care strategies to cope with her frustrations. In terms of occupational self-care, Erica intentionally sought work-life balance and employed work-life balance strategies she learned from a teaching podcast, such as "only staying one day late and then leaving at contract hours" (EOY). She reasoned, "I'm still getting the work done, or, like the bulk of the work done" (EOY). Erica also practiced several emotional self-care approaches. She explained how she "started seeing a therapist because stress from work [was] really getting to me, and I was having … panic attacks" (EOY). Additionally, Erica tried to have a "growth mindset" about teaching (Pre), "keep a level head" during stressful teaching moments (Post-Obs), "expect the unexpected" (Post-Obs 1), and "just [roll] with it and not [take] things too personally" (Ref). Erica used physical self-care to mitigate stress, explaining how "just staying consistent with my workouts—it's always a really good outlet for me" (EOY). Additionally, she took up boxing because "it's hard to punch something for 45 minutes and feel stressed after" (EOY).

To a lesser extent, Erica relied on care from others and avoiding/boundary-setting self-care approaches. She sought care from others by relying on a co-teacher friend and "being able to talk to her about things" (EOY). Using an avoiding/boundary-setting approach, when she encountered "negative Nancies," she "tried to stay away from them" because "this profession is hard enough" (EOY).

Henry: Low Need, Medium Practices

Henry, a first-year high school science teacher, worked in a difficult-to-staff rural school. He believed his school was grateful to have him and expressed confidence in his ability to impart knowledge and make the best use of limited material resources for his science classes. Henry was fortunate to be teaching courses he had taught as a student teacher, which gave him a collection of previously developed and usable instructional materials. He displayed confidence in his ability to "overcome challenges and keep teaching" but made subtle mentions of being overwhelmed. In his words, "I can overcome challenges and keep teaching. It doesn't necessarily have to mean that you're not overwhelmed with challenges in teaching" (EOY).

Henry's self-care practices predominately fit within the occupational, physical, and emotional self-care categories. Among these categories, Henry emphasized occupational self-care in the form of work-life balance. He explained, "Last year, I spent most of my weekends and, Sundays especially, lesson planning. This year, I've done that hardly at all" (EOY). By leveraging his student teaching lesson plans, Henry greatly improved his ability to balance work and personal life, enabling him to spend his weekends "running a lot and doing fun stuff outside of school to keep me kind of balanced in life and positive about what I'm doing." He reasoned, "that helps mentally with being just generally happy and optimistic" (EOY). To a lesser extent, Henry responded to challenges by using emotional self-care

16 Shannon L. Navy et al.

strategies. For example, when a failing chemistry student complained about an assignment, Henry explained, "I just brushed it off. I don't let comments like that bother [me]" (Ref).

Christopher: Low/Medium Need, Low Practices

Christopher was a fourth-year science teacher at a suburban high school in a low-income area with a large population of refugee students who struggled academically. He described "so many challenging situations" from students "not doing the work," "Googling" all of the answers, and "mindlessly copying word for word" (Pre). In these situations, Christopher reflected,

> Those are challenging, and I get frustrated … And it does make me feel as though I'm failing them by not teaching them what they need to know in class. And at the same time, I'm frustrated that they don't say, "Hey, I have trouble with this" and ask me how to fix it. (Pre)

Despite some challenges within his school, Christopher had an overall low need for self-care. His positive outlook on challenges and teaching partially contributed to his emotional self-care overall. He mentioned, "When you have these challenging situations, you just feel defeated … But again, you have to take them with a grain of salt, remember some of the good times" (Pre). He also stated, "I, of course, have bad days and my teaching goes way downhill. So yes, positive emotion as I'm teaching is paramount to being able to explain and being able to connect with the students" (Pre). He also discussed the importance of occupational self-care in the form of work-life balance and finding "some sort of outlet" (EOY) such as a recreational self-care strategy of gardening.

Occupationally, Christopher had supportive peers, colleagues, and administrators at his school. This gave him some additional care from others. As he mentioned,

> I have several different teachers and administrators and guidance counselors that I talk to at the school. There are some that I get together with pretty much every week. And we discussed what was going on and decompressed and figured that out. That's a huge help. Even though it's more of a social support, it is so important for my teaching. (Pre)

Another person who provided care and support for Christopher was his wife. Without his wife, he would have difficulties surviving in this job; as he commented, "If I didn't have my wife, there was no way" (EOY).

Natalie: Low Need, High Practices

Natalie was a first-year high school science teacher in a highly diverse school. Her need for self-care was more self-imposed as she believed her teaching demands were manageable. She explained,

> Because I was new, I felt like there are always eyes on you, making sure that you're doing what you're supposed to be doing. And, so, the expectation I had for myself was probably a lot higher than the expectation other people have. And that probably added more stress than was necessary (EOY).

Natalie engaged in numerous emotional and occupational self-care practices. Emotional self-care practices included having self-compassion, maintaining positivity, pushing through, practicing deep breathing, and showing humility. Natalie even participated in a book study on resilience for teachers and subsequently learned techniques to "have compassion for yourself and support yourself as an educator" (Pre). When she hit challenges in teaching, she reflected on these techniques. She also considered herself a highly optimistic person who tried to instill optimism in her students: "The biggest thing, my Pollyanna attitude that's constantly optimistic with expectation of positive outcomes" (EOY). She explained that she and her students "talk a lot about dissecting our internal scripts and rewriting our own narratives so that we have the outcomes that we want." She reasoned, "It's important to not just be optimistic, but actually I try to train my students to be optimistic as well" (EOY).

Natalie believed in staying present in the moment, especially in moments of chaos:

If you can just be ... in the middle of the chaos, at least you're there. You get to make decisions ... my philosophy is, if you could just take a couple of deep breaths, and just be here. It's like, what's the worst that can happen? ... I just think that you have to have a high threshold for chaos. And then when the chaos ensues, you have to just be really adaptable ... I think I've done a lot of adapting through chaos. (Pre)

For occupational self-care practices, Natalie focused on prioritizing work and setting work boundaries. A mentor at her school encouraged her to have a maximum of 10-hour workdays which has helped her "set boundaries between what I take home emotionally and even physically in terms of work when I leave school" (EOY). She stated,

My determination to be good at my job, and my ability to detox when I leave work, so that whatever I've got going on doesn't impact how I feel when I come in the next day ... Yeah, those belief systems, I have are very, very strongly ingrained in me. I think they're my saving grace (EOY).

Natalie also received care and support from others. Some of this support came from the science department team at her school and some came from the Noyce scholarship and induction program. When talking about the program, she mentioned, "So the Noyce has been one of the biggest ones because some of my peers in the Noyce program have been really supportive with sharing resources with me" (EOY). This program also kept her connected to her preparation program and the university community.

Cross-Case Discussion

Across the five cases of NHSTs, there were variations in the need for self-care and the practice of self-care. The teachers' need for self-care was indicative of the gap (or not) between their current self-care practices and the practices that would better help them navigate and thrive in their work life. Figure 1.1 portrays the position of each participant on the quadrants of these two intersecting factors (need and extent of practice).

This quadrant cross-case synthesis helps answer the overarching questions of this study. The first question asked was "To what extent do newly hired science teachers express the need for self-care?" There are at least two dimensions to consider when answering this

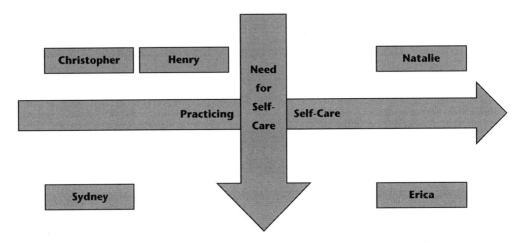

FIGURE 1.1 Representation of Teachers' Need for Self-Care and the Extent of Self-Care Practices.

question. The first dimension is the need for self-care and the second dimension is the extent to which a teacher engages in self-care practices. Two first-year teachers, Natalie and Erica, actively engaged in and practiced self-care strategies to navigate the demands of teaching. However, Erica expressed a higher need for self-care than Natalie. The support environments were also different between the two. Natalie relied on her science department team and the Noyce community for additional support and resources, whereas Erica did not rely on care from others and even avoided some people as a self-care strategy. By contrast, Sydney, a third-year teacher, noted a great need for self-care but struggled to engage in self-care practices. Her overall school environment was challenging and she did not have support from people in the school. She also avoided some people in her self-care practices. Christopher and Henry, fourth- and first-year teachers respectively, also had fewer self-care practices but they also expressed a lower need for self-care.

Teachers articulated their need for self-care in response to the challenges they encountered in their teaching environments. These five teachers experienced many of the stressors previously documented in the literature, including overwhelming workloads, lack of agency, student behavior, personal factors, and secondary trauma (Baker, 2020; Jennings et al., 2017; Miller & Flint-Stipp, 2019; Murphy et al., 2020). Student apathy and teacher perfectionism were other sources of stress identified within our sample. School-level stressors, like negative co-workers (Sydney and Erica) and loss of planning time (Erica), contributed to feelings of overwhelm and lack of agency.

Three of the four quadrants in Figure 1.1 represent neutral or positive outcomes. For instance, Erica's high need for self-care and high self-care practices might create a neutral outcome where one (self-care practices) balances the other (need for self-care). The quadrant with the most concern of a negative outcome for teachers and students is that of high need for self-care and low engagement in self-care practices, aligned with findings from Herman et al. (2018). In this study, Sydney occupies this quadrant and, like teachers in other studies, recognized a need for self-care but did not regularly engage in self-care practices (Miller & Flint-Stipp, 2019).

The second question in this study asked, "How do newly hired science teachers characterize self-care practices for themselves as teachers?" Using the six original categories from Noddings (2005), some were more prevalent than others. For instance, emotional and occupational self-care practices were demonstrated across all cases, but intellectual and spiritual self-care never occurred in these data. Likewise, physical and recreational self-care practices were apparent in only some cases.

In this study, self-care practices were individualized and unique to teachers' preferences and contexts. Some of this depended on personality traits, such as being an optimistic person or letting go of perfectionism, while others depended on what the teachers enjoyed doing outside of work, such as going for a run or gardening. Years of teaching experience may also factor into a teacher's self-care practices. Two first-year teachers, Erica and Natalie, had the highest engagement in self-care practices while the third- and fourth-year teachers, Sydney and Christopher, had the lowest engagement in self-care practices. However, these data are exploratory; more research needs to be conducted to determine if there is a relationship between self-care practices and years of teaching experience.

Many of the self-care practices in this study are supported by previous literature (e.g., Baker, 2020; Glazzard & Rose, 2020; Murphy et al., 2020). One practice that seems to cut across all the participants is that of work-life balance and setting work boundaries. For some teachers, this involved not taking work home, and, for other teachers, it was limiting the hours in a day one works. More research is needed regarding how teachers maintain work-life balance and how schools and systems can support work-life balance amid ever-increasing teaching demands.

Implications

The findings in this study have implications for science teachers, schools, teacher education, and induction programs. First, those who work in teacher education and induction programs should include self-care training in their programming. Teachers are experiencing increased demands, stress, and burnout post-COVID-19. The options to develop self-care approaches should be varied and appropriate to the career level of the teachers.

Second, schools should consider providing self-care time and spaces for teachers, especially teachers in the induction years. This could include teacher well-being days built into the school calendar and/or physical spaces in the schools for teachers to relax and reduce their stress. Schools could also offer self-care training programs and use self-study to identify the ways their policies and culture contribute to teacher stress.

Finally, teachers need to self-assess the alignment of their own self-care needs and practices. If a teacher has a high need for self-care, the teacher should try to engage in self-care practices to reduce some of the stress. Mentor teachers can work with new teachers in the induction years to help them assess the balance of their self-care needs and practices. Teachers give so much to students, schools, and communities; there must be time for them to also invest in themselves.

Acknowledgement

This study was made possible by the National Science Foundation under grant #2050145. The findings, conclusions, and opinions herein represent the views of the authors and do not necessarily represent the views of the National Science Foundation.

References

Baker, L. (2020). Self-care amongst first-year teachers. *Networks: An Online Journal for Teacher Research, 22*(2). 10.4148/2470-6353.1328

Baumgartner, J., Carson, R., Apavaloaie, L., & Tsouloupas, C. (2009). Uncovering common stressful factors and coping strategies among childcare providers. *Child and Youth Care Forum, 38*(5), 239–251.

Baumgartner, J., Ota, C., DiCarlo, C., Bauer, R., & Carson, R. (2021). Using ecological momentary assessment to examine the relationship between childcare teachers' stress, classroom behaviors, and afterhours professionalism activities. *Child Care in Practice*, 1–20. 10.1080/13575279.2021.1962247

Bellocchi, A., & Amat, A. (2021). Emotion and science teacher education. In J. A. Luft & M. G. Jones (Eds.), *Handbook of research on science teacher education* (pp. 426–438). Taylor & Francis.

Ciuhan, G. C., Nicolau, R. G., & Iliescu, D. (2022). Perceived stress and wellbeing in Romanian teachers during the COVID-19 pandemic: The intervening effects of job crafting and problem-focused coping. *Psychology in the Schools, 59*(9), 1844–1855.

Cleofas, J. V., & Mijares, M. F. (2022). The role of professional self-care practices in lowering anxiety among Filipino teachers enrolled in graduate studies. *Teacher Development, 26*(2), 206–220.

Davis, E. A., Petish, D., & Smithey, J. (2006). Challenges new science teachers face. *Review of Educational Research, 76*(4), 607–651.

Desouky, D., & Allam, H. (2017). Occupational stress, anxiety and depression among Egyptian teachers. *Journal of Epidemiology and Global Health, 7*, 191–198.

Gillani, A., Dierst-Davies, R., Lee, S., Robin, L., Li, J., Glover-Kudon, R., Baker, K., & Whitton, A. (2022). Teachers' dissatisfaction during the COVID-19 pandemic: Factors contributing to a desire to leave the profession. *Frontiers in Psychology,13*, 426–438.

Glazzard, J., & Rose, A. (2020). The impact of teacher well-being and mental health on pupil progress in primary schools. *Journal of Public Mental Health, 19*(4), 349–357.

Grise-Owens, E., Miller, J. J., Escobar-Ratliff, L., & George, N. (2018). Teaching note—Teaching self-care and wellness as a professional practice skill: A curricular case example. *Journal of Social Work Education, 54*(1), 180–186.

Herman, K. C., Hickmon-Rosa, J., & Reinke, W. M. (2018). Empirically derived profiles of teacher stress, burnout, self-efficacy, and coping and associated student outcomes. *Journal of Positive Behavior Interventions, 20*(2), 90–100.

Herman, K. C., Reinke, W. M., & Eddy, C. L. (2020). Advances in understanding and intervening in teacher stress and coping: The coping-competence-context theory. *Journal of School Psychology, 78*, 69–74.

Jennings, P. A., Brown, J. L., Frank, J. L., Doyle, S., Oh, Y., Davis, R., Rasheed, D., DeWeese, A., DeMauro, A. A., Cham, H., & Greenberg, M. T. (2017). Impacts of the CARE for Teachers program on teachers' social and emotional competence and classroom interactions. *Journal of Educational Psychology, 109*(7), 1010.

Luft, J. A., Dubois, S. L., Nixon, R. S., & Campbell, B. K. (2015). Supporting newly hired teachers of science: Attaining teacher professional standards. *Studies in Science Education, 51*(1), 1–48. https://doi.org/10.1080/03057267.2014.980559

Marshall, D. T., Shannon, D. M., & Love, S. M. (2020). How teachers experienced the COVID-19 transition to remote instruction. *Phi Delta Kappan, 102*(3), 46–50.

Miles, M. B., Huberman, A. M., & Saldaña, J. (2014). *Qualitative data analysis: A methods sourcebook.* Sage.

Miller, K., & Flint-Stipp, K. (2019). Preservice teacher burnout: Secondary trauma and self-care issues in teacher education. *Issues in Teacher Education, 28*(2), 28–45.

Murphy, T. R. N., Masterson, M., Mannix-McNamara, P., Tally, P., & McLaughlin, E. (2020). The being of a teacher: Teacher pedagogical well-being and teacher self-care. *Teachers and Teaching: Theory and Practice, 26*(7–8), 588–601.

Navy, S., Luft, J. A., & Msimanga, A., (2022). The learning opportunities of newly hired science teachers. In J. A. Luft & M. G. Jones (Eds.), *Handbook of research on science teacher education* (pp. 245–256). Taylor & Francis.

National Education Association (NEA). (2020). *Social-emotional learning should be priority during COVID-19 crisis.* https://www.nea.org/advocating-for-change/new-from-nea/social-emotional-learning-should-be-priority-during-covid-19

Noddings, N. (2005). *The challenge to care in schools: An alternative approach to education.* Teachers College.

Park, N., Song, S., & Kim, J. E. (2020). The mediating effect of childcare teacher's resilience on the relationship between social support in the workplace and their self-care. *International Journal of Environmental Research in Public Health, 17*(22), 8513.

Ray, J., Pijanowski, J., & Lasater, K. (2020). The self-care practices of school principals. *Journal of Educational Administration, 58*(4), 435–451.

2

HOW NOVICE TEACHERS VIEW THEIR TEACHER PREPARATION EXPERIENCES RELATED TO CARE IN THE CLASSROOM

Catherine Scott, Richard H. Costner, Heather Hagan, Jamia Richmond, and Kristal Curry

As teacher educators, we recognize that preservice teachers sometimes have difficulty identifying specific strategies for enacting care in the classroom. However, we wonder how their views of care might change once they enter the classroom. Do induction teachers explain what it means to show care in the same way they did as preservice teachers? Will they feel that their programs prepared them to enact care in the classroom, and will we see those elements of care while watching them teach? Understanding their perceptions provides opportunities for teacher educators to better enact care during teacher education programs in response to induction teachers' expressed needs and to further develop strategies to support graduates as they transition from coursework into teaching.

Conceptual Framework

Building positive relationships with students is at the heart of caring pedagogy (Moen et al., 2020; Noddings, 2012). As noted by Barek et al. (2023), caring pedagogy is "an approach to teaching based on an ethic of care as both a moral imperative and pedagogical necessity" (para 4). When enacting care in the classroom, teachers engage in dialogue with students to get to know them and their needs, build relationships, and determine how they can best meet those needs (Barek et al., 2023; Goldstein & Lake, 2000; Noddings, 1984). The dialogue must be reciprocal: Students should be able to contribute ideas and articulate what they feel they need to be successful, and teachers should be able to respond accordingly. Care is not a one-size-fits-all approach; rather, it varies based on what is needed by and works best for each student.

Learning how to care in meaningful ways can be challenging for new teachers, given their limited experience working with students. Often, novice teachers hold an oversimplified and romanticized view of caring built on paradigms associating women with care and teaching (Goldstein & Lake, 2000). For example, in a previous study, teacher candidates frequently associated caring for students with showing the students that "they are loved above everything else" (Scott & Allen, 2022); however, they were often unable to articulate *how* to demonstrate care beyond saying that they "love" them. Scott and Allen (2022) share that

DOI: 10.4324/9781032707471-4

"when using [these] paradigms to shape their own views of caring (particularly due to their lack of experience), they might sometimes find that their own views of how to enact care diverge from the realities of classroom practice" (p. 80).

The pandemic upended the ways in which teachers initially showed care to students, making strategies such as proximal contact and face-to-face interactions no longer feasible. Additionally, the shift to online learning, restricted access to schools for field experiences, and concern about one's own well-being changed how programs prepared their candidates. Concerns arose regarding the "difficulty [novice teachers] have in establishing and maintaining relationships with their students" (Carter Andrews et al., 2021, p. 267). These difficulties stemmed from preservice teachers' limited opportunities to engage with students during their teacher education program because of restrictions from COVID-19. Research shows that teachers already struggle in the induction years, due to a lack of resources, experience, and support (Dias-Lacy & Guirguis, 2017; Fantilli & McDougall, 2009). Coupled with preservice teachers' naïve views of care, these challenges present a unique opportunity to learn more about new teachers' transition to the classroom, their views and enactments of care in the induction years of teaching, and their preparation as it relates to care.

Methodology

This mixed methods study addressed three research questions: 1) What do novice teachers believe about ways of caring? 2) How do novice teachers perform on measurements associated with care in the classroom? and 3) To what extent do teacher education graduates feel their program prepared them to enact care in the classroom?

The study used a case study approach since the site was bound by place, length, and activity (Creswell & Poth, 2016). Only graduates from the university's initial licensure programs participated. The fifteen participants graduated between spring 2020 and spring 2022 and were thus considered induction teachers by the state, where induction is defined as the first three years in the classroom after graduation. All teachers were observed and interviewed once between February and March 2023, prior to state testing for their students. The PI observed all teachers and the other four researchers completed observations based on their areas of expertise (e.g., the special education faculty member observed those teaching in special education classrooms). The five observers included two early childhood/elementary professors (grades PK-6), one elementary professor (grades 2–6), one secondary social studies professor, and one special education professor.

Context and Graduates

This study occurred in the partnering districts of a mid-sized liberal arts institution in the southeast United States. At the institution, teacher candidates can earn an initial licensure certificate in early childhood (PreK-3), elementary (2–6), middle level (5–8), physical education (PK-12), and special education (PK-12). Candidates in the undergraduate initial licensure programs spend the first two years of their academic program completing liberal arts coursework and prerequisite program courses. In the second two years of the program, candidates complete methods courses and field experience work. Candidates earning initial licensure degrees in English, mathematics, science, and social studies secondary education

24 Catherine Scott et al.

TABLE 2.1 Participant Information (All Names are Pseudonyms)

Participant	Program	Graduation Semester	Grade Taught	Subject/Content Area
Anna	Early Childhood	Spring 2020	1	General Ed
Elaine	Early Childhood	Fall 2021	2	General Ed
Corinne	Elementary	Spring 2020	5	General Ed
Beth	Elementary	Fall 2020	4	General Ed
Brittany	Elementary	Fall 2020	6	Science
Eliza	Elementary	Spring 2021	4	General Ed
Alice	Elementary	Spring 2021	4	General Ed
Delaney	Elementary	Fall 2021	4	General Ed
Wendy	Elementary	Fall 2021	5	General Ed
Cora	Elementary	Spring 2022	4	General Ed
Kara	Elementary	Spring 2022	2	General Ed
June	Secondary	Spring 2022	6–8	ELA
James	Secondary	Spring 2022	9–12	Social Studies
Michael	Secondary	Spring 2022	9–12	Social Studies
Suzanne	Special Education	Spring 2022	PK-3	Resource

(grades 9–12) complete a four-year degree in the content area and an additional 18 months in pedagogical courses to complete a Master of Arts in Teaching degree. Historically, over 55% of graduates from the institution's initial licensure programs are hired by the two partnering districts in the study. These districts serve as the primary locations for all field experiences while candidates are enrolled in the initial licensure programs.

To identify participants, the principal investigator first contacted the district office for one partnering district to gain consent to conduct the study. The district granted permission to contact the institution's graduates at one local elementary school, which hired 12 induction teachers soon after they completed their programs. Of those graduates, seven agreed to participate. Additionally, the researcher contacted a second partnering district and a local charter school, which also granted consent to contact all recent graduates (e.g., the last 30 months). A total of 15 teachers agreed to participate. All but one worked in public Title I schools; the remaining graduate worked in the charter school. Demographics are in Table 2.1.

Data Collection

Data were collected from four sources: a pre-observation survey completed by all teachers, an observation of each participant's teaching, a post-observation interview with the teacher, and an interview with their principal. Once teachers identified a time they could be observed, they were asked to complete the pre-observation survey and to identify a time when they would be able to post-conference with the principal investigator. Approval from the institution's Institutional Review Board was gained prior to beginning the study.

Pre-observation Survey

The pre-observation survey, completed via Google Forms prior to the lesson, provided general information about the teacher's school context, including grade level, number of students, description of the lesson being taught, and assessments used to measure student understanding. The form also included an open-ended question for teachers to share any information that they thought the researchers should know about their class (e.g., class theme, student behaviors and characteristics, changes in schedule). The pre-observation survey took teachers approximately 10 minutes to complete.

Observation

Two researchers simultaneously observed each teacher for 30 minutes, taking running notes and using the Danielson Framework (2013) to score each graduate's performance. The Danielson Framework generates ratings of teaching across 22 components, organized into four domains: 1) Planning and Preparation, 2) Classroom Environment, 3) Instruction, and 4) Professional Responsibility. A score of 1 is considered unsatisfactory and a 4 is distinguished (Danielson, 2013). Each domain includes facets associated with the reciprocal nature of care. Domain 1 includes student choice and input in lesson activities and assessment practices, which allows for student input and teacher adjustment in the learning experience. Domain 2 includes student involvement in risk-taking, management, and adjusting the classroom environment, which focuses on attributes of care such as feeling "safe" enough to take risks, relationships built upon respect, and responding to student needs. Domain 3 includes student initiation of learning and contribution to assessments (a reciprocal activity), and Domain 4 includes involving students in communication with families.

Each researcher scored the graduate on Domains 1–3, then met to discuss their ratings. Domain 4 was scored after the observation and an interview with the school principal to evaluate teachers' scores regarding professional responsibilities. Observations took place between February and March 2023, after the winter break and prior to end-of-year student testing.

Post-observation Conference

Finally, the participants met with the principal investigator to discuss the observation and the teachers' perceptions of their undergraduate program preparation. Interviews were semi-structured with a guiding set of questions for teachers to respond to (e.g., What are areas where you feel that your program was helpful in preparing you, as it relates to creating an effective classroom environment?; What does it mean to care for students?; How do you show your care for your students?), with the opportunity to ask follow-up questions as needed. Teachers were provided the choice to interview in person or via Zoom. All but one interview occurred via Zoom, and all were recorded and transcribed.

Principal Interview

When possible, researchers met with the principal to review the Danielson Framework's Professional Responsibility Domain as the principal would have a deeper knowledge of the teachers' work with their colleagues, students' families, and the community. Each interview took 10 to 15 minutes to complete. Principals were asked to provide feedback on the teachers' abilities to plan, implement, and assess instruction, their abilities to build relationships with their students, and other areas of general strength and weakness. If the principal was unable to meet with the researchers, an email conversation occurred where principals were asked to rate the teachers on the Professional Responsibility domain and to provide general information about their work performance. Three of the five principals met or emailed with the researchers and provided information about graduate performance.

Data Analysis

Following each observation, the researchers met to discuss their respective scores from the Danielson Framework and arrive at a consensus. Qualitative data from the pre-conference form, field notes, post-observation conference, and principal interviews were used to support the scores across each domain. Qualitative data from these sources were analyzed by chunking into coding categories, which were based on the research questions and literature on care-based practice in the classroom. Coding categories were developed using themes from the data sources (Yin, 2003) (see Table 2.2 for examples).

Findings

Our findings indicate that, as induction teachers enter the field, they begin to identify specific ways in which they build relationships and enact care. In this section, we address each research question and how participants felt that their teacher education program supported them, or could better support them, in enacting care.

What Induction Teachers Believe about Ways of Caring

When compared to our previous research on preservice teachers and their beliefs about ways of caring (Scott & Allen, 2022), we found that novice teachers held more specific views of what it meant to care for students and how to do it. Receptive engagement was more visible, with 14 out of 15 teachers heavily emphasizing the value of building relationships with students. Twelve teachers also provided clear examples of the steps they took to show students that they cared about them, such as attending students' athletic, cultural arts, or other events outside of the school day.

The teachers also emphasized the importance of giving students a "voice" in the classroom. As Eliza noted, "Caring for them is including them. It's not just your classroom, that doesn't work for me. When they have a role, they feel like they matter, and their opinion is important" (Post-observation conference). She was able to support her statement with examples of how students shared their opinions and how instruction was adjusted to meet student goals and needs. James, a secondary teacher, explained that he worked hard to put the students' work on the walls and to adjust activities to do things students enjoyed and wanted to participate in, based on their feedback (Post-observation conference). This differed from our original study of student teachers who indicated that allowing student choice and voice were important but were unable to provide examples of where they did this in their instruction (Scott & Allen, 2022).

Novice teachers also noted that accountability was an important part of showing students care, with 11 explaining that students needed boundaries and to know that accountability comes from wanting students to be successful. Delaney, a fourth-grade teacher, explained that she learned quickly that accountability and high expectations were as important for her

TABLE 2.2 Coding Categories and Examples for Support

Initial Codes	Examples to Support	Final Code
Academic needs	I mean, yeah, care is more than just loving kids … it's also holding them accountable for themselves. I know all your teeth are falling out, but you can't get out of my line, you can't just get up, that tiny bug bite is not going to kill you … You have to set boundaries because they will cross them all day. We have things we have to learn!	Actionable methods for showing care
Social needs	I talk to them, and I'm like guys, you don't know that the people you don't get along with are the people that you have the most in common with. Y'all need to just sit and talk about your personal lives, so you can just see.	
Emotional needs	I had to change my plans. We've had two former students pass away recently, and my students were at the funeral for one of them. They needed to be there.	
Relationship Building	We are a family! We love to joke around, play, learn, and collaborate together. It is very comforting when you walk in.	Receptive Engagement
	Building relationships with my students is important to me … I talk to my students about my life, and they are more inclined to open up to me.	
	I also have a student and a teacher mailbox for students to share information that they might not want to say out loud.	
	We are having this meeting because I love you. We want you to be a better version of yourself.	
Time outside of the classroom	I show interest in their hobbies, jobs, and interests outside of class. I've attempted to make the classroom inviting by displaying their work, remaining consistent with procedures, and having materials available to them if needed.	
	I try to find resources that go along with their interests and keep them engaged. I also attend many of their after-school events.	
	I try to go to at least one game and at least one practice.	
Student autonomy	Caring for them is including them. It's not just your classroom, that doesn't work for me. When they have a role, they feel like they matter, and their opinion is important.	

students as "loving them" and shared that she was sure to let students know accountability was a part of care:

My students are able to come to me, comfortably, about anything. I have a couple that aren't afraid to tell me something personal or to come to me about something academic. They feel comfortable saying "Help me lady!" … I don't think my students feel like "If I say the wrong thing, she's going to snap at me." Sometimes they might tell me a little too much, but I'm glad they are comfortable with that. And, when they aren't doing what they need to do, we talk about it. I let them know that I love them, and that the next day

28 Catherine Scott et al.

is a new day, but that we have to meet with their parent or adult and work things out. I share that "We want you to be a better version of yourself" because we love you. (Post-observation conference)

Even though many of the induction teachers recognized that relationship-building was a critical part of care in the classroom, one teacher struggled. When asked about her experiences with students, Cora was quick to point out that they did not seem to be engaged in anything she wanted them to do and she felt they just "didn't care." The principal explained that Cora's struggles were due not to the students themselves but, rather, to her inability to connect with them on a more personal, meaningful level:

She knows something is different in the other rooms, but she hasn't quite figured it out yet. She can see that her colleagues don't have as many behavior issues. She's almost there, but she's got to see the role that she plays in that. (Principal interview)

Overall, the induction teachers were better able to provide examples of how their versions of care are built on relationship-building, more so than we found in our study of preservice teachers (Scott & Allen, 2022). One area where teachers needed to grow was in considering reciprocity in care. Although two were able to explain how they actively solicited input from students on instructional practices, lesson ideas, and other classroom factors that impact student relationships, 13 assigned students a more passive role. Often, they would ask students about their interests or ideas and work them into the lessons but they did not necessarily ask students if what they were doing actually made the students feel cared for. Given their status as induction teachers, this was not entirely surprising. Dias-Lacy and Guirguis (2017) note that new teachers are challenged due to their limited experience addressing students' academic and behavioral needs, limited access to resources, and lack of professional development on such topics.

Novice Teacher Ratings on Danielson Rubric Indicators Associated with Care

As noted earlier, observers used the Danielson Framework (2013) to score the participants' teaching. Within the aforementioned domains, the rubric includes several indicators associated with characteristics of care, as seen in Table 2.3 and described below.

In Domain 1, Planning and Preparation, two indicators aligned with reciprocal views of care: opportunities for student choice in the lesson (1e. Designing Coherent Instruction) and opportunities for students to assist in the assessment development process (1 f. Designing Student Assessments) (Danielson, 2013). The induction teachers earned a lower mean score for Designing Coherent Instruction (2.77) due to limited opportunities for student choice. They also earned lower mean scores for Designing Student Assessments (2.85) due to the lack of student opportunity to engage in developing the assessments and minimal adaptations to assessments based on student needs.

In Domain 2, three indicators aligned with practices associated with reciprocity and care: all students feeling valued and comfortable with taking risks (2a. Creating an Environment of Respect and Rapport), student opportunities to engage in the management of routines, materials, and supplies (2c. Managing Classroom Procedures), and student opportunities to adjust the classroom environment to meet their needs (2e. Organizing Physical Space)

How Novice Teachers View Their Teacher Preparation Experiences 29

TABLE 2.3 Danielson Framework Rubric Indicator Mean Scores (n = 15)

Domain	Indicator	Mean Score	Standard Deviation
Planning and Preparation	1e. Designing Coherent Instruction	2.77	0.39
	1 f: Designing Student Assessments	2.85	0.39
The Classroom Environment	2a: Creating an Environment of Respect and Rapport	3.46	0.66
	2c: Managing Classroom Procedures	3.38	0.51
	2e: Organizing Physical Space	3.38	0.65
Instruction	3c: Engaging Students in Learning	2.77	0.60
	3d: Using Assessment in Instruction	2.92	0.49
	3e: Demonstrating Flexibility and Responsiveness	2.77	0.60
Professional Responsibilities	4c: Communicating with Families	3.38	0.51

(Danielson, 2013). The teachers earned their overall highest mean scores across Domain 2, with mean scores of 3.46, 3.38, and 3.38, respectively.

Domain 3, Instruction, includes three indicators associated with care. Engaging Students in Learning (3c) addresses reciprocity by ensuring that students have opportunities to initiate inquiry, contribute to content, and serve as resources for their peers, while Using Assessment in Instruction (3d) includes opportunities for students to assist in developing assessment criteria. In Demonstrating Flexibility and Responsiveness (3e), teachers are recognized for building on students' interests and adjusting and differentiating instruction to meet student needs (Danielson, 2013). As with Domain 1, where scores are based on providing opportunities for student choice and differentiation, the induction teachers earned lower mean scores for both 3c and 3e (2.77 for each).

Finally, in communicating with families (Domain 4, Indicator 4c), teachers are rated based on their abilities to respond to family concerns, with opportunities for students to contribute to the communication process (Danielson, 2013). Based on principal feedback, the induction teachers earned an overall mean score of 3.38 for the indicator. Overall, they earned higher scores in areas focused on respect, rapport, and classroom environment but lower mean scores in areas associated with engaging students in decision-making processes. This aligns with the findings from research question one and the findings from previous research (Dias-Lacy & Guirguis, 2017).

Teachers' Feelings of Preparedness to Enact Care

All novice teachers felt their teacher education programs taught them how to enact care. However, a few suggested that programs and districts could do more to better support both preservice and newly hired teachers. When discussing care, 13 teachers specifically discussed their program's emphasis on relationship building and the classroom environment. Twelve of the 15 provided examples from their coursework to support their views; for example, Kara noted,

> I wanted them to be excited for school and come in … how I act is going to be how they act. That is one thing that I vividly remember from Dr. H … when we came in, she was

behind the shield, it was Covid, but she was so excited to be there, and so we were excited to be there. Also, little things, you know, I think about everything that you all have done and said a lot, little things, like how you brought up my pet duck the other day, those personal connections. I love that because I got to start a conversation with my class about something that you remembered about me. I try to take that, what you've done, and use it … (Post-observation conference)

Elaine brought up the value of learning about routines, consistency, and engaging with families to best meet student needs:

I had to do a lot of reaching out to people, and reaching out to his family, and working with his family … I learned *him*. I did get a relationship with him, I learned about him. I held him accountable. We had a structure. And I couldn't let it change the next day, we learned the importance of structure at [Institution]. We had to learn the structure, but it really paid off. (Post-observation conference)

Novice teachers felt their field experience coursework helped to prepare them for how to advocate for students, including developing ways to engage students in the decision-making process. Seven also provided examples of how they used student interests in their lesson plans, how they assessed student feelings for each day through morning meetings and daily check-ins, and ways in which they allowed student involvement based on what they learned in their courses. As previously noted, however, most opportunities for student engagement were passive, not active. Other than Eliza, only Wendy shared a specific example of how she advocated for student needs versus school expectations:

I talked with the kids about it [15-minute small groups], and they said that they feel rushed. So, I talked to my principal and said, "The 15-minute small groups isn't working for my kids, I need to do the two 30-minute groups for a longer time." (Post-observation conference)

While novice teachers, overall, felt their programs provided the experience needed to enact care in the classroom, there were still areas where they felt programs could continue to improve. For example, several, particularly from the early childhood and elementary programs, felt that they needed more training on how to deal with atypical child behaviors, including significant behavior issues and challenges with parents. Five shared that they needed more support with classroom management, providing examples of times when a student's behavior was disruptive enough to impact the entire classroom environment or when they struggled to build a relationship with a family. As Wendy explained, "When you have parents of those children, who see no wrong in their child, that transitions to the classroom" (Post-observation conference). All five indicated that, although they recognized that some things could not be experienced until they were in the classroom, holding conversations about such scenarios and how to handle them would help:

But you can talk about it, and have scenarios, but you can't really do it until you *do* it. You have to figure out how to build relationships with them. I will say that management has been more difficult to figure out. Because like, there's a lot of behaviors that we have to learn: where they come from, like why are behaviors a certain way, and how their brains function to survive in their home environment. If they kick and scream at home to get attention, they are going to kick and scream at school ... and at first, I didn't know what to do with that. (Anna, Post-observation conference)

Overall, novice teachers recognized the need to establish relationships with students and could provide examples of how their coursework prepared them to enact care in the classroom. Their strengths included being able to provide specific examples of how they enacted care, which aligned with what was observed while in their classrooms. Interviews and observations also provided insights into areas where further support was needed for induction teachers, including learning how to involve students in decision-making related to planning and assessment to ensure that student needs were really being met as teachers attempted to enact care in the classrooms.

Implications

Observing novice teachers' classrooms and conducting interviews regarding their time in our teacher education programs provides insights for teacher education and teacher induction. First, while induction teachers do recognize more nuanced ways of showing care for their students, there are still areas where further support would aid them through the induction period.

The novice teachers demonstrated strengths in identifying strategies used to build relationships with students, particularly compared to the suggestions provided by preservice teacher candidates (Scott & Allen, 2022). These strategies were based on their experience in the classroom as they learned about their students and how to engage with their families. Those working with early and elementary-aged children wanted better support to know how to work through challenging student behavior and other classroom situations, similar to the teachers in Dias-Lacy and Guirguis' (2017) study. Many teachers felt that they needed to know more about the causes of misbehavior and students' social or emotional challenges so that they were better able to meet student needs.

These challenges are becoming more prevalent post-COVID as the nation deals with challenges in schools, including the stripping of funding related to issues of cultural awareness and social-emotional well-being (Lieberman, 2023; National Center for Educational Statistics, 2022). Preservice programs and those working with novice teachers should consider ways in which to include training on such scenarios for candidates so they feel better prepared when entering the classroom. Additionally, administrators and district staff should actively involve induction teachers in determining what type of training is needed, engaging in a reciprocal relationship that values their needs and adjusts accordingly. For example, after recognizing that our candidates felt there were areas needing more support, we asked them where they needed help and then based subsequent professional development opportunities around their requests. We adjusted based on their feedback and continue to check each semester with candidates to make sure we provide what they would like to have for programming and support; this could also happen during the induction phase.

Novice teachers also made recommendations for how institutions of higher learning could better support them through the induction years. As teacher educators, we should be soliciting their feedback and developing the supports that best meet their needs, rather than offering a one-size-fits-all program option. For example, the induction teachers we observed wanted more training in classroom management and small group instruction after graduation. They felt that classroom management workshops could support managing atypical student behaviors or interactions with parents. Teachers also indicated that workshops on small group instruction would allow them to better meet student needs. We would also recommend that induction teachers receive training on how to engage students in the planning and instruction processes so that teachers can truly use a reciprocal approach to caring to make sure student needs are met.

Finally, although the novice teachers generally felt their districts supported them as new teachers, they lamented the redundant trainings or workshops on topics already covered in their teacher education program or during their new teacher orientation. Beginning teachers also felt that districts should back off and not put too many demands on new teachers, expressing concerns similar to those found in previous studies (Dias-Lacy & Guirguis, 2017; Fantilli & McDougall, 2009). As Cora shared,

> I'm trying to learn how to teach, let alone do whatever extras the district wants me to do. I am trying to tread water here. And I have to spend time in a workshop on something we've already covered, when that is time I could use to grade, or plan, or figure things out. (Post-observation conference)

If we truly want teachers to enact a caring, reciprocal relationship, those who work with induction teachers must find out what those teachers need and adjust their support accordingly. Moreover, as we would expect in their own classrooms, we must engage induction teachers in decisions about their own training.

References

Barek, H., Namukasa, I., & Ravitch, S. M. (2023). *Pedagogies of care in precarity.* https://www.methodspace.com/blog/pedagogies-of-care-in-precarity.

Carter Andrews, D. J., Richmond, G., & Marciano, J. E. (2021). The teacher support imperative: Teacher education and the pedagogy of connection. *Journal of Teacher Education, 72*(3), 267–270.

Creswell, J. C., & Poth, C. N. (2016). *Qualitative inquiry and research design (4th ed.).* Sage.

Danielson, C. (2013). *The framework for teaching evaluation instrument, 2013 instructionally focused edition.* http://www.nysed.gov/common/nysed/files/danielson-teacher-rubric-2013-instructionally-focused.pdf

Dias-Lacy, S. L., & Guirguis, R. V. (2017). Challenges for new teachers and ways of coping with them. *Journal of Education and Learning, 6*(3), 265–272.

Fantilli, R. D., & McDougall, D. E. (2009). A study of novice teachers: Challenges and supports in the first years. *Teaching and Teacher Education, 25*(6), 814–825.

Goldstein, L. S., & Lake, V. E. (2000). "Love, love, and more love for children": Exploring preservice teachers' understandings of caring. *Teaching and Teacher Education, 16*(8), 861–872.

Lieberman, M. (May 2, 2023). Schools could lose funding as lawmakers spar over the national debt ceiling. *Education Week.* https://www.edweek.org/policy-politics/schools-could-lose-funding-as-lawmakers-spar-over-the-national-debt-ceiling/2023/05

Moen, K. M., Westlie, K., Gerdin, G., Smith, W., Linner, S., Philpot, R., Schenker, K., & Larsen, L. (2020). Caring teaching and the complexity of building good relationships as pedagogies for social justice in health and physical education. *Sports, Education, and Society, 25*(9), 1015–1028.

National Center for Educational Statistics. (2022). *More than 80 percent of U.S. public schools report pandemic has negatively impacted student behavior and socio-emotional development.* https://nces.ed.gov/whatsnew/press_releases/07_06_2022.asp

Noddings, N. (1984). *Caring: A feminine approach to ethics and moral education.* University of California Press.

Noddings, N. (2012). The caring relation in teaching. *Oxford Review of Education, 38*(6), 771–781.

Scott, C. & Allen, M. (2022). Seeing beyond the plexiglass: Enacting a vision of caring during COVID. In M. Shoffner & A. Webb (Eds.), *Reconstructing care in teacher education after COVID-19: Caring enough to change.* Routledge. pp. 79–90.

Yin, R. K. (2003). *Case study research: Design and methods.* Sage.

3

"I WASN'T PLANNING ON YELLING"

Beginning English Teachers and Pandemic-Inflected SEL Curriculum

Katie Nagrotsky

The COVID-19 pandemic significantly altered the educational and labor experiences of students and teachers. Since the pandemic and its associated shifts to remote teaching and learning, both students and teachers are facing issues adjusting to a confusing mix of old and new difficulties and policies. These frustrations contribute to what the media characterizes as "teacher shortages" (Schwartz et al., 2021), though critical teacher educators characterize the phenomenon more as a slow protest or strike (Dunn, 2020). Teacher shortages can exacerbate the difficulties both students and teachers are facing even more.

This chapter builds from previous scholarship studying teachers' emotions by emphasizing how English teachers navigate their first semester in schools that have adopted social emotional learning (SEL) programming in response to COVID-19. Emerging as a research-based field in the 1990s, SEL is defined as "the process through which all young people and adults acquire and apply the knowledge, skills, and attitudes to develop healthy identities, manage emotions and achieve personal and collective goals, feel and show empathy for others, establish and maintain supportive relationships, and make responsible and caring decisions" (Collaborative for Academic, Social and Emotional Learning [CASEL], 2020). Dunn and Garcia (2020) point out that teachers are not often conditioned to think of their own needs; instead, they are led to think first of their students' needs and often act as facilitators of SEL for their students. This is particularly true in literacy classrooms, where English teachers witness students' expressions of emotions through personal writing (Dutro, 2019) and teachers and students engage in verbal and written affective responses to literature (Dunn, 2021).

Framing the Study

I began supervising student teachers as a doctoral student, and supervision remains the most interesting, difficult, and exciting work that I do as faculty. I first met the teacher participants in this study when they were enrolled in my student teaching seminar course at a private university in the northeast in the fall of 2021. This study, then, stems from research into my teaching during the 2021–22 academic year.

DOI: 10.4324/9781032707471-5

During one of our seminar sessions, I found myself fighting back tears as teacher candidates discussed their reactions to a reading I had assigned on trauma-informed teaching, role clarity, and boundaries (Venet, 2019). Reading over their reflections again later, I kept returning to how many students seemed to be uncertain about dealing with and responding to the trauma they perceived their middle and high school students to be carrying and processing in their student teaching placements. Along with questions about the responsibilities of care for their students, many also commented on feeling unsure about how to inhabit an empathetic stance while also confronting signs of their own personal burnout. I noticed that a few used language referring to detaching or distancing themselves as a form of self-preservation:

> My question relates to how to not let these traumatic things impact you? The one student that was discussed today in our meeting brought up an instance that shocked me to the core. I feel so bad when I look at this student and my heart breaks for her. How do you not let it faze you and keep it separate in a sense?
>
> (written reflection, seminar #4)

These were questions that I could not answer. They stayed with me as I sought to articulate boundaries for myself as a caring instructor and mentor, so I pursued the following research question: How do beginning English teachers describe the challenges of caring for their students amidst the ongoing pandemic in schools that have adopted SEL initiatives?

Care Theory and the Presumption of Need

Following Shoffner and Webb (2022), I write from the perspective that the COVID-19 pandemic and its effects must be included in any discussion of teacher education and care. Furthermore, this chapter relies on Noddings' (2012, 2019) notion of presumed and expressed needs to better understand teachers' experiences.

According to Noddings (2005), a caring teacher is sensitive to the academic, social, and emotional needs of students and is compelled to address those needs. Noddings (2019) writes that as teachers, we have to ensure that we do not "fail to engage the other in genuine dialogue and, simply because we assess certain needs as legitimate and important, we assume that others also have these needs" (p. 772). Further, Noddings (2012) suggests we have to engage in dialogue with those we are caring for to encourage them to convey their needs and to act on those expressions instead of defaulting to presumed needs. Otherwise, we end up relying on our own perceptions and assumptions about what they might need, instead of truly listening for expressed needs.

In Webb and Baumgartner's (2023) study, novice teachers explained how they received substantial professional learning opportunities related to the use of technology for distance learning, when in fact they felt quite comfortable with technology and some supported their mentor teachers in this area. Further, they found that these teachers were aware of the emphasis on their own "self-care" but suggestions to care for themselves and work towards a work-life balance often proved untenable. Education and induction should listen to new teachers to develop support based on their expressed needs rather than presumed needs. Unfortunately, new teacher induction programs are often based on presumed needs and are standardized such that they cannot be responsive to beginning teachers' expressed needs.

Social Emotional Learning (SEL)

Thirty-eight states referenced SEL in their response plans to the pandemic (Yoder et al., 2020). Numerous positive outcomes are associated with SEL and skill development, such as improving students' ability to integrate thinking, feeling, and behaving to achieve important tasks throughout their lives (Zins et al., 2004). The CASEL framework delineates five competency clusters: self-awareness, self-management, social awareness, relationship skills, and responsible decision-making.

The CASEL conceptualization of SEL, however, does not prioritize the sociopolitical dimensions of teaching and learning (Simmons, 2017), and therefore many SEL models do not account for historically marginalized students and their intersectional identities (e.g., race, ethnicity, gender, sexuality, ability). Instead, the SEL curriculum can reinforce racial oppression. The goals and skills for SEL programs in schools serving historically marginalized students are designed to develop students' compliance and emotion management while SEL programs in predominantly white schools are designed with college preparation in mind (Lin et al., 2023). It is necessary to engage an antiracist understanding of SEL (Simmons, 2017), one in which teachers and students are encouraged to develop a critical consciousness that allows them to recognize and challenge social inequalities and injustices at the core of developing social-emotional competencies.

Many inservice teachers recognize that factors like poverty, racism, ableism, and other structural inequalities increase students' levels of toxic stress and are therefore relevant to students' SEL and well-being. In addition, many inservice teachers have expressed a desire to develop competencies around mental health, culturally responsive behavior management, and student engagement (Donahue-Keegan et al., 2019; Schonert-Reichl et al., 2017; Waajid et al., 2013). Education leaders believe that K-12 students benefit from SEL because of the challenges associated with the return to in-person classrooms, so-called "learning loss," and interpersonal conflict students are struggling with after extended quarantine periods and remote schooling (Lehman et al., 2021). The SEL curricula developed for teachers to implement under CASEL, while focused on addressing these "losses" or presumed deficits, have not been complemented by similar measures to support teacher well-being.

Methods

This chapter presents findings from an instrumental case study involving a group of individuals who experienced the phenomenon under study. Stake (2005) holds that an instrumental case study permits researchers to gain more insider insight into an examined issue.

Teacher Participants

After the students in my student teaching seminar course graduated in the spring of 2022 and I was no longer their instructor, I obtained Institutional Review Board (IRB) approval for the study and sent all 21 secondary education program completers from my seminar course a recruitment email through their university email accounts. Of these, five beginning English teachers opted into the study. Four participants identified as white females; one identified as a white male. All five teachers worked in predominantly white suburban schools in the northeastern United States.

This chapter focuses on two focal teachers' experiences. Isabelle completed her senior year of college through online teacher education courses and engaged in her clinical practicum observations remotely. She shared that she always knew she wanted to be a teacher and completed her student teaching placement during her master's year in 7th grade English at a suburban middle school. After graduation, she accepted a position at the suburban high school where she had gone to school to teach English to 9th, 10th, and 11th graders. Ryan comes from a family of educators. Originally interested in a career in media production, he student taught in a high school in the same district where he went to school. He accepted a position to teach as a long-term substitute at that same high school in the fall of his first year as a teacher of record, teaching Freshman English classes.

I selected Isabelle and Ryan for analysis because they demonstrated two instances of beginning teachers' experiences in schools where the public health crisis and ongoing racial injustice had encouraged district and school-level commitments to discuss new ways to meet the presumed SEL needs of K-12 students in the return to in-person schooling. At the time of the study, both teachers worked in districts that used federal Elementary and Secondary School Emergency Relief Funds, established as part of the Education Stabilization Fund in the Coronavirus Aid, Relief, and Economic Security Act, to support SEL initiatives to address COVID-19's impact on schools.

Additionally, both Isabelle and Ryan were participating in the same two-year new teacher induction mentoring program required by the state's Department of Education to advance to professional certification. While the structure and emphasis of new teacher induction programs vary (Howe, 2006; Ingersoll, 2012), this program is designed to support beginning teachers as they transition from their teacher education program to their roles as teachers and provide regular opportunities to meet with an assigned mentor.

Positionality

As I reviewed my field notes and interview and focus group transcripts, I realized that there were considerable limits to my empathetic listening (Dutro, 2019) because my past personal experiences were not foregrounded in the collective and individual trauma of the COVID-19 pandemic. I am a white woman and former English teacher, and the experiences and concerns I remembered and shared with the teacher participants were different from my students' experiences and concerns. For example, one of the middle schools I taught in was a hard-to-staff school serving students of color where teachers were regularly expected to cover additional classes due to staffing issues. Another school I taught in served a predominantly white student population in a more affluent area and rarely saw the same kind of teacher turnover or urgent need for substitutes. I discussed the different layers of racialized privilege underneath this disparity in staffing with the teachers and they described how they were all noticing increased vacancies and coverages in their schools, including those that served privileged families. Some of the experiences and primary concerns of the teachers in this study were about making sense of colleagues' comments about "learning loss" and worrying about how to handle unprecedented absenteeism in their classes.

Data Collection and Analysis

Data collected during Isabelle's and Ryan's first semester as teachers of record included transcripts from individual semi-structured interviews (Merriam, 2009) and focus group sessions I conducted in the fall of 2022. The interviews addressed teacher beliefs about teaching SEL lessons, their interactions with students, and their perceptions of their own emotions and feelings in the classroom, specifically with respect to how they cared for their students. I conducted and recorded the interviews on Zoom. I interviewed both Isabelle and Ryan twice; each interview lasted about an hour. The larger group of five teachers also met twice for approximately an hour each in two focus group sessions after school, also via Zoom.

I revisited the interview and focus group transcripts to ask how teachers were "responding to the needs of diverse students for friendship, self-esteem, autonomy, self-knowledge, social competence, personal identity, intellectual growth, and academic achievement" (Gay, 2018, p. 62). From there, I labeled segments of the data where I noticed the teachers were discussing the support they strove to provide to their students and care for them.

This led me to consider the support that the teachers received, i.e., their presumed needs, or wished they were given, i.e., their expressed needs. Teachers expressed the need for non-evaluative spaces to discuss teaching incidents and authorization of their struggles to implement SEL, for example; they were presumed to need support for instructional planning, communicating with parents, and learning school norms. As I analyzed the data, I began to notice discrepancies between the role of the teacher in being sensitive to students' SEL needs and the discomfort teachers faced when presented with SEL curriculum that did not engage with students' identity markers as salient to their SEL development.

Findings

The beginning English teachers in this study noticed that their students struggled with stress management but, paradoxically, felt that they had to suppress their own emotional responses to their difficulties implementing SEL lessons authored by others. Teachers feel obligated to suppress their feelings for fear of being perceived and marked as unprofessional (Dunn, 2021) but teacher vulnerability can also be subversive (Dunn & Garcia, 2020). This study provides insight into an important related need for beginning teachers: New teachers of record, particularly those engaged in the emotional labor of school-wide SEL initiatives, seem to feel this tension more acutely.

Isabelle and Ryan taught in schools that situated SEL instruction in an advisory period distinct from core academic subjects, and they experienced challenges associated with its implementation. In Isabelle's school, advisory group lessons varied monthly and were themed. She was often asked to cover for absent colleagues and was provided with an SEL-focused lesson plan, PowerPoint slides, and student handouts. Ryan's school extended the homeroom period at least once a month during which teachers were expected to teach an SEL lesson the principal planned.

Both teachers felt a responsibility to discuss stress management and frequently used opportunities during their English classes to address the SEL needs their students were expressing. Isabelle, for example, explained how she facilitated deep breathing exercises with her students to acknowledge their worries. Isabelle did not wish to avoid what she felt were signs of student stress and anxiety. She had a talk with her students during which she emphasized, "You're a human in here and you're an individual first before a student. Yes, we learn, but I also want you to take away things from this class." Ryan described how he began to ask his students to write down two things that were "stressing them out this week" and share them with a partner as one of his classroom routines.

One dilemma emerged when Isabelle was asked to cover a class period of a small group of 8th graders during the school's designated advisory period. Isabelle described how the white male students in the advisory class began targeting an Indian classmate, making derogatory comments that included denigrating stereotypes; Isabelle, frustrated by the cruelty of the racist behavior and the students' refusal to hear her demands for an apology to their classmate, began crying during the class period. She noted that she felt she should not cry and attempted to hide her tears because she feared her students and colleagues would not respect her.

In this and other representative moments, Isabelle shared her concerns about how her expressions of emotion might be perceived, even as she engaged with SEL programs and advisory curriculum designed to support students' presumed SEL needs (Hargreaves, 2000). Mindfulness and deep breathing can be effective strategies for students to learn how to manage stress more generally but this example illustrates how any SEL curriculum without a racial justice lens is incomplete. Lin et al. (2023) write that current SEL definitions and practices are at risk of perpetuating a "one size fits all" approach that emphasizes the false concept of "neutrality" and assumes that everyone's emotions are perceived and welcomed equally, ignoring the impact of systemic oppression on those who have been consistently marginalized. Despite the proliferation of SEL programming and heightened awareness of teachers' responsibility of care, Isabelle felt unprepared to address the racism at the root of the classroom conflict.

It is also important that Isabelle felt she did not know these students well enough to attempt this work with them. There is a degree of vulnerability and skill required to work with students on self-reflection and effectively encourage the development of their racial literacy (Sealey-Ruiz, 2011). Without existing closeness and trust amongst teachers and students, it is unfair to expect teachers—like Isabelle, in this situation—to be brave and vulnerable in facilitating these kinds of lessons, particularly when authored by someone else.

Ryan, too, was concerned about how his emotional responses might be perceived, but he was worried about how administrators and students' parents might interpret his feelings, whereas Isabelle was worried about the reactions of her students and colleagues. Ryan, for instance, shared an account of how he became angry when a group of students began bullying a neurodivergent student, remembering his frustration when they teased her and how he felt guilt that he was unable to prevent the behavior:

I wasn't planning on yelling. But they started arguing back and I really started to yell. And I definitely would not have done that again, because I was nervous about it. I felt like I'd done the wrong thing. I felt like I was gonna get in trouble with the administration, because I really shouldn't have yelled like that. You know, you bite your tongue, and you pocket it, I probably wouldn't have even had them stick around, maybe just to get [the students'] names and just told them to go away. But I wanted to confront them about it.

In describing his yelling and the subsequent concern that his reaction would be seen as outbursts, Ryan showed a conflicting desire to care for and protect his student and how that was complicated by the uncertainty of his role as a new teacher. Ryan felt that he was not supposed to express anger towards his students, even though he characterized their behavior towards a peer as cruel and inexcusable. Ryan demanded an apology from the bullies yet he told me multiple times that he felt his outburst would be viewed as unprofessional. Ryan, much like Isabelle in interactions with her students, felt he had to veil his emotions from students and colleagues for fear of losing respect and authority in the classroom. His comments support previous research that suggests teachers' "outlaw emotions" are inscribed by notions of "appropriateness" (Dunn & Garcia 2020; Neville, 2018) and, interestingly, align with his district's emphasis on the SEL tenets of emotional regulation according to the CASEL framework.

Additionally, Isabelle and Ryan both expressed frustration with the learning loss narrative that some of their more experienced colleagues mentioned when discussing challenging student behaviors. While administrators in these teachers' schools had developed resources and materials centering on high school students' assumed SEL needs, Isabelle and Ryan wanted assurance that they could present the full range of their emotions, including sadness, anger, and frustration, without repercussions, whether from parents, administrators, or students themselves.

Both teachers spoke about how their professional development sessions at school focused on the national mental health crisis of adolescents and provided lessons to teachers to address these presumed needs. Yet little attention was given to the emotional support that Isabelle or Ryan might need to feel authorized to admit to difficulties they encountered in being themselves in these lessons. For example, Isabelle wished she could have a "consistent" meeting with a mentor where she could voice concerns about emerging issues in her teaching weekly. Both Isabelle and Ryan explained that because these issues were not purely curricular concerns, they did not feel it was appropriate to air them in their regularly scheduled professional learning community meetings or with their assigned mentors.

Implications

We cannot presume to know what beginning teachers like Isabelle and Ryan need in schools since the onset of the COVID-19 pandemic unless we listen to their stories. As teacher education faculty, I recognize that I have not undergone similar experiences as the beginning teachers that I teach. This is all the more reason that faculty, school administrators, and more experienced teachers supervising teachers like Isabelle and Ryan in their induction years must listen carefully to new teachers' expressed needs and resist projecting needs on them based solely on prior experiences with beginning teachers or on their own personal past needs remembered from their induction years.

Many assume that novice teachers who completed teacher education programs during the COVID-19 pandemic require additional support due to the alteration and disruption of their training, especially reduced in-person and emergency remote clinical placement opportunities. Yet these beginning teachers also possess unique perspectives, having been both students and teachers during the pandemic. This duality can attune them to their own K-12 students' needs in generative ways (Darling-Hammond & Hyler, 2020).

Researchers have noted that beginning teachers typically encounter multiple identity tensions but induction programs do not prioritize these tensions. For instance, teachers may want to care for students but, in doing so, do not keep enough distance, wanting to present as a competent teacher to their students and colleagues but still feel like a student themselves in many ways (Schellings et al., 2023). The issues my participants faced are not typical classroom management issues but issues of confronting oppression in action.

Their stories lead to multiple opportunities for policymakers. Teachers, beginning teachers included, should be given the opportunity to develop their own approaches to SEL. Isabelle and Ryan, for example, would benefit from release time to work with colleagues on SEL as an integrated part of their ELA curriculum. CASEL's current delineation of SEL competencies suggest that SEL is a uniform set of skills that can be taught in the same way to all students (Simmons, 2017), however uniform SEL curricula undermine the relational responsiveness of an ethics of care.

One option is to integrate SEL programming into English classes through project-based learning since those classrooms are already spaces where students read, think, talk, and write about their emotional responses to literature; teachers can intentionally design project-based instruction that attends to the affective needs of teachers and students (Boardman et al., 2021). This integration of SEL into English classes would support collaboration and has the potential to improve racial literacy outcomes as students practice their literacy skills in the service of learning to write and talk about race and racism.

Further, we need to alter new teacher induction programs, including mentorship programs, to meet beginning teachers' emotional needs as they navigate teaching prescriptive SEL curricula. Acknowledging how difficult the first three years of teaching are, the induction program and accompanying modules that Ryan and Isabelle were working on calls for mentors to monitor their mentees for fatigue and disillusionment, which is excellent. However, the majority of the program focuses on basic school functions (e.g., parent-teacher conferences, report cards, standardized testing). Not only do these programs need to include preparation for effectively teaching the SEL curriculum, they should also demonstrate care for teachers' well-being. Moving forward, antiracist SEL should be a priority, as should teacher education courses, professional development, and mentoring communities around antiracist SEL in the inductive years.

References

Boardman, A. G., Garcia, A., Dalton, B., & Polman, J. L. (2021). *Compose our world: Project-based learning in secondary English language arts.* Teachers College Press.

Darling-Hammond, L., & Hyler, M. E. (2020). Preparing educators for the time of COVID … and beyond. *European Journal of Teacher Education, 43*(4), 457–465.

Donahue-Keegan, D., Villegas-Reimers, E., & Cressey, J. M. (2019). Integrating social-emotional learning and culturally responsive teaching in teacher education preparation programs. *Teacher Education Quarterly, 46*(4), 150–168.

Dunn, A. H. (2020). "A vicious cycle of disempowerment": The relationship between neoliberal policies and teachers' reports of morale and pedagogy in an urban high school. *Teachers College Record, 122*(1), 1–40.

Dunn, M. B. (2021). When teachers hurt: Supporting preservice teacher well-being. *English Education, 53*(2), 145–151.

Dunn, M. B., & Garcia, A. (2020). Grief, loss, and literature: Reading texts as social artifacts. *English Journal, 109*(6), 52–58.

Dutro, E. (2019). *The vulnerable heart of literacy: Centering trauma as powerful pedagogy.* Teachers College Press.

Gay, G. (2018). *Culturally responsive teaching: Theory, research, and practice.* Teachers College Press.

Hargreaves, A. (2000.) Mixed emotions: Teachers' perceptions of their interactions with students. *Teaching and Teacher Education, 16*(8), 811–826. doi:10.1016/S0742-051X(00)00028-7.

Howe, E. R. (2006). Exemplary teacher induction: An international review. *Educational Philosophy and Theory*, *38*(3), 287–297.

Ingersoll, R. M. (2012). Beginning teacher induction what the data tell us. *Phi Delta Kappan*, *93*(8), 47–51.

Lehman, C., Orange-Jones, K. C., & Lacy-Schoenberger, E. (2021). Lose the language of "learning loss." *Voices from the Middle*, *28*(4), 26–29.

Lin, M., Olsen, S., Simmons, D. N., Miller, M., & Tominey, S. L. (2023). "Not try to save them or ask them to breathe through their oppression": Educator perceptions and the need for a human-centered, liberatory approach to social and emotional learning. *Frontiers in Education*, *7*, 1044730. 10.3389/feduc.2022.1044730

Merriam, S. B. (2009). *Qualitative research: A guide to design and implementation*, (2nd ed.). Jossey-Bass.

Neville, M. L. (2018). "Sites of control and resistance": Outlaw emotions in an out-of-school book club. *English Teaching: Practice & Critique*, *17*(4), 310–327.

Noddings, N. (2005). Identifying and responding to needs in education. *Cambridge Journal of education*, *35*(2), 147–159.

Noddings, N. (2012). The caring relation in teaching. *Oxford Review of Education*, *38*(6), 771–781. doi: 10.1080/03054985.2012.745047

Noddings, N. (2019). Concepts of care in teacher education. In J. Lampert (Ed.), *The Oxford encyclopedia of global perspectives on teacher education* (pp. 139–150). Oxford University Press. https://doi.org/10.1093/acrefore/9780190264093.013.371

Schellings, G., Koopman, M., Beijaard, D., & Mommers, J. (2023). Constructing configurations to capture the complexity and uniqueness of beginning teachers' professional identity. *European Journal of Teacher Education*, *46*(3), 372–396.

Schonert-Reichl, K. A., Kitil, M. J., & Hanson-Peterson, J. (2017). *To reach the students, teach the teachers: A national scan of teacher preparation and social & emotional learning*. Collaborative for Academic, Social, and Emotional Learning (CASEL). https://eric.ed.gov/?id=ED582029

Schwartz, H. L., Diliberti, M. K., Berdie, L., Grant, D., Hunter, G. P., & Setodji, C. M. (2021, May 11). *Urban and rural districts show strong divide during the covid-19 pandemic*. RAND Corporation. https://www.rand.org/pubs/research_reports/RRA956-2.html

Sealey-Ruiz, Y. (2011). Learning to talk and write about race: Developing racial literacy in a college English classroom. *English Quarterly Canada*, *42*(1), 24–42

Shoffner, M., & Webb, A. W. (Eds.). (2022). *Reconstructing care in teacher education after COVID-19: Caring enough to change*. Routledge.

Simmons, D. (2017). Is social-emotional learning really going to work for students of color? *Education Week*. https://www.edweek.org/tm/articles/2017/06/07/weneed-to-redefine-social-emotional-learning-for.html

Stake, R. (2005). Qualitative case studies. In N. K. Denzin & Y. S. Lincoln (Eds.), *The Sage handbook of qualitative research* (3rd ed., pp. 443–466). Sage Publications Ltd.

Venet, A. S. (2019). Role-clarity and boundaries for trauma-informed teachers. *Educational Considerations*, *44*(2), 1–9. https://doi.org/10.4148/0146-9282.2175

Waajid, B., Garner, P. W., & Owen, J. E. (2013). Infusing social emotional learning into the teacher education curriculum. *International Journal of Emotional Education*, *5*(2), 31–48.

Webb, A. W., & Baumgartner, J. J. (2023). So much new to learn and so much unknown: Novice teachers' experiences during COVID-19. *Journal of Educational Research and Practice*, *13*(1), 237–250. https://doi.org/10.5590/JERAP.2023.13.1.17

Yoder, N., Posamentier, J., Godek, D., Seibel, K., & Dusenbury, L. (2020). From response to reopening: State efforts to elevate social and emotional learning during the pandemic. *Collaborative for Academic, Social, and Emotional Learning*. https://files.eric.ed.gov/fulltext/ED610659.pdf

Zins, J., Weissberg, R. W., Wang, M. C., & Walberg, H. (Eds.). (2004). *Building academic success on social and emotional learning: What does the research say?* Teachers College Press.

4

RESHAPING TEACHER INDUCTION THROUGH CARE AND COMMUNITY

Allison Wynhoff Olsen

There is a damaging clause often lobbed at teachers when negotiating salaries and workdays: "It's about the kids." When education stakeholders put "the kids" first, they seem to forget one key component of teaching and learning: teachers. If internalized, teachers may push away their own needs and build a complicated relationship with work, often resulting in staying where and when they are unwell. Teachers feel guilty for taking a personal or sick day (Wynhoff Olsen et al., 2022), stressed that their financial burdens are growing, and increasingly isolated (Petrone & Wynhoff Olsen, 2021). To quote one high school teacher in my network: "How many hours must a teacher work before they can comfortably say they worked enough?" She added, "I feel guilty every day, because every day I could be better if I put in more time, but I don't want to put in more time. How much time is a good amount of time?"

I take such questions to my preservice teachers (PSTs) so we can layer in emotional elements of teaching alongside the curricula. Starting these conversations when we are on campus also affords opportunities for me to return to affective topics when PSTs are in their induction years—busy, often frazzled, excited, and typically willing to pour themselves into their job as they find their way within the profession. Affective, caring conversations also offer continuous pathways of support that can reshape teacher induction and fuel teaching careers.

Building communities of practice (Lave & Wenger, 1991) during teacher education increases PSTs' confidence and plays a role in their growing identities as teachers (Mitchell et al., 2019). Unfortunately, the peer support that prompts confidence and provides a physical togetherness naturally dissipates as PSTs move into the induction years, accept jobs, and move into teacher vacancies across school districts. Thus, a focus on moving from teacher preparation into teaching, via acts of care, is necessary.

This chapter draws from a structured reflection over the past 10 years in my role as a teacher educator in an English education program in the western United States. To illustrate my response to the current teaching context in the United States, I use a collection of notes and emails from preservice teachers, my own reflective writing, and induction teacher responses from a survey on teachers' sense of belonging in their schools and communities (Wynhoff Olsen et al., 2022). Specifically, I focus on how teacher educators can harness this moment to reshape the induction years of teaching in affective ways.

DOI: 10.4324/9781032707471-6

Representative Induction Experiences

Agatha and Andy are pseudonyms for teachers in my network; I highlight their trajectories as early-career teachers because they well represent their peers within my English education (EE) community. Of course, each person uniquely maneuvers their way into and through the field yet their experiences make visible a pattern of need that warrants attention.

Agatha and Andy were high school English teachers completing their third year of teaching in their respective school districts. They had a few English teacher colleagues in the building, taught multiple course preparations, and coached speech and debate. From the beginning of their careers, Agatha and Andy built relationships with students, recognizing that knowing their interests, strengths, and struggles would afford insight into programming curricula in their high school programs and, possibly, impact students as readers and writers outside of the classroom. To outside observers, Andy and Agatha were successful. Their students engaged with them and one another and were making solid progress as readers and writers. Their curricula were creative, challenging, rich with varied texts, and aligned with school district expectations. Their speech and debate teams competed well, traveling the state making friends and gaining important experiences. Agatha and Andy also networked, attending their state's annual teacher conference, sustaining relationships with their university's EE community via social media, and reaching out to building colleagues and administrators with questions. Agatha and Andy explored graduate school options and believed education was the right field: Students were their passion!

And yet, on a teacher survey exploring a sense of belonging in school and community (Wynhoff Olsen et al., 2022), both shared difficulties in their responses to the open prompt: Anything more you'd like us to know? Agatha wrote,

> I really do love teaching and know my school needs teachers like me [Agatha identifies as a member of the LGBTQ+ community]. I'm sure my community doesn't believe they are hostile to me; however, that doesn't make it any less hard.

Agatha's survey and social media posts over the years suggested that they felt excluded and unhappy at times. Interactions with students were mostly positive and, yet, the experience of living as a teacher in that community was hard.

Similarly, Andy's response to the same open prompt indicated a need for time and reflection:

> I have had a rough go of it this year and am considering finding a new profession at the end of the school year, at least for a little while. I think I need to find some perspective elsewhere in order to try to truly enjoy teaching again.

When he completed his survey, Andy was a husband and a dad; the complexities of his new familial roles, while working as an English teacher, were becoming overwhelming, reshaping his teaching identity and sense of belonging in the field and in his community.

Community

While I used to consider our PST community a bridge into the field, I now position it as a sustained relationship that needs more intention (Beach, 2022), particularly during teachers' induction years when they are experiencing so much newness and change. Throughout our shared time, PSTs like Agatha and Andy accept invitations to respond to our world and human experiences with diverse texts, dialogue, and layered assignments, while being surrounded by others experiencing a common foundation (e.g., signature assignments, required courses). Over the years, PSTs also experience acts of care and tangled personal connections (e.g., cohort members, cooperating teachers, professors) if they choose to participate. They move into their student teaching experiences and teaching jobs with creative ideas, confidence, and a healthy level of trepidation.

During traditional induction years, teachers experience a flood of emotions and life experiences as they learn how to be teachers in place. These induction years extend or return as teachers change jobs. Regardless of how many years someone has taught, the time they need to "start over" is as significant as when they started year one of teaching—a significance emphasized when we lean into teachers' emotions and wellness. In our rural state, most communities have one high school with one English teacher, requiring a move to a new town and sometimes, to a new state to find another teaching job. Though they begin their next job with experience, teachers who seek belonging begin anew and explore the school and community values and routines, figuring out how (if) they belong. Small, rural communities do not respond well to an outside professional who assumes knowledge; rather, teachers need to establish themselves in the new place and learn anew how to *do English* in their particular place. Additionally, if they shift roles from a position where they are the sole English teacher for grades 7–12, with 25–50 students total, and accept a position as an English teacher with departmental colleagues, teaching 1–3 grade levels or an elective course with 20–35 students in class, they begin learning to teach and be a teacher all over again. Teachers who move districts do not typically receive credit for all their years of experience toward their salaries, either: a concrete cementing that the movement within a teaching career is not upward, professional mobility but, rather, a series of restarts. With multiple inductions in a career, we need more attention toward teachers' mental load in order to co-construct ways to support how teachers feel and create networks that center affect across the profession.

Layers of Emotion

Teachers need not mute their emotional intelligence when they receive their teaching licensures; rather, as a field, we can build communities of care to promote emotional capacity and invite PSTs and teachers to participate with us as professional human beings who teach. Marc Brackett (2019), a scholar on emotional intelligence, poses a question that suits a reshaping of teacher induction years: "Is there something missing in the school environment as it's been constructed over the course of decades and centuries—something both students *and* teachers need?" (p. 414). Yes: care and emotion.

Shifting Pride

When I began teaching high school in 1998, I was proud to be a teacher. Throughout my college coursework, fieldwork, and early career, I experienced solid support for teachers and teaching. It is certainly plausible that my experiences were self-induced: My mother and sister were teachers, my father valued education, and my parents' closest friends had jobs in education or service-related fields. I also had numerous teacher friends across the United States. School was and remains a second home to me: a place I experience comfort and a high sense of social and cultural capital. Now, as a tenured professor of English education, the profession feels different. My role has taken me out of the secondary English classroom so I do not interact with youth and high school politics each day; however, the difference is more pronounced than a shift in position and teaching responsibilities. The difference is within the affective realm: the general feelings about teachers, teaching, and experiences with youth and English language arts curricula in public schools in the United States. Twenty-five years into the profession, I remain proud to be a teacher, yet my pride is now interlaced with worry.

Brave Willingness

Within the local EE community built during our undergraduate degree program, I have experienced teachers—particularly those in their induction years—willingly sharing teaching stories with our PSTs (one of their first professional communities). Reflecting on interactions with the induction teachers, I question: What is it about the community that made space for their brave willingness to share their failures and fears alongside their aha moments and how could I play a more intentional role in cultivating the health of this community? In response to both questions, I assert what my heart innately recognized: intentional care for PSTs, teachers, and our field across the teacher lifespan. We show up for one another, we build relationships, and we work to stay connected as PSTs graduate and move through their induction years. We discuss how we feel in place and how that shapes our curriculum as well as our permanence (or lack thereof) in the job/profession, giving teachers in the induction years opportunities to articulate and grow in their affect as well as their craft and/or career.

As an incoming teacher educator in this local EE community, I was drawn to the teachers' willingness to emote as they shared stories. Reflecting back, their emotions stuck out to me because I experienced them as courageous, vulnerable, and relatable. Listening to their stories, I immediately returned to my own induction years as a teacher and could feel the burden of working all day, well into the night, to learn my curriculum and become a part of my new community.

Yet, I don't think I was as brave as these new teachers. Instead of sharing my experiences and my raw emotions, I built an armor that allowed me to go into my classroom each day and return the next. I was not cold to my students or colleagues; rather, I was selective in what I was willing to notice about my feelings, my belonging, and my well-being. I reached out for curricular help and received wonderful support from my mentor, now a dear friend, yet I did not fully bring myself to the classroom. I did not look for a confluence of cognition, behavior, and emotion (Bracket, 2019) for myself or my students; rather, I assumed that the academic work should be of primary importance. Fortunately, time, generous students, graduate school mentors, and loss have helped me reorient myself as a teacher throughout my 25-year career. I recognize that emoting is not just a sign of bravery; rather, it is something that teachers and students need (Shoffner & Webb, 2022).

Control and Love

Public schools in the United States are divisive, particularly around the values communities and school boards allow teachers to take up in their classrooms. There is distrust toward educators; there are political moves and campaigns built on controlling and censoring texts (e.g., *Gender Queer* by Maia Kobabe [2019]) and topics (e.g., equity). To illustrate, in the state in which I educate teachers, there is a House Bill seeking to open "public schools, libraries, museums and their employees to criminal liability for displaying or disseminating to minors material deemed 'obscene'" (Kuglin, 2023, para 1). Librarians and teachers who share a book title or offer expansive library selections have been threatened and are at the mercy of any parent/guardian who takes issue or has a different set of values. Another topic that has been challenged is social emotional learning, with parents claiming that emotions are to be taught in the home. Conflicting messages confuse the roles of teachers in schools as well as pose damage to children and youth who need help. Yet, "when teachers work to affirm the emotional well-being of students, we are doing the work of love" (hooks, 2003, p. 133). Love should be present in our classrooms, for with a love relation, "the intersection of academic striving meets the overall striving to be psychologically whole" (hooks, 2003, p. 136).

As a teacher educator, whose students become teachers, I lean into hooks' ethos. Of course, I want my students to be "psychologically whole," and yet, I recognize that being in a love relationship takes time. Caring for teachers in the induction years means meeting those people where they are when they enter our programs as PSTs. And right now, many PSTs are faced with lingering mental health crises heightened by altered schooling during the COVID-19 pandemic (Shoffner & Webb, 2022). Finding ways to take care of PSTs while they are university students and simultaneously prepare them for the challenges in the teaching field (Smith et al., 2022) can feel insurmountable. Layer on the need to sustain relationships with those PSTs as they move into their induction years and throughout their careers, and the whole endeavor seems far too extensive.

And yet, recognizing the affordances a community relation brings mitigates some of the strain: "Research shows that our emotions and moods transfer from one person to another and from one person to an entire team—both consciously and unconsciously. It's called 'emotional contagion'" (Brackett, 2019, p. 445). Collectively, we can boost the mood or dampen a moment; more often than not, exploring teachers' emotional capacity helps showcase how they feel about teaching and how they feel while teaching in place; together, we give words to how we are feeling, find commonalities, remark on the distinctions. Being in a relationship with others over time creates space for varied emotions. We hold space for one another to reflect and give voice to our emotions rather than carry, and likely bury, them on our own.

Throughout my experiences, I have become more comfortable sitting alongside others in their—or my—discomfort and pain, while learning new ways to encourage them and be encouraged by them. So, "as we develop emotion skills, hopefully we become more aware of how we are actively creating emotional contagion and understand its impact on others" (Brackett, 2019, p. 446). I show up in our local EE community with love. In community together, we support one another. Yes, we share curricular ideas and help one another with management strategies as we lead new groups of students. Yet, if we want to be consciously daring, we must double down on being transparent and vulnerable (Brown, 2018): We must say no to armor even though the easier move is to self-protect, as I did at the beginning of my career. hooks (2000) reminds us, "We are not born knowing how to love anyone, either ourselves or somebody else. However, we are born able to respond to care" (p. 53). After all, "everyone wants to be received" (Noddings, 2005, p. 17). To keep moving forward, we have to refuel our emotional tanks.

Teacher Voices

To better understand the emotional landscape of teaching professionals, this section elevates teacher voices. Examinations of teachers' stories, survey responses, and affirmation writing I have collected over the past 10 years indicate a willingness to express emotional capacity, particularly as they move into and through induction years. When we listen to their messages as well as how they craft them, we gain a deeper understanding of how teachers creatively engage and endure the profession (or not). All names in this section are pseudonyms.

Lack of Trust

As an illustration of willingness, I return to the open survey prompt: Anything more you'd like us to know? (Wynhoff Olsen et al., 2022). High school teacher Jessica used the open prompt to describe her induction years:

> I *was transferred* [from one high school to another one in the district] *against my will.* I was made to feel as if I had a choice to make as a professional and valued member. *I was misled.* When I was transferred to XHS, *I was given a classroom and had it taken away* at the last minute ... *The whole process left me feeling used, betrayed, and leery* of administration and anything they say to me.

In examining her response, the phrases in italics are most telling. Through passive voice constructions, Jessica offers a sequence of events that led to her negative emotions and sense of instability in her job. To attempt healthy gains in her position and career, Jessica needed support—support that her district could not provide. Her wider survey responses (Wynhoff Olsen et al., 2022) suggested that she wanted to be heard yet could not speak with anyone; rather, she shared her experiences and feelings with those she could trust: her PST community.

Miscommunication

First-year teacher Alice experienced "situational discomfort" related to students' behaviors and administrators. As she tried to align her disciplinary practices with school policies, she noted "miscommunication between the instructional coach and the vice principal that made the situation worse." Rather than find people at school to help or to listen, Alice "shut down." Alice shared that she did not have the emotional capacity nor willingness to remain in a school that lacked support for her as a teacher: "I'm not feeling very encouraged to continue teaching."

While, Alice willingly shared her story with me when asked, she did not reach out while she was in teaching in pain. She left the profession after year one.

Systemic Strain

Teacher education programs are experiencing low enrollment numbers (Fuller, 2023) given, in part, to an unrelenting, negative discourse around the teaching profession in the United States. Hans, amid the second induction of his career (i.e., beginning anew in a new state in a larger school district), speaks to this moment with emotional awareness:

There's a whole section of TikTok called TeacherQuitTok about teachers leaving their jobs, finding new careers, changing things. And there's all this noise around the profession, to the point where sometimes I think, "Am I missing something to still love it? Or are my experiences just so different from theirs?" I want to validate their experiences, their feelings, but it's not something I relate with … . I do think that if some systemic things don't change, education is going to become really tough.

Hans is one of the few teachers in our community who is able to turn down the "noise" and find gratitude; most others express that their students bring them joy but the surrounding noise is deafening, wearing them down in ways that have them reaching out for support. Hans leans in, hears the concerns, and wants to "validate" others yet he does not relate. He alludes to the need for "systemic" change but appears to have high resiliency.

Relatedly, Clara—a teacher in her third induction phase—tapped into her emotional capacity and describes herself as "*numb* to any public or private criticism of how I do my job" and thereby, feels "free." During her first induction years, Clara attended to detail with abandon, noting that she was "overcompensating" because of a felt need to mitigate how others viewed teaching; she "developed a health problem," quit, and moved out of state. Within months, she accepted a part-time teaching job, "recovered," and is "much happier." Perhaps most notably, she is moving out of her induction phase into her career no longer feeling obligated: "I'm not responsible for the shortcomings of a school system that don't support good teaching." She shared that she has "a circle of people who understand teaching," encourage her, and "recognize why I take my job seriously." She focuses on those who support her, free to ignore the voices that exhausted her into a health issue during her first induction years.

Teacher Gratitude

Teaching is a profession that requires intelligence and heart, yet this particular cultural moment has a flavor of sadness and fatigue that lands in a dissonant context, rife with a cacophony of voices and forces that demand to be heard. Too often in this noise, teachers' voices are not amplified or welcomed. To illustrate, I offer high school teacher Erin's brief and affirming words on the open survey prompt: Anything more you'd like us to know? (Wynhoff Olsen et al., 2022). Erin wrote, "Thanks for working to give teachers a voice in this matter!" Erin's appreciation indexes that her voice—a teacher's voice—is often muted or erased "in this matter" of discerning how teachers experience their job. Her phrase "working to give" also suggests that she experiences a devaluing of teachers' experiences in schools and communities and recognizes that a shift toward valuing teachers is not a sanctioned right in the field.

It is also the case that teachers mute themselves out of fear for their jobs and their safety; others are muted by administration and school boards; others find no need to speak up because their focus is within their classroom—a place where they feel the most able to make a difference.

And yet, as a field, we need teachers' voices amplified if we aim to respond to this moment and care for those induction teachers educated in our programs.

Across the last decade, I have received notes of affirmation, social media posts, and in-person hugs from PSTs and induction teachers. One undergraduate PST wrote, "I have been stretched in my thinking and understanding of how teachers ought to lead their students." Another, after traveling with me and presenting her work at an annual convention expressed, "... going to NCTE [National Council of Teachers of English] this year was one of the best experiences of my college career. It totally changed the way I view English Education." Another, appreciating my encouragement, shared, "You were one of the first people to ever tell me that I belong in this field and that I have the ability to be a change maker for youth." This same student made a point to lean in further, bringing her mom to a graduation social to meet her community. For each of these women, there was reciprocal beauty in taking time to sit down, write her feelings, and share them. Each note represented the culmination of a stage in their career and the time taken to reflect on their belonging with gratitude.

Teacher Partnerships

Sometimes, we need to reach out and collaborate with teachers during their induction years, even when we cannot predict how the experience will unfold. I collaborated with a high school teacher from our program whom I had never met; my teaching partner shared how amazing she was as a PST and, so, when I was seeking a school partnership for a methods class, we built a writing mentorship with her high school writers and my PSTs (see Wynhoff Olsen, 2019, for more details on this collaboration). Ms. Maverick was an innovative teacher and served as a mentor to PSTs in my class: She modeled feedback language and showcased how her knowledge of students merged with her goals for their writing. In addition, Ms. Maverick was experimenting with a new curriculum so she openly asked for feedback on her assignments. At the culmination of our partnership, Ms. Maverick sent me a thank you note:

> I'm not sure I can fully say thank you for agreeing to mesh an entire year's curriculum with a brand new high school class, with a high school in a totally different state, with a teacher who had only taught for one year and you had never met. Thank you for taking such a giant risk ... Thanks for investing in me as an educator and coaching me to become a better teacher. Thanks for investing in my students as writers and learners.

She offered amazement that I positioned her and her students as people worthy of our attention: people who had knowledge and gifts to share. She also appreciated the opportunity to grow as a professional, particularly since she had "only" taught for one year. Early induction years are transformative. Sometimes, teachers hit their stride and find belonging. Other times, they face exhaustion, and worry, and seek out community. It was my extreme honor to work alongside Ms. Maverick as she experienced the range of these feelings and more.

Conclusion

The busier we become, the more people need time to sit with their feelings and reflect on what they (don't) know. Teachers, particularly those in their induction years, need validation that how they experience their work is important; their professional lives are not just "about the kids." When we invite teachers across induction experiences to lean into affective experiences and consider their emotional capacity (or lack thereof), their stories and feelings complexify how we understand teacher induction(s) and the role of care in the teaching field.

Care and love are two emotions on which we can act, two feelings and actions that breathe life and humanity into our classrooms, opening people up for a range of emotions and risks because "to love is to be vulnerable" (Brown, 2018, p. 22). Teachers are vulnerable as learners and leaders daily. Since vulnerability, like connection, is cultivated over time, the care we infuse within induction years should begin during teacher education programs.

To sustain my relationship with the teachers in my local EE community, I send encouragement and ask if they need support both by email and on our social media page. My most recent message read:

I believe that you are a brave, vulnerable, smart leader. I also believe that teaching is beautiful, raw, and exhausting. Are there any kinds of conversations, check-ins, visits, and/or experiences you would like to see me offer as a way to continue supporting you?

We sustain our relationship through the responses and, most often, the teachers emote. One stands out in its simplicity: "I really like the occasional 'how are things' posts in the Facebook Page." Another offered gratitude: "Thank you for continuing to be such a compassionate, thoughtful leader in education."

From the time my students are PSTs, we work to build a community. We lean into one another. We learn, we fail, we worry, and we celebrate. We also agitate (sometimes one another) and advocate for the issues that matter to each of us. Together, we press for ways to invite youth into hard conversations regarding texts and human issues. And then, as our PSTs graduate, we move together into their teacher induction years, helping them find new footing in our intergenerational, local EE community.

With each induction, I encourage teachers to share a description of their teaching position with our community; practically, this allows us to stay connected and find one another as they shift schools. More than that, we (their professional community) get a glimpse into how teachers understand their roles. We use technology (e.g., a shared group in a social media platform, emails, and text messages) to our advantage and ask questions, share resources, seek advice, and hold space for one another. I also invite teachers to local writing project events, professional conference proposals, and back into the university classroom to talk with pre-service teachers. At random times, I check in and ask how teachers are feeling. I send notes of encouragement. I remind them that they deserve to feel safe and belong, and if at any point they do not, it is okay to pause and figure out why. I also assert that they, as teachers, deserve to be attuned to their emotions (Brackett, 2019) so they can pay attention to how they feel in order to be able to respond and take care of themselves. Across our community, we discuss ways to repair relationships, shift expectations, and align values.

Leaning into local communities of practice (Owen & Whitney, 2022) and extending them outside of our finite teacher programs can help bolster teachers' feelings of acceptance and belonging (Wynhoff Olsen et al., 2022) and be a part of continued, increasing care of educators—particularly, during their induction years. As hooks (2000) reminds us, "To live our lives based on the principles of a love ethic (showing care, respect, knowledge, integrity, and the will to cooperate), we have to be courageous" (p. 101). It takes courage to care for teachers; even more, it takes courage for teachers in their induction years to take care of themselves.

References

Beach, C. L. (2022). Care beyond COVID as a teacher and teacher educator. In M. Shoffner & A. W. Webb (Eds.), *Reconstructing care in teacher education after COVID-19: Caring enough to change* (pp. 159–168). Routledge. DOI 10.4324/9781003244875-18.

Brackett, M. (2019). *Permission to feel: Unlocking the power of emotions to help our kids, ourselves, and our society thrive*. Celadon Books.

Brown, B. (2018). *Dare to lead: Brave work. Tough conversations. Whole hearts*. Random House.

Fuller, E. J. (2023, May). *Trends in enrollment in US teacher preparation programs: 2009–2021 programs*. Penn State College of Education.

hooks, b. (2000). *All about love: New visions*. Routledge.

hooks, b. (2003). *Teaching community: A pedagogy of hope*. Routledge.

Kobabe, M. (2019). *Gender queer: A memoir*. Oni Press.

Kuglin, T. (2023). Bill criminalizes 'obscene' material to minors by school libraries. *Independent Record*: https://helenair.com/news/state-regional/government-politics/bill-criminalizes-obscene-material-to-minors-by-schools-libraries/article_33105a35-ca5f-5050-9631-b31dd7b795d3.html

Lave, J., & Wenger, E. (1991). *Situated learning: Legitimate peripheral participation*. Cambridge University.

Mitchell, R., Wynhoff Olsen, A., Hampton, P., Hicks, J., Long, D., & Olsen, K. (2019). Rural exposure: An examination of rural fieldwork opportunities and methodologies in three universities in the U.S. and Australia. *The Rural Educator, 40*(2), 12–22.

Noddings, N. (2005). *The challenge to care in schools: An alternative approach to education* (2nd ed.). Teachers College.

Owen, C. & Whitney, A. (2022). Learning communities as caring communities during COVID: Caring as relation that empowers teacher education. In M. Shoffner & A. W. Webb (Eds.), *Reconstructing care in teacher education after COVID-19: Caring enough to change* (pp. 236–246). Routledge. DOI 10.4324/9781003244875-26.

Petrone, R. & Wynhoff Olsen, A. (2021). *Teaching English in rural communities: Toward a critical rural English education*. Rowman & Littlefield.

Shoffner, M. & Webb, A. W. (Eds.). (2022). *Reconstructing care in teacher education after COVID-19: Caring enough to change*. Routledge.

Smith, R., Sutton, P., & Tierney, G. (2022). Redefining care in teacher education: Responding to teacher candidate needs after COVID. In M. Shoffner & A. W. Webb (Eds.), *Reconstructing care in teacher education after COVID-19: Caring enough to change* (pp. 25–35). Routledge. DOI 10.4324/9781003244875-4

Wynhoff Olsen, A. (2019). Tensions in ELA field experiences: Service learning in rural contexts. In H. Hallman, K. Pastore-Capuana, & D. Pasternak (Eds.), *Methods into practice: New visions in teaching the English language arts methods class* (pp. 145–158). Rowman & Littlefield.

Wynhoff Olsen, A., Fassbender, W., Long, D., & Olsen, K. (2022). Teachers, schools, communities: How rural sense of belonging holds impact for English teachers in place. *Australian and International Journal of Rural Education, 32*(2), 108–125. 10.47381/aijre.v32i2.330

5
ENCOURAGING AND UPLIFTING NEW TEACHERS BY DEMONSTRATING CARE AND FOSTERING GROWTH MINDSET TO BUILD RESILIENCE

Amanda Steiner, Julie Bell, and Chris Wilcoxen

Teachers are leaving the profession at a rate faster than ever before. For some, the reason is money; for others, it is support; and attrition was only exacerbated by the COVID-19 pandemic (Olson Stewart et al., 2021). Eadie and colleagues (2021) found that well-being impacted early childhood educators' decisions to leave teaching and supportive structures lowered teachers' risk of leaving. Kraft et al. (2020) also found that teachers needed to feel successful to stay, and they were influenced by working conditions. Knowing that support structures have helped bolster resilience during difficult times (Wilcoxen et al., 2022), in this chapter we reflect on the practices and supports utilized to create positive environments for beginning teachers through induction.

Teaching was stressful prior to the pandemic (Desrumaux et al., 2015; Wilcoxen et al., 2020) with job demands, discipline problems, emotional exhaustion, time constraints, and low self-efficacy (Collie et al., 2015; Skaalvik & Skaalvik, 2018). Support is necessary to minimize stress including physical, emotional, or psychological implications. These factors negatively impact efficacy and, in turn, teachers' resilience, which correlates with teachers' mental health (Daniilidou et al., 2020; Yu et al., 2015). Teachers' well-being is highly dependent upon feeling safe and being built up through supportive growth-focused approaches instead of accountability-driven systems (Netolicky, 2016).

The pandemic impacted opportunities to collaborate with colleagues, changed mentoring practices, and minimized opportunities for professional development. With teacher retention dependent on engagement, well-being, care, and satisfaction, the impact of the pandemic needs to be contemplated to develop teacher education and the cultural competence necessary for collaboration and learning in the profession. Heynoski and colleagues (2022) argued in favor of a focus on well-being as one way to address the national educator shortage, including "strengthen[ing] educators' sense of purpose, belonging, and connection" (p. 22). Beyond the pandemic, teachers have been negatively challenged by other factors outside their control, such as teacher evaluations that are focused on accountability instead of professional development (Guenther, 2021).

As schools continue to navigate their return post-pandemic, it is imperative they create cultures of care that foster resilience in veteran and beginning teachers to help mitigate

DOI: 10.4324/9781032707471-7

attrition, since "resilience is the ability to bounce back from setbacks ... in the face of adversity and struggle" (Helmke, 2022, p. 48). Although hard to define, a culture of care is one that recognizes the whole person (Noddings, 2005), encourages relational development, and prizes listening to others (Noddings, 2012). Beginning teachers must be cared for, encouraged, and supported in building resilience to overcome professional, academic, and personal challenges and crises. Our reflection on The Career Advancement and Development for Recruits and Experienced [teachers] (CADRE) Project is grounded in existing literature about crisis, care, and building resilience in beginning teachers. The intention of this reflection is to improve our induction program and provide recommendations for other induction programs.

Responding to Crises

Anytime there is a "disruption of the norm," there is a crisis (Houwer, 2011, p. 110) and an opportunity for the people involved to learn from the situation. At the same time, people need guidance and time to learn from crises (Houwer, 2011); too much pressure to immediately return to previous structures can magnify crises' impact. Houwer (2011) additionally argued that people in crises either take action (i.e., are subjects or agents) or are acted upon (i.e., are objects) (p. 110). Feeling like an object instead of a subject, or the inability to act and make strategic changes in the face of a crisis, can delay the opportunity for growth after trauma. The last few years have been difficult and placed educators as subjects and objects—at times, simultaneously.

Growth mindset is an indicator of a teacher's ability to problem-solve and work through adverse situations. Teachers exhibiting a growth mindset perceive teaching as a malleable practice and welcome opportunities to grow in their craft, which fosters engagement and enjoyment in teaching (Frondozo et al., 2022). Furthermore, this mindset supports developing positive relationships with colleagues, improving practice through professional learning, and accomplishing goals (Nalipay et al., 2022). The use of goal setting is essential as it promotes improvement and mastery of a teacher's skill set.

Fostering a growth mindset and building resilience in beginning teachers necessitates carefully structured mentoring/coaching practices. Educative mentoring supports teachers in acclimating to the school and engages teachers in reflecting on their practice to help evolve their teaching (Bradbury, 2022; Feiman-Nemser, 2001; Wilcoxen et al., 2022). Similar to educative mentoring, instructional coaches provide on-site professional development and one-on-one support to help teachers improve their practice (Aguilar, 2013; Knight, 2021). A blend of mentoring/coaching can best support beginning teachers (Steiner et al., 2022). Mentors/coaches can wear many hats. Their varied roles may consist of data, literacy, or instructional coaches, among others (Killion, 2009; Steiner et al., 2022). The mentor/ coach's ability to connect with others is at the heart of their work.

The relationship that must exist between a mentor/coach and a teacher can be actualized through Noddings' (2013) *ethic of care*. Care ethics support the idea that the mentor/coach is attentive and receptive to what the teacher is feeling and expressing. Additionally, Shoffner and Webb (2022) noted, "Care must acknowledge the context and lived experiences of all parties, which requires us to see the whole rather than the part put forward in the moment" (p. 7). The development of relationships where beginning teachers feel valued, connected, and cared for creates a platform for teachers to grow in their practice.

The CADRE Project

The CADRE Project is a 14-month induction program that has helped foster resilience in beginning teachers for more than 25 years (Wilcoxen et al., 2020) by providing coaching and mentoring support to beginning teachers. School districts select mentors/coaches (i.e., Associates) who support two beginning teachers 10 hours a week, work for their districts 20 hours a week, and work in reciprocity with the university 10 hours a week. Throughout this collaboration, beginning teachers also complete a master's degree while working full-time as a first- or second-year teacher. Associates support master's degree work by facilitating university seminars. The project has proven to support beginning teachers' well-being (Wilcoxen et al., 2020), and nearly 95% of participants (beginning teachers and Associates) remain in education (Bell et al., 2021). As Ronfeldt and McQueen (2017) found, beginning teachers who received induction support were less likely to move buildings or leave the field. They noted mentoring, seminars, collaborative time, and supportive communication from school leaders were the most impactful in induction support.

As a high-intensity induction program, the CADRE Project provides a positive environment and supports a growth mindset and resilience. Building upon Dishena and Mokoena's (2016) framework, the CADRE Project implements both high-intensity and low-intensity practices. High-intensity practices require time and money to support induction (i.e., mentoring, observations, offering resources, professional development) while low-intensity practices (i.e., orientation, emotional support, providing information) can be implemented quickly with minimal effort (Dishnena & Mokoena, 2016).

The CADRE Project aligns with the structures identified by Dishena and Mokoena (2016) and we have found it has positive outcomes, similar to those found by Ronfeldt and McQueen (2017), such as minimizing teacher migration and attrition (Steiner et al., 2021).

CADRE Associates use a blend of mentoring and coaching to support teachers by holding reflective conversations (Bell et al., 2022; Steiner et al., 2022). In the CADRE Project, Associates and teachers partner throughout induction and select supports from a high-intensity induction practices strategies menu. These strategies are used throughout the year to support the growth of the new teacher, Associate, and PK-12 students. The menu includes the following: making procedures into routines, modeling effective teaching practices, co-planning and co-teaching, problem-solving classroom management concerns, managing individual behaviors, analyzing student performance/data, collecting evidence through observation, navigating the school culture, building a professional reputation, general tasks, and supporting social-emotional needs.

Reflection on the CADRE Project

The author team consists of the CADRE Project Director (Wilcoxen) and two university faculty members (Steiner and Bell) who teach graduate-level coursework taken by the beginning teachers. Our reflection is guided by dialogue captured by Wilcoxen, 36 beginning teachers completing their first or second year of teaching and 17 Associates. All three of us reviewed notes from the conversations and reflected on the practices and supports Associates used to create positive environments that encourage and uplift teachers. We then aligned selected quotes from the conversations with the high-intensity induction practices menu to identify trends for program improvement.

Making Procedures into Routines

As former elementary and secondary teachers, we know disruptions during instruction can impact learning and a teacher's confidence. Associates help CADRE teachers plan for this in advance, which builds independence, supports resilience, and provides strategies to help problem-solve through classroom structures. When reflecting, teachers noted they appreciated the time they had in seminars to plan for routines and procedures and to create classroom materials. Associates provided support and guidance so classrooms could run smoothly. A teacher said they valued the time to process routines and procedures with peers and Associates before the year started. One Associate commented it is important to "internalize curriculum and management routines—which leads to them [teachers] being confident in their daily/hourly teacher decisions that they make based on truly knowing their students."

Modeling Effective Teaching Practices

Teachers need models of great teaching. Within our program, this can take many forms, such as an Associate modeling an entire lesson or a small portion of a lesson (e.g., instructional strategy) or observing another teacher's classroom. The act of modeling supports the attainment of new skills, attitudes, and behaviors within the classroom. As noted previously, a goal of the CADRE Project is to foster a growth mindset. Teachers with a growth mindset understand that abilities are malleable and are developed and improved over time.

Associate modeling was an important aspect of promoting a growth mindset in beginning teachers. One teacher remarked, "I struggled with having deeper conversations with students [who acted out]. [My Associate] facilitated conversations with students about how they were feeling, what they could do next time, and how to create a friendship rather than fighting all the time." Another teacher noted,

> My Associate is my favorite part of this whole process. I think it was so helpful at the beginning because she was able to step in and help with lessons and bring new ideas … but it's also cool to see the growth [in myself]. I don't have to ask her to step in for lessons anymore because she was able to help so much in August, September, and October, and I now take those strategies and implement them.

We also noticed modeling supports self-efficacy. When teachers saw others successfully performing a task or behavior, they were likely to believe they could also implement the practice in the classroom. One teacher noted, "I liked getting ideas from other teachers that I can use in my classroom." Additionally, teachers enjoyed the time together to learn from each other: "I collaborated with many colleagues to gain new ideas that would help me and my students in the classroom." Teachers and Associates utilized the year-end showcase to celebrate strategies, structures, and procedures that work effectively in the classroom.

Co-planning and Co-teaching

An extension of modeling that promoted a growth mindset was co-planning and co-teaching. The most important part of co-planning is collaboration, which we acknowledge is a high-intensity practice that requires time. Co-planning includes metacognitive practices where the teacher and Associate share their thinking through planning a lesson. This allows the pair to name strategies and work through challenges in real time, including small group instructional support and planning for pause days after assessments to provide time to analyze the results. Other co-planning methods include long-range planning, double planning (i.e., planning for instruction and planning for classroom management), planning for error, and partnering for co-teaching. Two teachers commented on the connection between data analysis and co-planning: "We did a lot of analyzing data together and co-planning. The two go hand in hand." Another teacher remarked, "We did co-planning, but I guess co-teaching too. We both would rotate around the room and stop and help students."

Co-teaching includes team teaching (e.g., co-delivery of a lesson), station teaching and alternative teaching (e.g., small groups), parallel teaching (e.g., splitting the class in half), one-on-one work with students, and micro-modeling within lessons. When the teacher and Associate work together to co-deliver the lesson, the lesson is co-planned to ensure the roles are clear, learning targets are defined, and both understand how the lesson is crafted.

One teacher reflected on the impact of co-planning. "My Associate was literally my rock." The teacher went on to explain the cadence of their weekly interactions:

We would co-plan and reflect. We'd take my goal each week and focus on planning that week. We did a little bit of co-teaching, but I found that I liked [my Associate] to co-plan with me so that I could attain my goals. Otherwise, I was noticing that I would go week after week after week and still have the same goal because I hadn't taken any specific action steps to get there. It really helped me. We would take an hour to reflect and then plan the next action steps.

Co-planning and co-teaching were powerful supports for fostering a growth mindset. Reflective conversations showcased how Associates demonstrated care through interactions, time, and guidance.

Problem-Solving Classroom Management Concerns and Managing Individual Behaviors

Mentors and coaches serve as thinking partners to create a caring environment that promotes a growth mindset, especially when beginning teachers encounter classroom and behavior management concerns. Teachers and CADRE Associates analyzed whole-class needs, such as routines and procedures, targeted management problems, transitions, and the creation of reinforcement systems and/or student motivation lists. Additionally, Associates and beginning teachers problem-solved how to manage individual behaviors, such as taking a break with a student, processing through systems of support, helping students stay on task, or planning for an intervention. Teachers appreciated support in these areas and Associates noticed their growth. Whereas teachers saw the support as an act of care, Associates saw a relationship between a growth mindset and teacher resilience. As one Associate stated, "They have both overcome the most challenging days with negative student behaviors with grace and dignity. They stayed positive and came back the next day. They have stayed calm under high pressure and have been very professional in how they handle themselves."

Another Associate spoke to teacher resilience in learning to deal with difficult behaviors when she said,

I have seen [my teacher] morph into this excellent teacher dealing with very extreme behaviors! She is calm at all times and has great words she uses to de-escalate students. I have also seen her develop those relationships that have helped ... I do not think either of my teachers expected these behaviors or expected that they would be so great in dealing with them!

The teacher affirmed, "My Associate assured me that what I was experiencing with behaviors was not my fault. She was the only other person seeing them as frequently and intensely as I was. She helped me take breaks for myself, too." Another teacher expressed, "Hearing others in the cohort were struggling at certain times helped me feel better when I was struggling, too." Collaborative problem-solving promoted teachers' growth in their abilities to manage the classroom and address behavior in a caring and positive manner.

Analyzing Student Performance/Data

Teachers enter the first years of teaching with varied experiences and levels of comfort with data analysis. As Associates and beginning teachers shared their reflections, we noted teachers found value in discussing student work/outcomes in relation to performance, using video to identify outcomes and needs, engaging in scoring calibration for formative/summative assessments (especially in writing), and receiving guidance in analyzing various forms of data (e.g., formative, summative, district assessments).

Associates and teachers collaborated to organize, analyze, and reflect on the data. A teacher shared that one Associate "helped me create a lot of pretests for math, and we'd make an item analysis for every topic ... getting to reflect over student data was helpful ... Just having her support - telling me no, you're doing the right thing." Another teacher commented,

> Analyzing data was huge. Not only collecting the data, but we would literally sit down at my table, open the reports, highlight, and go through specific skills. I don't think I would have even thought to do that if I didn't have her organizing it that way.

Collecting Evidence through Observation

Mentors and coaches typically observe beginning teachers, which is an essential part of their support. Associates collected evidence of beginning teachers' growth through observations, which included multiple coaching and mentoring tools. This allowed teachers and Associates time to reflect on what was happening, why it was happening, and set goals for the future. One teacher described what the process looked like for them:

> We did a lot [with evidence]. She would just do running observation notes, and I found that really helpful. She would take a lot of pictures and videos ... I think she knew I would take the time to go through those notes.

Another teacher expressed, "I think what pushed me to grow the most was when she and I would reflect afterwards ... talk about lessons and what had gone well that week or what had gone wrong." Observation with evidence can also be ongoing: "My Associate always checks in on me and my day. She let me express my stress or concerns, but would quickly move me toward a solution focused conversation."

Observation data and reflective conversations promoted a growth mindset and resilience. Through these interactions, teachers noted they felt cared for as their Associates took a specific interest in their well-being by genuinely asking how they were doing and using questioning to help teachers reflect on their practice.

Building a Professional Reputation and Navigating the School Culture

Navigating school culture and helping new teachers feel welcome is essential to their success, yet beginning teachers may find it difficult to join a new professional culture. This transition from student to teacher can cause new teachers to put a lot of pressure on themselves. Sometimes, someone reminding them they are good enough and helping them celebrate small successes they may not see is all they need. As one teacher said,

> It's like you're proving yourself to your district, to your principal, to your colleagues, to your team, and to your students. It puts a lot of pressure on you. I've been very fortunate to realize that I just have to be me.

Another teacher phrased it like this: "I saw myself grow a lot this year professionally. I think my confidence in myself grew because of CADRE Project and it really made me feel good about myself." A sentiment echoed by multiple teachers was noting their Associate was a rock for them: "She supported me in being the best teacher I could and helped me focus on things I was doing right rather than wrong."

Associates also provided guidance to support teachers in navigating the nuances of school culture, such as communicating with the principal or other leadership, engaging with dynamic teams, and interacting with families and other professionals. Teachers found that reinforcement and modeling were all they needed at times. Associates became a sounding board from which to work through concerns and needs, and address difficulties. This form of caring promoted positive outcomes and demonstrated care for the teachers' progress and development.

General Tasks and Supporting Social-Emotional Needs

General tasks include anything that is done to support productivity and organization or things that take an Associate away from students. For example, tasks may be making copies, creating bulletin boards, finding resources, entering grades, or preparing lesson materials. At times, these tasks support the social-emotional needs of the teacher. Social-emotional support creates a safe space for teachers to express themselves and share their feelings without fear of judgment. For Associates, this includes being a "tear catcher" and listening to overwhelming feelings, showing empathy with statements such as, "I know this is hard," or providing positive reinforcement.

One teacher remarked, "My Associate was constantly encouraging me to set boundaries in order to spend time doing things that were enjoyable to me." Another teacher explained,

60 Amanda Steiner et al.

I liked that [my Associate] did not look at things from a math teacher point of view. This helped me see things I don't see. I don't think I would have made it through if I did not have the emotional support. I'm a human, and I'm not going to be perfect. I'm a first-year teacher. I just need support as another adult human that makes mistakes, and that's what helped me survive.

Teachers also noted the importance of being part of a cohort and how this provided additional social-emotional support. One teacher stated, "The cohort was a daily reminder that I was not going through this alone … so it helped to feel like we were all in this together."

When individuals feel cared for, they are better able to cope with challenges and setbacks. An Associate commented on the growth seen in two teachers:

Interestingly, both of my teachers struggled with self-affirmation and acknowledging successes. Recently, they both are more apt to name what they are doing well and identify areas of opportunity and growth … Through a growth mindset, not a deficit model. The level of flexibility and professional inquiry to grow is always astounding. Teachers are incredible at what they do and are excelling exponentially as a result of the program and its support.

Implications and Conclusions

Induction is one approach to developing resilience and a growth mindset in beginning teachers. In the absence of a structured induction program, the authors suggest considering high-intensity induction practices to demonstrate care, foster a growth mindset, and build resilience in teachers to mitigate attrition. Although we recognize that the CADRE Project has been in existence for more than 25 years and includes release time for Associates, many induction practices can be implemented with minimal cost by creating a culture of care and providing opportunities to network and collaborate with other educators. In situations where mentors/coaches are available, high-intensity induction practices can take a variety of forms, such as co-planning, co-teaching, observation, modeling effective teaching practices, analyzing student data, and engaging in reflective dialogue. These interactions can support teachers in feeling cared for and supported as they enter the profession and begin working in schools.

Creating a culture where individuals feel valued, seen, and supported is essential to beginning teachers growing in their resilience. We suggest mentors/coaches assist in creating a culture of care by beginning the year with building relationships with teachers and connecting them to resources and support networks. A foundation for creating a culture of care is building trust between the mentor/coach and the beginning teacher. Mentors/coaches should be intentional at the beginning of the school year in engaging in conversations to get to know beginning teachers as individuals and as educators. Teachers also need opportunities to connect with other educators. Teachers find it powerful to network with beginning teachers who are experiencing similar feelings, emotions, and challenges. Additionally, networks of support provide opportunities for teachers to mentor/coach each other by sharing ideas, teaching strategies, and celebrating each other's successes. Opportunities for collaboration create a symbiotic relationship for beginning teachers.

Establishing a culture of care works best through mentoring/coaching. Mentoring/coaching can help beginning teachers navigate initial teaching experiences, reflect on their practice, and approach challenges with a solution-based lens. The care and support of a mentor/coach can help foster resilience and meet the social-emotional needs of the beginning teacher. To foster a growth mindset and help teachers persevere in the face of challenges, provide collaborative opportunities for mentors/coaches to co-plan or co-teach with beginning teachers. These opportunities allow for each party to learn with and from each other. Co-planning and co-teaching encourage reflective conversations with caring dialogue. Through conversation, beginning teachers can examine the realities of their teaching and set goals for growth. Additionally, mentors/coaches provide support to beginning teachers by serving as thought partners, cheerleaders, and connectors. Mentors/coaches assist in developing a growth mindset by helping teachers determine action steps that align with their goals.

Care can take many forms, including emotional support, encouragement, and practical assistance. Creating a culture of care, connecting beginning teachers with mentoring/coaching support, and providing opportunities to network and collaborate with other educators can help foster resilience and meet social-emotional needs, while a growth mindset can help teachers persevere in the face of challenges. The success of implementing high-intensity practices is dependent upon dedicated time to allow mentors/coaches and beginning teachers to collaborate. Additionally, mentors/coaches must consider support structures and practices they can offer to develop a caring relationship, promote growth, and build resilience in teachers.

References

Aguilar, E. (2013). *The art of coaching: Effective strategies for school transformation.* Wiley.

Bell, J., Wilcoxen, C., & Steiner, A. (2021). Teacher induction that works: Empowering, retaining, and developing teacher leaders. In B. S. Zugelder (Ed.), *Empowering formal and informal leadership while maintaining teacher identity* (pp.227–257). IGI Global.

Bell, J., Wilcoxen, C., & Steiner, A. (2022). Mentoring and coaching through induction to develop reflective practices in beginning teachers. *The New Educator, 18*(4), 281–305.

Bradbury, L. U. (2022). Recent trends in science education research on mentoring preservice teachers. In J.A. Luft & M.G. Jones, *Handbook of Research on Science Teacher Education,* (pp.132–144). Routlage.

Collie, R. J., Shapka, J. D., Perry, N., & Martin. (2015). Teacher well-being: Exploring its components and a practice-oriented scale. *Journal of Psychoeducational Assessment, 33*(8), 744–756.

Daniilidou, A., Platsidou, M., & Gonida, S-E. (2020). Primary school teachers' resilience: Association with teacher self-efficacy, burnout, and stress. *Electronic Journal of Research in Educational Psychology, 18*(3), 549–582.

Desrumaux, P., Lapointe, D., Ntsame Sima, M., Boudrais, J. S., Savoie, A., & Brunet, L. (2015) The impact of work demands, climate, and optimism on wellbeing and distress at work: What are the mediating effects of basic psychological need satisfaction? *European Review of Applied Psychology, 65*(1), 179–188.

Dishena, R., & Mokoena, S. (2016). Novice teachers' experiences of induction in selected primary schools in Namibia. *Eurasian Journal of Educational Research, 66,* 335–354.

Eadie, P., Levickis, P., Murray, L., Page, J., Elek, C., & Church, A. (2021). Early childhood educators' wellbeing during the COVID-19 pandemic. *Early Childhood Education Journal, 49,* 903–913.

Feiman-Nemser, S. (2001). Helping novices learn to teach. *Journal of Teacher Education, 52*(1), 17–30. https://doi.org/10.1177/0022487101052001003

Frondozo, King, R. B., Nalipay, M. J. N., & Mordeno, I. G. (2022). Mindsets matter for teachers, too: Growth mindset about teaching ability predicts teachers' enjoyment and engagement. *Current Psychology, 41*(8), 5030–5033. 10.1007/s12144-020-01008-4

Guenther, A. R. (2021). "It should be helping me improve, not telling me I'm a bad teacher": The influence of accountability-focused evaluations on teachers' professional identities. *Teaching and Teacher Education, 108*, Article 103511. 10.1016/j.tate.2021.103511

Helmke, S. (2022). Encourage a growth mindset in teachers. *The Learning Professional, 41*(4), 12–14.

Heynoski, K., Douglas-McNab, E., Khandaker, N., Tamang, T., & Howell, E. (2022). *Shortage to surplus: 5 shifts to address the national educator shortage.* American Association of School Personnel Administrators. https://www.aaspa.org/national-educator-shortage

Houwer, R. (2011). Learning freedom: The pedagogical potential of crisis. *Journal for Activism in Science and Technology Education, 3*(1), 109–117.

Knight, J. (2021). *The definitive guide to instructional coaching: Seven factors for success.* ASCD.

Kraft, M. A., Simon, N. S., & Arnold Lyon, M. (2020). Sustaining a sense of success: The importance of teacher working conditions during the COVID-19 pandemic. (EdWorkingPaper: 20-279). Annenberg Institute at Brown University. 10.26300/35nj-v890

Nalipay, M. J. N., King, R. B., Mordeno, I. G., & Wang, H. (2022). Are good teachers born or made? Teachers who hold a growth mindset about their teaching ability have better well-being. *Educational Psychology, 42*(1), 23–41.

Netolicky, D. M. (2016). Coaching for professional growth in one Australian school: "Oil in water." *International Journal of Mentoring and Coaching in Education, 5*(2), 66–86.

Noddings, N. (2005). What does it mean to educate the whole child? *Educational Leadership, 63*(1), 8–13.

Noddings, N. (2012). The caring relation in teaching. *Oxford Review of Education, 38*(6), 771–781.

Noddings, N. (2013). *Caring.* University of California Press.

Olson Stewart, K., Rotherham-Fuller, E., & Liou, D. (2021). Beginning teacher support model: Elementary teachers' resilience and retention in Arizona. *International Journal of Modern Education Studies, 5*(1), 49–74.

Ronfeldt, M., & McQueen, K. (2017). Does new teacher induction really improve retention? *Journal of Teacher Education, 68*(4), 394–410.

Shoffner, M., & Webb, A. W. (2022). Introduction: Care after COVID: Moving forward as caring teacher educators. In M. Shoffner & A. W. Webb (Eds.), *Reconstructing care in teacher education after COVID-19: Caring enough to change* (pp. 1–12). Routledge.

Skaalvik, E. M., & Skaalvik, S. (2018). Job demands and job resources as predictors of teacher motivation and well-being. *School Psychology of Education, 21*, 1251–1275.

Steiner, A., Bell, J., & Wilcoxen, C. (2022). Mentoring blended with coaching: A recipe for teacher growth. *Delta Kappa Gamma Bulletin, 88*(3), 27–34.

Steiner, A., Wilcoxen, C., & Bell, J. (2021). The CADRE Project: Developing high-quality connections among teachers for over 25 years. *The Chronicle of Mentoring & Coaching, 1*(13), 521–525.

Wilcoxen, C., Bell, J., & Steiner, A. (2020). Empowerment through induction: Supporting the well-being of beginning teachers. *International Journal of Mentoring and Coaching in Education, 9*(1), 52–70.

Wilcoxen, C., Steiner, A. & Bell, J. (2022). New teachers thrive with induction support through the phases of a first-year teacher. In B. S. Zugelder & M. L'Esperance (Eds.), *Handbook of research on the educator continuum and development of teachers* (pp. 289–312). IGI Global.

Yu, X., Wang, P., Zhai, X., Dai, H., & Yang, Q. (2015). The effect of work stress on job burnout among teachers: The mediating role of self-efficacy. *Social Indicators Research, 122*(3), 701–708. 10.1007/s11205-014-0716-5

PART II

CARE THROUGH MENTORSHIP AND FORMAL INDUCTION

6

NEW BEGINNINGS

Making Connections and Navigating Transitions for Enacting Care in Secondary Mathematics Classrooms

Jennifer A. Wolfe and Elaine Saunders

The COVID-19 pandemic underscored deep disparities within the mathematics teacher education community. This, combined with escalating instances of violence and biased laws against Indigenous, Black, Asian, LGBTQIA+, and immigrant populations, has ignited a pressing call to revisit and reform mathematics teacher preparation. Amidst these adversities and the professional and personal losses, teachers are challenged with enacting caring practices that recognize and address students' lived experiences.

Therefore, as we re-envision mathematics teacher education, it is not just the academic or pedagogical techniques that demand attention; the human connections foundational to effective teaching are equally critical. During the induction phase, the emphasis on fostering genuine relationships is paramount. It's not just about mathematics or pedagogy; it's about seeing and caring for each other as full human beings. Genuine interactions act as bridges, linking mathematics methods coursework with the realities of the classroom and presenting a more complete perspective of teacher preparation and induction. It is through this lens that we can understand how caring practices are adapted and manifested by new teachers in real classroom settings. Assessing these transitions is crucial, helping to determine which changes in teacher preparation have the most tangible impact on the classroom practices of beginning educators.

In this chapter, we highlight the role of an ethic of care in a secondary mathematics classroom through our narrative. We also explore how an induction process, grounded in this ethic of care, supports beginning teachers, especially against the backdrop of the challenges introduced by the COVID-19 pandemic.

Our Positionality

Jennifer (she/her), the first author, is a biracial Asian American cisgender woman, and the proud daughter of a Thai immigrant. As a first-generation college graduate, she has dedicated over 20 years to mathematics teacher education. Elaine (she/her), the second author, wears many hats: a mom, a biracial Korean American, a first-generation college graduate, an esports coach, and a cherished friend. Currently in her first year of teaching,

DOI: 10.4324/9781032707471-9

Elaine has Jennifer, her mathematics methods professor, as an invaluable guiding force and an informal mentor during her teacher induction phase.

This chapter emanates from our shared pedagogical philosophy. We view ourselves as perpetual learners, educators ever evolving. Our collaboration, whether amongst ourselves or with our students, consistently circles back to two introspective questions: 1) How can we collaboratively foster learning communities underpinned by belonging, inclusion, love, and care? and 2) How do we conjointly shape experiences that beckon us to pause, reflecting on our path towards more humanizing, equitable, and just pedagogical actions? (Wolfe, 2021, 2022; Wolfe & Amidon, in-press).

In our exploration of teacher induction, we champion a community-centric approach to teaching and learning, one that draws inspiration from scholars such as hooks (1994). This approach emphasizes the importance of collective endeavors in "creating and sustaining a learning community" (hooks, 1994, p. 8). However, the heart of our endeavor lies in our commitment to care, a concept deeply rooted in the works of Venet (2021), Gay (2018), and Noddings (2002).

Venet's (2021) perspective on *unconditional positive regard* forms the bedrock of our mentorship relationship. An unconditional positive regard entails an unwavering acceptance and respect for one another, irrespective of differences or challenges. It is the essence of fostering a nurturing and inclusive learning environment between mentor and mentee and mentee with their students. Gay's (2018) work extends our understanding of care by emphasizing the importance of *caring for*, not just *caring about*, one another. The distinction is pivotal, as it underscores the significance of actively engaging in actions and behaviors that demonstrate our commitment to the holistic well-being of our teacher induction relationship as well as the mentee teacher's relationship in supporting her students. Noddings' (2002) philosophy of care involves a genuine and reciprocal relationship where both mentor and mentee are attentive to each other's needs. The idea goes beyond surface-level interactions and delves into the profound connections that foster growth and learning for both mentor and mentee.

Incorporating these perspectives into our work not only aligns with our commitment to creating caring learning spaces but also serves as the foundational understanding that underpins our exploration of teacher induction. Care, as defined by Venet (2021), Gay (2018), and Noddings (2002), was the guiding principle as we embarked on this teacher induction mentoring relationship. In the subsequent sections, we illustrate how these concepts of care manifest in practice and why they are essential in supporting beginning teachers through teacher induction.

Mathematics Methods and Mentorship: Elaine's Journey

Entering Jennifer's methods course as a 35-year-old transfer student from the University of Texas-San Antonio and mother of two, I was filled with a mix of anticipation and uncertainty. Being in a new school, in a new state, and among a secondary mathematics cohort nearing the end of their program, I pondered my place within the group. Jennifer eased my worries via a one-on-one video chat at the semester's start that cast the first lifeline. Her genuine warmth, authenticity, and care for my well-being provided an anchoring assurance.

Our initial class focused on group discussions, unearthing deep conversations around our identities. The emphasis was clear: Listening to one another and being present supported a focus on learning from and with one another. This initiation, undergirded by the *Learning to Listen and Listening to Learn* protocols (Wolfe & Safi, 2022), although daunting at first, subtly wove the first threads of camaraderie and care in our cohort.

Under Jennifer's guidance, we engaged in self-exploration through an *archeology of self* (Mentor & Sealey-Ruiz, 2021), unearthing the intricate connections between our own identities and our future roles as teachers. This introspective journey illuminated the mosaic of student identities, underscoring the imperative to respect and embrace this diversity in our impending classrooms. This formative experience recalibrated my teaching philosophy, prompting critical introspection. Was I prioritizing the well-being and identities of my students over the curriculum's rigidity? It also crystallized a conviction: Teaching transcended mere content delivery, encompassing a holistic emphasis on student identity and well-being.

This exploration became a guiding framework for my teaching practice, igniting deep reflection on the equity and inclusivity of my instructional choices. Are my practices equitable? Will they benefit every student in the class? Am I inadvertently perpetuating inequities? Above all, I contemplated how I wanted my students to feel within the walls of my classroom. This introspection led to a powerful realization that, while mathematics holds importance, the well-being and identities of my students must take precedence over rigid adherence to a predetermined curriculum pacing calendar. Investing significant time in understanding the role of identities in mathematics teaching and learning highlighted the fundamental belief that the personal growth and development of my students are of utmost importance. The exploration of identity solidified my understanding that fostering a safe and inclusive learning environment, where students can authentically express themselves, lies at the heart of impactful mathematics education. This transformative perspective shifted my focus, reinforcing the notion that teaching mathematics encompasses far more than the mere transmission of content. It embraces a holistic approach, centering student well-being and affirming their unique identities in every aspect of their learning journey.

Throughout this methods course, Jennifer's embodiment of unconditional positive regard became a model for how I envisioned what I wanted my teaching to sound and feel like for my students. Her adaptability, effort to spotlight our mental well-being, and leeway to reflect, revise, and grow were a testament to the spirit of mentorship and underscored the essence of care in pedagogy.

One example of Jennifer's humanizing and caring approach was her policy for submitting assignments past the due date. She would always grant extensions, accompanied by a heartfelt statement:

> Of course, you can have an extension. Please take the time you need to turn in work that you would feel proud to submit. It's important to allow yourself the necessary time so that I can provide you with timely, educative, and constructive feedback that will support you on your journey to becoming a reflective and thoughtful teacher.

Furthermore, she always gave us opportunities to revise and resubmit our work, prompting us to then reflect on how the revision process helped us grow and learn. I appreciated this as it was in alignment with a rough draft approach to learning mathematics (Jansen, 2020); revising is part of the process, and our in-progress ideas are valued.

Through her teaching approach, Jennifer validated that understanding and growth take time, happen through reflection and revision, and take precedence over strict adherence to timelines or inequitable grading practices. This perspective, deeply rooted in the principles of care as framed by Venet (2021), Gay (2018), and Noddings (2002), led me to reflect on the policies I may or may not want to adopt in my own classroom, prompting me to question their purpose: Are they primarily aimed at fostering compliance or do they genuinely support student learning? Jennifer's teaching approach sparked a critical examination of school-wide practices and policies, particularly in terms of how they contribute to or challenge systemic inequities. It empowered me to consider how to leverage my power, privilege, and sphere of influence as a new teacher to create classroom-level changes that disrupt the intentional harm historically and presently marginalized students often face.

When we engaged in mathematics lessons in our methods course, I had the unique opportunity to experience them as both a student and a future teacher. As a student, I found myself comfortable sharing my ideas and appreciated the impact of hearing my peers' initial thoughts. This experience was unlike any I had in a math class before—it was collaborative, uplifting, safe, and filled with joy. It was at this moment that I realized my aspiration: to create a learning environment where my future students could feel this way as frequently as possible. This realization instilled in me a profound sense of responsibility. I am committed to fostering a space where students feel safe, cared for, and free to share their initial ideas, embracing their true selves without fear of judgment based on their perceived math abilities.

Teacher Induction: Building Our Collaborative Partnership

The teacher induction process is traditionally marked by clear mentor-mentee roles. In our collaborative partnership, we ventured to transform this paradigm, challenging conventional power dynamics, and emphasizing genuine interpersonal connections. Building trusting relationships and community is a deliberate and gradual process consisting of small, everyday moments that pave the way for meaningful connections. True relationship building doesn't happen during scripted or contrived activities but rather through the genuine interactions that occur naturally between people. These often-imperceptible moments may seem insignificant but they accumulate over time and become the building blocks of relationships characterized by trust, understanding, and empathy.

Enactments of Care: Detour Conversations

While our discussions spanned from light-hearted TV show chats to culinary adventures, these "detour conversations" laid the groundwork for a deep bond. Not just distractions, they served as connectors, bridging personal interests with our shared passion for educating students. These seemingly casual talks often circled back to classroom practices, enriching our professional dialogue. This ability to comfortably switch between personal and professional topics fostered a fluidity that became the hallmark of our collaborative partnership. We discovered these tangents added richness to our discussions about pedagogy and caring classroom practices. They provided informal spaces for us to share anecdotes, reflect on our own experiences, and find inspiration to explore innovative teaching strategies grounded in an ethic of care and mutual respect. Such interactions are often missing from standard teacher induction programs, yet they hold the potential to create more effective and empathetic educators.

Intentionally Shifting Power Dynamics

Despite the typical challenges of mentor-mentee dynamics, our close age range proved to be a distinctive asset. It softened traditional power dynamics, seamlessly blending both friendship and mentorship. This nuanced relationship nurtured a bond built on trust and vulnerability, setting it apart from conventional hierarchical mentor-mentee induction models.

In the classroom, Jennifer's role transcended that of a mere observer. As a collaborative partner and mentor, we adopted a transformative approach to teaching and learning, rooted in the principles of care that are essential for effective teacher induction. In our co-teaching approach, we implemented a unique strategy. Elaine took the lead in planning content-driven lessons, drawing from her expertise, while Jennifer focused on designing team-building and group-worthy tasks that fostered a caring and inclusive learning environment. When we implemented these lessons, Elaine would typically launch the lesson but the dynamic shifted as both of us fully engaged with the students, guiding the lesson together.

Jennifer's role transcended traditional observation; she actively engaged with diverse student groups, modeling effective teaching strategies and fostering student engagement. As a mentee in the early stages of her teaching journey, Elaine closely observed Jennifer's interactions, swiftly adopting similar strategies. This real-time feedback loop allowed us to adapt our teaching methods to meet the evolving needs of each student group, all while placing a strong emphasis on the principles of care, a cornerstone of effective teacher induction.

By actively listening to our students' mathematical ideas and building upon them, Jennifer not only exemplified active caring strategies but also demonstrated how such approaches can be integral to the mentorship process. Her guidance was instrumental in nurturing an inclusive learning environment that prioritized the well-being and growth of each student. This practice of unconditional positive regard for students' learning and well-being, instilled through mentorship, is a vital aspect of teacher induction that we believe should be central to the development of caring educators.

This hands-on collaborative teaching approach starkly contrasts with the traditional model, where one teaches while the other passively observes. Much of Elaine's induction experience was within a traditional observer-only model, which she felt inadvertently established a performative environment. Under this setup, she felt under a microscope, as if every instructional decision and move would be scrutinized and judged, making it difficult to be her true teaching self. The resultant atmosphere leaned less towards open exploration and more towards showcasing knowledge.

Our approach facilitated immediate dialogue, fostering adjustments during live teaching sessions and emphasizing teamwork. This shift from individual-centric views to collective goals emphasized the creation of an environment where students felt nurtured and supported. The post-lesson debriefs reflected this collective approach. As co-participants in the teaching process, our discussions revolved around shared experiences rather than isolated observations. This dynamic encouraged mutual ownership over teaching outcomes, prioritizing the students' collective learning journey over individual performance metrics.

Ultimately, our emphasis wasn't on how Elaine performed on any given day but on our joint aspiration of nurturing a sense of community and care within students' mathematical learning. Such a partnership, built on mutual collaboration, paves the way for more enriching classroom experiences, moving beyond traditional assessment-centric models.

Teaching is about embodying our beliefs. If we advocate for a caring and collaborative learning atmosphere, then why shouldn't we exemplify a hands-on mentor/mentee teaching approach? As experienced by Elaine, the observer-only model can inadvertently emphasize correctness over shared understanding, potentially stifling students' willingness to express unfinished thoughts. An unengaged observer can cast a shadow of mistrust, discouraging students from venturing out of their comfort zones. Collaborating, however, showcased the richness of learning through shared dialogue and mutual involvement.

In the context of teacher induction, mentors—whether they are formal administrators, instructional coaches, department mentors, or school mentors—play a pivotal role. Limiting their roles to mere observation misses an opportunity to engage with students across diverse contexts. This limits their understanding of students' skills, behaviors, and unique perspectives, and restricts students' opportunities to assert their expertise. This interaction holds particular significance for mentors who may not specialize in subjects like mathematics. Immersing themselves in students' learning processes allows them to dismantle biases and genuinely appreciate students' capabilities. Elaine found it difficult to fully embrace educative and constructive feedback from mentors who relegated their role to just merely observing her classroom teaching, as they did not fully interact with her students.

Teacher induction aims to seamlessly integrate teacher education with classroom realities by infusing mutual respect, open dialogue, and joint teaching experiences. The future of teacher induction lies in re-envisioning partnerships centered on an ethic of care. As illustrated in our mentor/mentee partnership, emphasizing genuine connections, shared responsibility, and balanced power dynamics fosters an environment conducive to mutual growth. As educators, our duty extends beyond our students to uplift one another, ensuring the shift from training to teaching is underpinned by an unwavering commitment to care, support, collaboration, and shared growth.

From Methods to Classroom: Fostering Care through the Mentor-Mentee Induction Dynamic

Jennifer's presence in Elaine's journey was pivotal. Our mentor-mentee relationship was more than just guidance; it was a dynamic partnership that fused experience with innovation, and theory with practice. Jennifer's teachings from the methods class instilled in Elaine the power of collaboration but it was our constant dialogue, mutual feedback, and shared vision that transformed these teachings into actionable classroom strategies.

At the start of the teacher induction journey, we worked together to develop a framework for the first few weeks of school that centered on building a sense of community and establishing a caring and inclusive classroom culture. We discussed various strategies and activities that would help create a positive and supportive learning environment from the very beginning. We wanted Elaine's students to experience a sense of belonging in the classroom and to feel that their voices were valued and respected. We sought to highlight the significance of embracing curiosity, rather than judgment, when it comes to approaching mathematics and each other. This approach fosters open communication in the classroom, encouraging students to actively listen, ask questions, and offer constructive feedback to one another. By fostering a culture of open communication, we aimed to cultivate an environment where students felt comfortable sharing rough draft ideas and engaging in meaningful discussions.

Setting the Groundwork: Co-Created Community Agreements

Taking a page out of bell hooks' (1994) philosophy, we embarked on a reflective journey in how Elaine would co-create community agreements with her students. This wasn't a top-down imposition of rules; it was a democratic, collective voice shaping the classroom's ethos. Students weren't passive recipients; they were active contributors, laying the foundations for a classroom culture rooted in mutual respect, understanding, and shared responsibility. Elaine facilitated the co-construction of community agreements, akin to her experience in the methods course (see Wolfe, 2022; Wolfe & Amidon, in-press). Throughout the process, she documented students' ideas, actively involving them in a collaborative rough drafting and revision journey. She continually encouraged students to contemplate the implications of the proposed agreements, fleshing out what they would entail in practice, both in terms of sound and action.

Co-creating community agreements signals our intent to collaboratively shape a space where everyone's needs can be met while also acknowledging the collective responsibility we hold for each other's learning. Elaine's first-hand experience of this approach during her methods course was impactful, showcasing how to draw upon students' previous mathematical learning experiences, incorporate revision and rough drafting into the learning process, and attentively shift power dynamics, enabling students to take the lead in shaping the classroom experience they wanted.

Advocacy and Care

Care extends beyond merely fostering academic growth. It encompasses the whole of a student's experience, incorporating their emotional and personal well-being as well. This holistic conception of care was not an abstract ideal; rather it was a reality that Elaine had witnessed first-hand in her methods class. Jennifer modeled an ethic of care that was grounded in honesty, transparency, accountability, and advocacy. She did not shy away when she made a mistake and, importantly, she showed how to apologize and take steps to prevent further harm. Jennifer shared experiences such as what to do when you unintentionally cause harm, for example, misgendering a student. She prompted us to acknowledge and deeply examine the distinction between one's intention and the real impact of the action taken. She also had us critically reflect on considerations for holding space and explicitly engaging in conversations around traumatic events in the community. She didn't just lead these discussions; she provided space for deep reflection on the potential impact of these events on students. She emphasized the need to consider the possible emotional and psychological effects and that when we choose not to address such events, our silence is complicity. This approach deeply resonated with Elaine, reinforcing the idea that care in teaching requires acknowledging students' humanity, their lived experiences both inside and outside the classroom, and holding space for challenging conversations for students' overall well-being.

Example of Impact versus Intent in Classroom Practice

Elaine found herself at a crossroads when her commitment to creating a safe and caring classroom environment was put to the test. During her sixth period class, she learned of a grenade threat and subsequent lockdown at a nearby high school, not through an official channel but via a student's Snapchat post. With no word from the administration to validate or refute the information, Elaine made a choice: to continue class as usual. When the threat and lockdown were confirmed after school—a situation thankfully resolved without physical harm—Elaine reflected deeply on her decision. It began to gnaw at her conscience, feeling more and more like a misstep from the path of care she was committed to treading. In this moment of introspection, she reached out to Jennifer, sharing her experience, the decision she had made, and her intent to apologize to her students. Jennifer, drawing from her personal experiences, such as her own reactions during 9/11, empathetically supported Elaine. She assured Elaine that her students would appreciate the transparency, displaying unconditional positive regard towards her. Even in the face of Elaine's perceived failure, Jennifer responded with understanding and trust, reinforcing her belief in Elaine's capacity to learn and grow from the experience.

Guided by Jennifer's support, Elaine addressed the situation head-on the next day. She created space for each class to discuss their feelings about the incident, acknowledging that many of her students had connections to the affected school. When the sixth period came around, she offered a sincere apology. She expressed regret for possibly exacerbating their stress and made a promise to prioritize their well-being over routine in future situations. Through these actions, Elaine demonstrated unconditional positive regard towards her students, showing them that her care extended beyond the confines of 'normal' situations.

This reflection and subsequent action highlight the substantial influence of Jennifer's lessons on honesty and transparency in her methods course and induction mentorship. It was through these modeling and induction conversations that Elaine learned to reflect intentionally on her actions and to hold space for her students. It emphasized the importance of acknowledging mistakes and learning from them, a principle Elaine came to recognize as "know better, do better." This experience served as a real-world application of the distinction between intention and impact, solidifying Elaine's commitment to fostering an environment where unconditional positive regard is the norm, not the exception.

Example of Advocacy in Classroom Practice

The process of reflection and self-examination following the grenade threat incident led Elaine to a deeper understanding of her role as an educator. She began to critically analyze her practices from an equity lens, asking herself questions: Are my practices equitable? Are they beneficial to every student in the class? Am I unknowingly perpetuating inequities? Over time, these introspective questions evolved into a proactive mindset: How can I make my practices more equitable? How can I ensure that my choices are beneficial to all students? How can I combat the inequities that I observe impacting my students? These reflective prompts centering care and responding to injustices are ones that are always at the forefront of our conversations and further support a reshaping of the traditional teacher induction mentor-mentee dynamic.

This transformation of thought motivated Elaine to leverage her position, power, and privilege to advocate for her students. A case in point was her response to students being placed in ACE (Alternative Classroom Experience or in-school suspension). Recognizing that these students were not only missing out on learning experiences but also that their peers were being deprived of their valuable contributions, Elaine lobbied for them to be allowed back into her class. She maintained the belief that, regardless of any behavioral issues or disciplinary action taken against them, these students had valuable thoughts and ideas to contribute and that their presence enriched the class.

A specific instance that highlighted Elaine's advocacy was her interaction with a student, Miguel (pseudonym), a kind, genuine, and creative spirit. Unfortunately, not everyone witnessed his talents as various carceral school policies and practices had Miguel frequently in and out of ACE. Most teachers had arguably given up on Miguel, as he had missed too many classes, and the invitations his teachers extended to come to extra tutoring hours were often unanswered. He was someone Elaine recognized for his potential and contributions to the class. Elaine worked alongside Miguel to help him catch up in her course; it was clear that Miguel felt lost as he was sent constant messages of "you are too far behind." Elaine, however, enacted an unconditional positive regard for Miguel, highlighting all the contributions he had made to class, recognizing that he was actively working to catch up and, together, they negotiated a manageable path forward where Miguel was not only learning mathematics but also building confidence in collaborating with his peers. Miguel's remarkable dedication and hard work became evident, to the extent that Elaine considered nominating him for the "student of the month" award.

Her actions showed not only her acknowledgment of Miguel's capabilities and contributions but also her dedication to challenging systemic issues that resulted in marginalized students of color, like Miguel, being underrepresented and overlooked. Elaine's efforts to include students placed in ACE and her intention to nominate Miguel affirmed the ethic of care she had adopted, displaying her commitment to not just teach her students but also to listen, understand, and advocate for them. This approach embodied a fusion of care, respect, and advocacy, championing a truly inclusive and equitable learning environment.

Through their induction relationship, Elaine took from Jennifer the idea that true care extends beyond academic guidance. It is about recognizing the students' holistic experiences, both within and outside the classroom walls. When faced with the challenge of the grenade threat, the difference between intention and impact became vividly clear. Elaine's reflection and subsequent actions, supported by Jennifer's empathetic guidance, reinforced the ethos of genuine care. It was not about merely addressing academic gaps but understanding and advocating for the emotional and psychological well-being of every student. Elaine's advocacy did not stop there, however. In her stance against punitive policies, Elaine showcased the depth of her care, ensuring that every student, irrespective of their past, felt seen, heard, and valued. Under the collaborative mentorship of Jennifer, Elaine transformed challenges into learning experiences, creating an inclusive environment that celebrated every student's uniqueness. Their partnership is a testament to the transformative power of shared vision and unwavering commitment, championing an educational ethos where every student felt truly at home.

Concluding Thoughts

In our shared journey of induction, the intricacies of establishing and nurturing caring communities within mathematics education emerge distinctly. Observations of a secondary mathematics teacher bridging the gap between theoretical coursework and the tactile challenges of the classroom emphasize the transformative nature of care in practice. Mentorship during induction should be a dynamic interplay of trust and collaboration as well as a profound commitment to collective learning and well-being. To this end, we share the following recommendations that were central to the success of our mentor-mentee relationship.

- **View the mentor/mentee relationship as a true partnership:** Emphasize the importance of a dynamic and collaborative mentor/mentee relationship that goes beyond traditional observation.
- **Shift from caring about to caring for:** Encourage mentors and mentees to transition from simply caring about each other to genuinely caring for each other, fostering a sense of community within the partnership.
- **Empower mentees as agents of change:** Inspire mentees to leverage their power, privilege, and influence as teachers to create classroom-level changes that disrupt historical and present harms marginalized students often face. Encourage them to advocate for equitable practices within their educational institutions.
- **Promote continuous communication:** Stress the significance of ongoing communication and feedback between mentors and mentees. Encourage open dialogue where both parties can express their needs, concerns, and aspirations.
- **Prioritize well-being:** Remind mentors and mentees to prioritize the mental and emotional well-being of themselves and their students. A care-centered mentorship should consider the holistic development of both educators and learners.
- **Model caring behavior:** Encourage mentors to model caring behavior in their interactions with mentees. Actions such as active listening, empathy, and support can set the tone for a nurturing mentor-mentee relationship.

The COVID-19 pandemic and contemporary societal challenges magnify the urgency of placing care, as defined by scholars like Gay (2018), Noddings (2002), and Venet (2021) at the heart of our teaching methodologies, especially within the realm of teacher induction. As we navigate these demanding terrains, it becomes paramount to reflect on and evaluate our pedagogical choices and their repercussions on student experiences, as well as the growth of novice teachers. For educators striving to create truly inclusive, equitable, and just classrooms, it's essential that our actions transcend mere articulation of care to authentically demonstrating it. Through the insights and practices shared in this chapter, we hope to embolden educators in their quest to incarnate an ethic of care in mathematics and beyond. By embodying the synergy of our mentor-mentee collaboration, we advocate for a departure from the superficiality of observation-only induction models. Our aspiration is to foster an educational community underpinned by trust, mutual reliance, and collective triumph.

References

Gay, G. (2018). *Culturally responsive teaching: Theory, research, and practice (3rd ed.).* Teacher College Press.

hooks, b. (1994). *Teaching to transgress: Education as the practices of freedom.* Routledge.

Jansen, A. (2020). *Rough draft math: Revising to learn.* Stenhouse.

Mentor, M. & Sealey-Ruiz, Y. (2021). Doing the deep work of anti-racist pedagogy: Toward self-excavation for equitable classroom teaching. *Language Arts, 99*(1), 19–24.

Noddings, N. (2002). *Educating moral people: A caring alternative to character education.* Teachers College Press.

Venet, A. S. (2021). *Equity-centered trauma informed education.* Norton.

Wolfe, J. A. (2021). A journey in becoming. *Mathematics Teacher: Learning and Teaching PK-12, 3*(114), 104–114. 10.5951/MTLT.2020.0378

Wolfe, J. A. (2022). Building caring communities in math methods: COVID and classrooms in teacher education. In M. Shoffner, & A. Webb (Eds.), *Care after COVID: Reconstructing understanding of care in teacher education* (pp. 104–114). Routledge.

Wolfe, J. A., & Amidon, J. (in press). Centering community care & love in the preparation of prospective secondary teachers: A collective responsibility approach to mathematics teaching and learning. In C. Koestler & E. Thanheiser (Eds.), *Building community to center equity and justice in mathematics teacher education.* Association of Mathematics Teacher Educators.

Wolfe, J. A., & Safi, F. (2022). Lesson 7.3 majority and power. In B. Conway, L. Id-Deen, M. C. Raygoza, A. Ruiz, J. W. Staley, & E. Thanheiser (Eds.), *Middle school mathematics lessons to explore, understand, and respond to social injustice* (pp. 141–151). Corwin.

7

EXTINGUISHING THE FLAME OF BURNOUT

Mentorship and Care to Support Teacher Induction

Crystal L. Beach and Leigh Anne Turner

Today, a mass exodus from the teaching profession continues to remind us that there is much work to be done in supporting teachers (GaDOE, 2022; Walker, 2018; Will, 2019). We acknowledge the support we give our students 180+ days of the year, and we believe that teachers should have that same support. Specifically, we recognize the significance of supporting induction teachers in order to support, retain, and professionally grow the next generation of people dedicated to leading public education and the young people they serve. This chapter provides a dialogue between a mentor teacher and a mentee teacher to share with readers the ways in which strong mentorship and a genuine focus on care can support teacher induction.

Crystal is a veteran secondary English language arts (ELA) teacher who has taught in both metropolitan and rural school districts. A former collegiate athlete, Crystal has also coached many young women over the years in a variety of sports. Her research interests focus on all areas of literacy education, including multimodality and digital literacies. As a part-time adjunct, she taught Leigh Anne, who was also a student-athlete in college, in a content area literacy course during her teacher education program in the Northeast Georgia mountains. Crystal then had the privilege to work as Leigh Anne's supervising teacher during her student teaching experience in her own ELA classroom at the height of the pandemic. The authors have continued their mentorship (and friendship) as Leigh Anne navigated the job market in spring 2021 and entered her own classroom in fall 2021; she is now an athletic coach herself and in her third year of teaching.

For us, care means recognizing and respecting the fact that we are all learning together no matter where we are on our journey of teaching and learning. This collaborative approach between mentor and mentee inspires hope; as Sieben (2015) reminds us, "Building hope in education shows caring and respect for our students, our classrooms, and ourselves as educators" (p. 7). This last part–focusing on ourselves as educators–is how we position our work together through a lens of care and where we have found collaboration, and a strong mentorship, to support our work on care through the induction years. Especially in the first few years of teaching, it is imperative for new teachers to feel a sense of belonging, and this is

DOI: 10.4324/9781032707471-10

best achieved when veteran teachers build a sound relationship with beginning teachers, based not on outcome but on care.

The forthcoming dialogue pulls from Leigh Anne's personal journals during her student teaching and induction years of teaching, and Crystal's experience currently leading her school's induction teacher program. We offer current reflections on how we directly (or indirectly) realized the importance of strong mentorship and the reciprocity that can form from a positive relationship that is focused on care. Through our dialogue, we highlight some of the ways both mentor and mentee learned, and continue to learn, together through a lens of care.

The Power of Planning and Intentional Design

In a school year, each teacher has 180 days to reach specific goals tied to state standards and proficiencies. It is especially necessary to have a comprehensive grasp of those expectations in order to plan intentionally over such a large span of time. Without a clear learning goal, teachers are often overwhelmed and underprepared for the day-to-day challenges of classroom management and student engagement. One way to mitigate teacher stress and student apathy is actively (and consistently) planning (and revising) to be intentional in designing lessons to help students achieve those goals.

The best way to begin a journey is to know where one is going so we offer the analogy of a marathon (as one might expect ELA teachers to do). We believe this analogy is helpful in showing how we facilitate the power of planning and intentional design to support induction teachers and the consequential positive effects on student learning.

Keh (2019) notes Eliud Kipchoge had a goal to run a sub-two-hour marathon, a feat which had never been accomplished. He did not wake up on the day of the marathon and figure out the mile splits he needed to accomplish his goal; he planned long before the day of the race. In fact, Kipchoge had runners alongside him helping keep the necessary pace of four minutes, 34 seconds per mile; he also painted lines on the course indicating the most efficient way to reach his goal. On an overcast day in Vienna, Eliud Kipchoge ran a marathon in one hour and 59 minutes.

In many ways, teachers are running a year-long marathon. We should know the split times and how to modify as needed to meet the unique needs of students. We should be painting the desired path for optimal outcomes through effective planning. We should run alongside those who have run before and run with an internal pace as we learn what works and what doesn't. Given the appropriate support and care, induction teachers can meet their classroom goal(s), too, so long as they know the goal and how to plan for it.

Leigh Anne: Lessons Learned in Induction Years

The school I currently teach in has a blended schedule of block days and "skinny" days. The week starts with one skinny day of 45-minute class periods, and it feels like nothing meaningful can be accomplished in such a short time. The following four days are block days. Block days are a special type of torture for most first-year/induction teachers; a 95-minute lesson feels like an eternity to fill when you are figuring out the duration of sufficient instruction and modeling.

In between meetings, grading, and making copies, the creativity required to make planning effective seems to dwindle. There were often times in the first year of teaching I found myself stretching activities to meet a 20-minute time frame. I became obsessed with time because there are few things as intimidating as unplanned and unorganized time with 30 teenagers staring at you. Yet, the days I focused on time were the days I managed time the worst. When my focus shifted from the learning goals to time management, I became bad at both: teaching and managing time.

The 45-minute class periods were a dream: review previous content, create a bellringer, and finish with an activity (Guhlin, 2022). However, double that time for a block day and it didn't seem such a simple task. My best course of action in the face of a block day was not to "fill time" but to make a goal. By the end of this lesson, what should they know and be able to do? By the end of this week, what should they be able to understand? By the end of the unit, what should they be able to create?

The time to plan did not magically appear. I relied heavily on the Georgia ELA standards to help determine the goals for the unit, which in turn determined the goals for the week. In reflecting on my time teaching with Crystal, I found notes that echoed the necessity of working with backward design (Wiggins & McTighe, 2005). She designed her units with goals in place which made it easy to work towards those goals. As I was reminded from my student teaching journals in January 2021,

[I] looked at the overall goal of the next week and how each day built up to that goal. I tried to mentally practice and organize the materials Dr. Beach had already prepared for the lessons. Through practicing the assignments and estimating times, I tried to work through the lesson and gauge the cadence of how the class would go.

From the beginning, her mentorship was leading me away from "clock management." I stopped racing against the clock and looked at block days as a building block into the grand scheme of the year's goal: equip students with the ability and opportunity to read a variety of informational and literary texts with the capacity to analyze and interpret themes and literary devices as well as communicate that knowledge with people around them. I was able to reframe the block period from a daily marathon to a single mile marker. Instead of desperately trying to race the bell, I instead aimed to hit a certain mile-split in order to keep pace with the year-long marathon of teaching ELA to teenagers. There was never a formal academic conversation that Crystal and I had regarding backwards design. My understanding and application of this strategy were rooted in our relationship and through our natural conversations. Our informal, organic, caring discussions of our profession are what most impacted my ability to implement backwards design effectively.

Crystal: Reflecting on Preparing and Supporting Induction Teachers

In working with Leigh Anne as a student teacher, it was important to me to model how planning allowed me to intentionally create engaging learning experiences for students in our classes. Her notes from the first day of observing my classroom teaching (dated January 6, 2021) included a focus on circular teaching with an emphasis on the foundational skills students need to use both in and out of the classroom. Leigh Anne was able to pick out key parts of my lesson focused on critical media literacy: prior knowledge activation, practice opportunities for both in and out of school, and application tied to students' popular culture examples, all of which furthered overall understanding and skill development. This lesson helped Leigh Anne understand that every minute of instructional time is focused on planning and intentional design to help me, as the teacher, understand where I needed to help students meet our learning goals.

In addition, she not only picked up on the core tenets of my planning efforts but noted the learning goals I had built into our lesson for that day. During our planning period, we were able to unpack what she saw and questioned, as well as go over the "why" behind my decisions. I attempted to scaffold not only for my students, but for her learning experience, too, so I could try to help her understand my choices. This discussion time was also important for me to explicitly reflect on my teaching practices.

As I reflect on that focus and her experiences as an induction teacher, I think it is valuable to point out that Leigh Anne recognized that, when she only focused on time management and not learning goals, she believed she became bad at both teaching and managing time. From my experiences, setting goals helps one create a clear path to improved student achievement because both teacher and student know the plan to get there, weaving together prior knowledge with real world connections and intentionally encouraging those connections in all that one does. The best way to support induction teachers is to allow them to "wobble;" as Fecho reminds us, "Teaching itself is learned by wobble" (Teachers College, 2017, para. 3). In other words, we learn how to become better teachers by being just uncomfortable enough that we reflect deeply on the anticipated goal we are hoping to achieve. In the case of induction teachers, showing you care by providing them with the opportunity to wobble *and* unpack that reflection with a mentor is instrumental on their journey—their marathon—to becoming a great teacher within their first years.

The Power of Feedback

We strongly believe that for learning to occur, feedback is necessary. Whether working with secondary students, student teachers, or induction teachers, we believe feedback makes us all better in whatever our role is. Research and personal experience prove that genuine and timely feedback not only assesses learning but also develops opportunities for more learning to occur (Wiggins, 2012). The necessity of feedback is inextricably intertwined with planning. Classroom feedback should be linked to a learning goal so that students can determine the accuracy of application to their learning target. As Wiggins (2012) notes, "the key is to gear feedback to long-term goals" (para. 30). Thus, there should be a clear link between what the student (or induction teacher) is accomplishing in a measurable goal and multiple ways to give timely and consistent feedback.

Leigh Anne: Lessons Learned in Induction Years

At the beginning of each school year, I ask my ninth-grade students what they want to gain from their literature course. For the majority of the students I teach, the feedback they (and their parents) most value is what goes in the grade book. They have been trained to believe that a number gives them more information than qualitative feedback. The learning process has become transactional. When the students acknowledge there is something they desire from class, however, they invest more in the feedback I give and I can orient the feedback towards the goal they have set out to accomplish. However, how that feedback is distributed should also reflect my value of their work.

As an ELA teacher, there are often too many things to assign. Students need lots of practice before they have the confidence to produce high caliber work. I became bogged down by all of the formative practice I felt needed a numerical value. However, Crystal shared critical advice that saved me many hours of grading and an opportunity to provide more authentic, goal-oriented feedback for my students. For example, from my journal, I noted,

> When giving out assignments and activities, don't always collect it for the sake of collecting it. Let the students use some of that work time and activities as practice. Let them create a community of work that peers review and allow them to develop a practice of creating without the carrot of turning it in.

If I graded every practice assignment that my students did, it would communicate that numerical values were the real goal. Instead, as my first year progressed, I felt freer to do writing assignments where students highlighted favorite sentences from their prose. After they turned in an assignment, I highlighted my favorite sentence and explained why based on the ELA standards and goals we were focused on in that specific writing assignment. There were no official grades or "participation" points but my students loved the opportunity to pick a favorite sentence and analyze why ours may have been different or the same. This was a critical area of growth for me in the first year as I saw the value in their authentic learning and my authentic feedback.

In my experience, first-year teachers (and especially those in ELA) grade homework nearly every night. This was a hard-fought lesson much to the benefit of my students and me, a lesson that was quickly learned not from years of sleepless nights but through the conversations with and mentorship from Crystal. She offered professional advice that demonstrated her care not just for my effectiveness in giving feedback but also for my work-life balance. Her care impacted more than just my classroom strategies by including a focus on my ability to balance a demanding workload.

Crystal: Reflecting on Preparing and Supporting Induction Teachers

Whether I am teaching a pre/in-service graduate course or a high school ELA class, I always offer opportunities for students to give me feedback on how I can help them achieve their learning goals. However, I have typically found that most people do not always like to take risks with their learning when a grade, an evaluation, or other high-stakes assessment is on the line. With that in mind, I have found it imperative to help induction teachers better understand the power of feedback and how it can help everyone be more successful in the end.

As Leigh Anne shared above, she recognized that her students needed lots of practice before developing the confidence needed to produce quality work. We know this to be true with induction teachers, too, as they learn to develop their craft. In my current role leading the induction program for my school, it is very important to me that I remember many of the points that Leigh Anne brings up, including the value of authentic learning and feedback.

What this looks like in action, then, is working with induction teachers to set up a goal for the month derived from Bambino's (n.d.) individual monthly action plan or I-MAP. This creates the opportunity for them to share with me what they want me to observe in their classrooms over the course of that time period in an area that they self-identify as needing improvement, which requires a pre-conference, observation, and post-conference. From there, rich discussions occur in which I ask many questions to help them discern if they did or did not reach their own goal based on my observations. This no-judgment zone provides an opportunity for them to reflect on their own practice while often identifying how I can help them continue to grow within the profession. After the month is up, they decide if they want to keep that goal or focus on a new one as we move ahead. The pacing allows for the specific feedback that the induction teachers need at that time in a way that is non-threatening and supportive.

The coaching cycle reminds mentors that they should be "particularly attuned to indicators of this period of development so they can provide adequate emotional support as well as capacity development" (Killion & Harrison, 2017, p. 93); however, it is also one in which mentors acknowledge "one of the greatest challenges is balancing support with developing capacity" (p. 93). Yet I have found that induction teachers are more willing to take risks in their own learning—to wobble—as they explore their craft. It is through these consistent routines, then, that expectations can be developed, appreciated, and reflected upon to help them best see how they can positively influence student achievement.

The Power of Routines

Developing routines in the classroom can help teachers maximize learning time and build a rapport with students. Routines not only help with student achievement; they also help students overcome challenges (Doll, 2013). From the opportunity to create differentiated activities to conferencing with students, the routine of a classroom can help with a myriad of goals that a teacher might have and is an important element to stress to induction teachers for their success.

Leigh Anne: Lessons Learned in Induction Years

Structure and routine in a classroom are beneficial for a multitude of reasons. As students enter the classroom, there is a mutual expectation that they are ready to contribute to a plan and structure designed by the teacher. Students have more success when they are aware of class expectations and routines. This was a lesson I learned through observation in Crystal's class. She was equipped to teach from bell to bell. The class began with an expected warm-up that either tied into the class period before or led into the content for the day, with everyone as a participant.

In starting my own classroom, I have found this to be one of the best ways to build my classroom management and connections with students. Structure and routine help both students and teachers. When developing my lessons and warm-ups, I consider backwards design and use activators at the beginning of class to review the previous day's work and build into the rest of the day's information. The students catch on to this and bring out their notes and activities from the previous day to help complete the warmup. While these actions may seem like a small measure of the success tied to routine and structure, they have been instrumental for my students to understand the scaffolding nature of class and how nothing we learn is in isolation. All of our activities, lessons, and units work together.

This practice of building routines and structure also helps me as the teacher. At the beginning of every class period, we start class with a bellringer, which is typically when I take roll. During this time, I check in with every student with a "good morning." It is not revolutionary; I am aware this is a common practice, yet this simple routine helps me get my feet under me for each class. This is also a great way to make and maintain relationships with students.

Crystal: Reflecting on Preparing and Supporting Induction Teachers

Managing a classroom is tough. Even veteran teachers can struggle as each class, each day, is a new learning environment. However, there are some consistent classroom management strategies I share with induction teachers to help alleviate what might feel like a roller coaster of events in their room. I encourage them to think, "Why does it matter?" After all, good classroom management helps keep a classroom safe and orderly. This means that all students can feel safe, valued, and respected, and come to the classroom ready to meet the learning goals of the day.

Some of the specific strategies focus on making a learning goal to help teachers effectively plan a lesson. When teachers plan effectively, there is less time for students to be off task, which is when behavioral issues can arise. Next, creating clear expectations with student input for how the learning environment in your room is respected by each member. The implementation of expectations and procedures creates a classroom climate and culture that fosters respect. The types of expectations themselves build parameters that help cultivate the success of the learning environment following the reverence of the co-created procedures helping reinforce the necessity of those boundaries and respect for them.

I remind induction teachers that they can also arrange the classroom in a way that effectively allows students to learn. I encourage them to sit in seats around the room to gain a better perspective. Also, if a student is continuously acting out, take time to talk to them before or after class. This shows the student you care about them and want them to be successful. Remind the student that each day is a new day, and you are excited for them to be a great learner and leader in your classroom!

As Leigh Anne noted above, nothing we learn is in isolation and I think a set routine helps with that notion. When students start to put together the pieces of the puzzle, planning, intentional design, feedback, and routines have done something right. However, we also have to remember to support induction teachers and remind them that they are not working in isolation. Planning, design, feedback, and routines can go wrong on one day, in one block or period, or for one student. We need to remember that we are all in this together, and the way we show care, the way we mentor, matters.

The Power of Humanity

In *The Gifts of Imperfection*, Brené Brown (2020) notes the following quote from theologian Howard Thurman: "Don't ask what the world needs. Ask what makes you come alive, and go do it. Because what the world needs is people who have come alive" (pp. 146–147). In education today, we believe this quote to be even more relevant as we need teachers *and* students to come alive and make the world a better place.

We call this the power of humanity, which we believe to be an imperative supporting factor in helping teachers, teacher educators, and induction teachers (as well as our students) be successful. Brown (2020) notes, "Research shows that perfectionism hampers success" as it is an "unattainable goal" (pp. 76–77). Thus, by being transparent in the ways we scaffold, revisit, grow, reflect, and reciprocate in our mentor-mentee relationships, we can accept what we don't know, feel comfortable asking questions when we need to, and, perhaps most importantly, admit when we are wrong without fear of judgment. Again, collaboration fosters care (Sieben, 2015), and we have found this approach to be mutually beneficial in helping both of us grow as educators and enact care in all that we do, especially when it means supporting induction-level teaching and learning experiences. When we build each other up and take every opportunity we can to learn from each other, our profession benefits and we work towards collective teacher efficacy, which Hattie's (2019) visible learning research suggests is a high indicator of student achievement.

Leigh Anne: Lessons Learned in Induction Years

The puzzling conundrum of induction mentorship is that too often the interactions are limited to bi-monthly meetings or Google Form check-ins. Mentorship programs, while well intentioned, are rarely organic, resulting in manufactured relationships that feel more like a checkbox and less like a genuine attempt to support new teachers. It doesn't feel like human connections but a systemized way to label and promote a school system that "cares about new teachers." One of my fondest memories and genuine experiences happened naturally over breakfast discussions with Crystal with a routine of Chick-Fil-A minis and sweet tea as we discussed the highs and lows of the week. It was a point of reflection and genuine feedback where my errors did not feel like career destroyers but rather an opportunity to discuss the difficult situations of classroom management and assessment.

The honest and sincere connection was not meant to check a box for funding or state requirements. She referred to me as Ms. Turner and continued to build my identity as a *contributing* teacher to the profession. Her guidance and encouragement were not one of convenience or mandatory participation; they were built from collaboration and care. Her support made tangible impacts that pushed me into the teaching profession as more than a mere vessel to convey information to students, but rather as an educator who strives to create and develop new resources and effective practices to best meet the needs of the unique learners in my classroom. Humanity in the induction years is having real, sometimes tough, conversations that show the vulnerability of both mentor and mentee in a safe space that promotes growth and collective teacher efficacy.

Crystal: Reflecting on Preparing and Supporting Induction Teachers

As I read Leigh Anne's words, one word comes to mind: grateful. During COVID-19, I didn't know what I was doing, let alone if I was doing her justice by highlighting every choice I made. And honestly, there were times I was afraid I might be too honest. Nonetheless, that nod to understanding our humanity and instilling that in the mentor-mentee relationship built on care allowed her to grow into a colleague. It allowed me to become better, too, and acknowledge that none of us are in isolation, ever.

It is also important for those in positions of assigning mentors or being a mentor to note the identity shift that should occur to make the mentor-mentee relationship a successful one. Mentors have to understand the full importance of their role in the new relationship. This success also comes from the support from leadership, whether from the university within the student teaching program or the school-level team. Yet, as Bullough (2005) points out, mentoring can be valued little in schools and universities. Furthermore, while induction programs are helpful and do have a positive correlation with teacher retention, there are still not always clear and consistent expectations of those programs and how they are implemented, which can be further complicated by a lack of administrative and university support (Bullough, 2012; Farrell, 2003; Ingersoll & Strong, 2011). From my experience, though, a strong induction program allows for opportunities for both parties to make each other better, just as I am from working with, and learning from, Leigh Anne.

Our Final Thoughts

The ability to come together as professionals can feel challenging when there are no mandated meetings or calendar invites. However, these moments are integral for battling the first-year hurdles. Adopting a routine of walking to the front office, making copies, or eating lunch together can create those natural patterns of mentorship. The reality of mentorship is that it is a human connection that, at its core is what teachers are built for, but it can be hard to manage those relationships on top of what feels like a laundry list of other duties. For this reason, we share an honest mentorship that takes intentional effort to develop and maintain especially as the miles between us grow. Nonetheless, as Sieben (2015) notes,

> we believe that through collaboration, we all have the power to foster student, educator, and school success ... Through dialogue, we share values and connectedness; through collaboration, we build collective hope. As connected educators, we listen to and learn from each other in order to offer students worthwhile educational experiences that foster hope for the future. (p. 11)

In other words, through our mentor-mentee relationship, we found the importance of care to be foundational in the development of induction teachers as we foster hope for our future.

Ultimately, we believe that induction teacher support is more like taking vitamins than having surgery. One massive change doesn't support day-to-day life in the classroom (and it definitely won't lead to that marathon success we discussed previously). Teachers need small supplements of support and care on a week-to-week (and sometimes daily) basis to feel the support necessary to continue and grow in the profession. In our own experience, this was true of our Chick-fil-A Thursdays, where natural conversations fostered honest reflections and positive reinforcement. As the research suggests, "a sense of professional identity will contribute to teachers' self-efficacy, motivation, commitment and job satisfaction" (Flores & Day, 2006, p. 220), which is another benefit of the strong mentor-mentee relationship.

Our hope is that this chapter provides support to teacher educators, teachers, and induction teachers through the lived experiences we shared. And while we acknowledge there are no perfect solutions and answers to the challenges our profession currently faces, our goal is to share our experiences and shed light on ways mentorship and care can and should be enacted within our profession. Similar to Eliud Kipchoge running his sub two-hour marathon, teaching requires that we run the race with others. He needed fellow runners and guides to indicate the shortest route and necessary pace. Teachers need this same support. We are running a marathon and it takes a lot of care to cross the finish line.

References

Bambino, D. (n.d.). Individual monthly action plan (I-MAP). *National School Reform Faculty.* https://www.nsrfharmony.org/wp-content/uploads/2017/10/imap_0.pdf

Brown, B. (2020). *The gifts of imperfection.* Random House.

Bullough, R. V. (2005). Being and becoming a mentor: School-based teacher educators and teacher educator identity. *Teaching and Teacher Education, 21*(2), 143–155. 10.1016/j.tate.2004.12.002

Bullough, R. V. (2012). Mentoring and new teacher induction in the United States: A review and analysis of current practices. *Mentoring & Tutoring: Partnership in Learning, 20*(1), 57–74. 10.1 080/13611267.2012.645600

Doll, B. (2013). Enhancing resilience in classrooms. In S. Goldstein & R. B. Brooks (Eds.), *Handbook of resilience in children* (2nd ed., pp. 399–409). Springer.

Farrell, T. S. C. (2003). Learning to teach English language during the first year: Personal influences and challenges. *Teaching and Teacher Education, 19*(1), 95–111. 10.1016/S0742-051X(02) 00088-4

Flores, M. A., & Day, C. (2006). Contexts which shape and reshape new teachers' identities: A multi-perspective study. *Teaching and Teacher Education, 22*(2), 219–232. 10.1016/j.tate.2005.09.002

GaDOE. (2022). *Teacher burnout in Georgia: Voices from the classroom.* https://www.gadoe.org/External-Affairs-and-Policy/communications/Documents/Teacher%20Burnout%20Task%20Force%20Report.pdf

Guhlin, M. (2022). *Bell ringers for improved retention and engagement. TechNotes Blog.* https://blog.tcea.org/bell-ringers-for-improved-retention-and-engagement/

Hattie, J. (2019). Visible learning: 250+ Influences on student achievement. Corwin. https://visible-learning.org/wp-content/uploads/2022/01/250-Influences.pdf

Ingersoll, R. M., & Strong, M. (2011). The impact of induction and mentoring programs for beginning teachers: A critical review of the research. *Review of Educational Research, 81*(2), 201–233. 10.3102/0034654311403323

Keh, A. (2019, Oct. 14). "Eliud Kipchoge breaks two-hour marathon barrier." *The New York Times.* https://www.nytimes.com/2019/10/12/sports/eliud-kipchoge-marathon-record.html.

Killion, J., & Harrison, C. (2017). *Taking the lead: New roles for teachers and school-based coaches.* Learning Forward.

Sieben, N. (2015). Collaboration fosters hope. *English Leadership Quarterly, 27*(4), 7–11.

Teachers College. (2017, June 15). Unconventional wisdom: Wobbling towards meaning. https://www.tc.columbia.edu/articles/2017/june/unconventional-wisdom-wobbling-towards-meaning/

Walker, T. (2018, January 1). Teacher burnout or demoralization? What's the difference and why it matters. *National Education Association.* www.nea.org/advocating-for-change/new-from-nea/teacher-burnout-or-demoralization-whats-di"erence-and-why-it.

Wiggins, G. (2012). Seven keys to effective feedback. *ASCD.* https://www.ascd.org/el/articles/seven-keys-to-effective-feedback

Wiggins, G., & McTighe, J. (2005). *Understanding by design.* Pearson.

Will, M.. (2019, December 3). Enrollment in teacher-preparation program is declining fast. Here's what the data show. *Education Week.* www.edweek.org/teaching-learning/enrollment-in-teacher-preparation-programs-is-declining-fast-heres-what-the-data-show/2019/12.

8

THE NEED FOR CARE

An Australian Perspective on Teacher Induction Post-COVID

Ceridwen Owen

The COVID-19 pandemic has had a profound impact on Australian schools, classrooms, and communities, and its effects will shape the experiences of teachers and students for years to come. The pandemic has altered parents' expectations of teachers and schools, students' behavior and needs, and teachers' responsibilities, which now include increased regulatory compliance and support for students and parents (Bulfin et al., 2023; Longmuir et al., 2022). Consideration at a school level must be given to how the context of education and the needs and experiences of teachers beginning their careers have changed to ensure school practices are fit for purpose.

Teacher induction practices within schools were inadequate before the pandemic (Owen, 2020) and have become even less effective in the post-COVID era. Inadequate induction practices have contributed to high levels of teacher stress and retention issues in Australia (Bulfin et al., 2023; Longmuir et al., 2022). In this chapter, drawing on three sets of data collected before, during, and after the pandemic in Victoria, Australia, I demonstrate the shortcomings of current teacher induction practices in schools before proposing that a care approach to teacher induction could address these shortcomings and better meet the needs of beginning teachers.

The first section of the chapter presents pre-COVID research on the needs, development, and experiences of early-career teachers (Owen, 2020). It highlights the inadequacy of institutional induction practices as teachers enter the profession. The second section draws on a narrative from a first-year teacher during remote teaching and learning, as well as my autobiographical experience of teaching during the pandemic to highlight the needs of teachers during a period of isolation and stress (Owen, 2020; Owen & Whitney, 2022). The third section discusses beginning teachers' post-COVID experiences and needs as documented through my experience working in higher education.

Through these sets of data, I argue that current teacher induction practices are institutionally driven rather than developed from the perspective of teachers as people. In Australia, and around the world, teachers' work is being reduced to "outcomes, effectiveness, performance standards, service delivery to 'clients', customer satisfaction and accountability" (Kostogriz, 2012, p. 398). This institutionally driven approach does not acknowledge that teaching is a "social profession" (p. 398), where the "lived experiences of teachers [are]

DOI: 10.4324/9781032707471-11

deeply relational, affective, and ethical" (p. 399). To address this issue, teacher induction practices need to be freed from the agendas of institutions to meet the needs of teachers more effectively (Owen, 2020).

The concept of care recognizes the relational dimension of human experience (Noddings, 2012; Shoffner & Webb, 2022), and integrates "intellectual needs with emotional and wellbeing needs" (Owen & Whitney, 2022, p. 237). Drawing on Noddings' (2012) concept of caring as a relation that involves listening, dialogue, critical thinking, reflective response, and thoughtful connections to discipline and life, I demonstrate how a care approach to teacher induction that recognizes the affective, relational, and ethical work of teaching can support the unaddressed needs of teachers.

Teacher Induction Practices in Australian Schools

Teacher induction practices in Australian schools are context specific and are generally decided by the leadership team in schools based on the assumed needs of newly hired teachers and the needs of the school. However, in Victorian schools, teachers are required to align their practice with a set of Australian government-endorsed standards, the Australian Professional Standards for Teachers (APST), developed by the Australian Institute for Teaching and School Leadership (2011). Throughout their careers, they will provide evidence that they have met these standards to the "standards-based regulator" the Victorian Institute of Teaching (VIT), the organization that oversees teacher registration (Victorian Institute of Teaching, 2023, p. 5). These standards are the same for all teachers, "regardless of the context in which they are working" (p. 5).

When teachers start in the profession, they have provisional registration, which means they have demonstrated through their higher education degree that they have met the Graduate level of the APST, which is the first career stage. Provisional registration is valid for two years. In these two years, teachers need to complete at least 80 days of teaching and demonstrate they have met the standards for the second career stage in the APST: Proficient. To meet the Proficient level and apply for full registration, teachers need to demonstrate their proficiency through the VIT's Inquiry Process (VIT, 2023). The VIT Inquiry Process is a school-based process that usually takes one year to complete, where teachers demonstrate their knowledge and practice through evidence of planning, teaching, assessing, and reflecting.

The APST and VIT Inquiry Process are focused on benchmarks and descriptors of what teachers should be able to do and what they should know at each stage of their careers and limits teacher development to evidence-based levels that can be measured (Allard & Doecke, 2014). Moreover, the APST outlines that teacher development is a linear process that correlates experience with ability. The lived experience of teachers and teaching, however, does not align with generic descriptors and a linear process (Owen, 2020). For the participants in my study, discussed below, the regulatory process of VIT registration and the APST requirements often led them to feelings of being under surveillance; they found them to be an inconvenience and detrimental to their process of becoming.

A Study on Early Career English Teachers Pre-COVID

In 2020, I completed my PhD on the becoming of early career English teachers (i.e., those teaching in secondary schools, grades 7–12, in the first five years of their careers) in Victoria,

Australia (Owen, 2020). The study examined the everyday work and ideological becoming of teachers within a standards-based reform agenda, where ideological becoming considers the developing views, values, and beliefs of teachers.

Using an ethnography-in-education methodology, the focus was the "human experience within social, cultural and structural patterns and regularities" (Owen, 2020, p. 70; see also Delamont, 2014; Green & Bloome, 2005; Hammersley, 2006; Selwyn et al., 2018; Troman & Jeffrey, 2004). Due to my experience as a teacher and teacher-educator, an ethnography-in-education methodology enabled the explicit recognition of my experience in the gathering of the data and the analysis. Rather than attempting to be an objective observer, I utilized my knowledge and expertise to work alongside participants. An ethnographic approach enabled me to examine "teachers' practice and the issues of everyday life in classrooms from the perspective of teachers" (Woods, 1996, p. 10). Within this broader focus, there was an examination of the teacher induction practices of schools and the participants' experience of these.

There were nine participants for the study, seven of whom were in their graduate year, which is their first year teaching post-higher education study, when data collection began. The other two had been in the profession for over two years. All participants (anonymized) had completed their higher education degree at the same university and the seven in their graduate year were known to each other prior to participating in the study. All were working in different schools across Victoria, including public (government-owned) and independent (privately-owned) schools.

Data collection was conducted over two years and included semi-structured interviews, focus groups, observations and fieldnotes, reflective writing with and apart from the participants, and artifact and document collection. Data analysis was narrative and thematic, enabling the discussion of experiences across participants as well as focusing on the stories of teaching.

Early Career Accounts of Induction

How schools induct teachers and implement the VIT Inquiry Process is up to them and, therefore, broad conclusions are difficult to make. However, the seven participants in their first year of teaching all reported that their school induction processes were mostly focused on informing them about school policy and procedures, schedules, systems, and the teams they would be working in. The focus was on accountability measures that the teachers had to align with, particularly the VIT process.

One of the participants, Hunter, described the induction programs as focusing mainly on the digital systems of the school, including the school management system. These programs were not run by the principal and assistant principals but by leading classroom teachers. He felt the programs were not focused on supporting teachers, bringing them into the school community, or considering their well-being and development. This made him feel that he could not connect with the leadership team, as they were managers rather than colleagues. He felt that the school agenda was focused on reputation and results rather than supporting teachers and students.

This view was shared by the other participants, however, not all the participants felt disconnected from their principal team. One participant of the seven, Theodore, described the open-door approach of the leadership team that he found when he entered his school:

They were like, "Look, you know, don't obviously come to us for where can I go to the bathroom. You can ask another staff member. But, if there's a question that you generally can't find the answer to, just come and ask us, open the door." (Owen, 2020, p. 97)

He felt the leadership team cared about his professional needs, which developed from their approachability and the open-door policy rather than the teacher induction program. As such, his sense of connection came from specific people in the leadership team rather than the teacher induction process.

Apart from Theodore, accounts from the participants show that the approach of the leadership team and the induction process impacted how they felt in their schools, resulting in feelings of disconnection and isolation. This is supported by Kostogriz's (2012) work where he argues that the negative implications of the shift to managerial and accountability approaches in schools are that the affective labors of teachers are no longer viewed as valuable, impacting teachers' sense of community and their ability to focus on and develop the relational work of teaching.

The importance of the affective labors of teachers is further highlighted when participants discussed their mentors. All seven participants in their first year of teaching were completing their VIT Inquiry Process. As part of this process, each school provided them with a VIT mentor. Generally, the role of this official school mentor was to assist with the everyday practicalities of the classroom and support the teachers in meeting standardized requirements, such as the VIT Inquiry Process. The participants felt there were limited opportunities with these mentors and within their schools to engage in genuine dialogic discussion about their developing practice, as meetings were focused on process and the formation of evidence to use in the VIT Inquiry Process. They contrasted this with their experience in higher education where dialogic discussions had been the norm. In response to this realization, all the participants formed unofficial mentor relationships with teachers in their schools and sought groups external to the school context where they could gain ongoing support, mentoring, and dialogic discussion:

> They found their first [two] years challenging and were looking for a place in which they could dialogically engage in sustained discussions about their teaching, especially discussions that were grounded in theory. (Owen, 2020, p. 170)

Further, they all reported that, while there were times that the VIT Inquiry Process gave them the opportunity to consider their classrooms and teaching, overall, the process made them feel that there was "an inherent distrust from schools and governments in their abilities" (Owen, 2020, p. 172). They felt they had to continually prove themselves as teachers and they were positioned as inferior to their colleagues who were at different career stages, according to the APST. The language of policy and how they were positioned by colleagues made them feel as if they were deficient and inexperienced. The participants were not arguing for the removal of accountability, as they explicitly stated that they "desired genuine accountability that enhanced their professionalism" (Owen, 2020, p. 172). They wanted accountability that linked to their professional and ethical responsibility for their students rather than "monitoring mechanisms" (Kostogriz & Doecke, 2011, p. 399).

Due to the needs of participants not being met, all nine participants (seven first-year teachers and two early career teachers) sought communities outside of school. There were two main communities that the participants engaged in: the English Education Praxis group, which had approximately 30 members, and English Education in the Secondary Years, which had approximately 200 members. The focus of both groups was members gathering to reflect on their teaching experiences and understandings in relation to an academic reading or a presentation from members of the group. There was also often a chance for members to write and discuss their writing with others. There were a range of members involved in the groups including preservice teachers, practicing and retired teachers, academics, and doctoral candidates.

Discussing their involvement in these learning communities, two participants reported that they enjoyed the range of experiences and ages in the group and, unlike in their schools, that they were not treated as "newbies" (Owen, 2020, p. 175). Another commented that the community "makes [her] feel like [she's] not alone," while another stated that she "comes, even though [she] feels tired, because [she] knows it's good for [her]" to share with "like-minded teachers" (p. 176). This is supported by Hobson's (2009) large-scale longitudinal study on preservice and early career teachers, where teachers were looking for people "willing and able to listen" (p. 306).

While the level of teacher induction support varied from school to school, generally, the induction processes experienced by these seven graduate teachers demonstrate that, rather than supporting them as they entered the teaching profession, the processes made them feel isolated, observed, and judged. The genuine support that they experienced came mostly from like-minded teachers within their schools and external learning communities that they took the initiative to find.

Teachers' Experiences in a Radically Different Education Context During COVID

Due to the COVID-19 pandemic, most Australian states and territories experienced school closures and home-schooling for varying lengths of time. Accounts of teachers during this time provide insights about the support they needed and continue to need beyond the pandemic. During part of the Victorian lockdown period, I was a secondary school English teacher as well as an academic researcher. From this position, in collaboration with five other secondary school English teachers, we wrote an article about our experiences (Owen et al., 2021). Of the five teachers, Emma was in her first year of teaching and her writing is the focus of this section.

Emma discussed the excitement of starting in the profession and then shifted to the difficulties of moving to remote learning. Within her description of starting at a new school, she commented that she was "handed the text list by the Head of English" which gave her "a legitimate reason to lock [her]self in [her] room and read" (Owen et al., 2021, p. 11). While this was a great opportunity for her to indulge her love of reading, Emma was left to engage with the texts she would be teaching for the first time in isolation, which provides insight into the teacher induction process of the school.

During lockdown and remote teaching, Emma commented that she was "crafting curriculum for the first time ever" and described the "balancing act of engaging education and accessible education" becoming her "biggest challenge" (Owen et al., 2021, p. 11). What was missing from Emma's experience was the presence of colleagues; after "eight weeks of teaching under [her] belt, [she] had to redefine [her] pedagogy and practice" (p. 11) on her own. Emma's experience echoes the experience of the seven first-year teachers from my study where the teacher induction processes of their schools focused on systems, policy, and curriculum, excluding the relational aspect of the profession (Owen, 2020).

I had just returned to secondary teaching before the second large lockdown in Victoria. I experienced that lockdown isolated from my colleagues and, apart from attending Zoom staff meetings and emails with updates to policy, I had no interactions with leadership in my school. My support came from outsiders, those that I had connected with during my PhD study, in particular, Joe, who had been part of a teacher praxis group I facilitated before the lockdown (Owen & Whitney, 2022). We regularly had late night chats once the children were in bed and our work had finished for the day:

> These chats became an important contrasting experience to day-to-day difficulties and monotony. At times hilarious, other times despairing, these conversations offered companionship and a way to engage in dialogic storying together … In a time when [we] were constantly receiving messages to put on a brave face and continue to show up for others, these conversations enabled [us] to be vulnerable, to support each other, and to practice self-care. (Owen & Whitney, 2022, p. 242)

Unlike Emma, I already had a teacher community to support me when the leadership team and colleagues at my school did not. Both Emma and I were new to the schools we were working in, although we had different levels of experience. Emma had completed her teaching degree the year prior, and I have over 15 years of experience in education. Despite this difference, our experience shares similarities, such as planning curriculum on our own and having very little daily communication with others beyond students. Luckily, due to my previous education experiences and connections, I had other teachers to turn to, but Emma did not.

The Ongoing Needs of Graduate Teachers after COVID

After the COVID-19 pandemic lockdowns, I moved from secondary school teaching back to working in higher education. In my current role, I bridge between schools and university. I work with preservice teachers at university and while they are placed in schools, and I support teachers in primary and secondary schools. My role also includes working closely with schools, the mentors of preservice teachers, and the leadership teams. In this section, I consider the ongoing needs of teachers as recorded in literature and from my professional experience and how these needs relate to teachers as they transition from university to the teaching profession.

An interim report on the experience of secondary school English teachers post-pandemic in Victoria shows that of the 179 survey responses received, "many respondents noted feeling support from immediate colleagues but not always from school leadership" (Bulfin et al. 2023, p. 2). Part of the reason for this was a "perception of misalignment between or a fracturing of relationships between classroom teaching staff and school leadership," potentially due to the "marketisation [sic] of education" (p. 2). While these teachers are not just first-year teachers, the views raised are like those expressed by six of the seven first-year teachers from my study, where only one participant felt care from the principal team. The suggestion here is that the issues experienced by teachers are not just due to the COVID-19 pandemic or its aftermath but rather they are an ongoing issue.

Speaking with preservice teachers on placement and with first-year teachers, the disconnect between leadership and classroom teachers is a common issue. These teachers are receiving support from their mentors and teaching teams rather than from school leadership. There is a sentiment that leadership does not understand the situation in classrooms and the difficulties that teachers are facing.

The issues teachers raised with me are like those reported across the education sector in Australia (Bulfin et al., 2023; Longmuir et al., 2022). Bulfin et al.'s (2023) interim report highlights "stress and pressure at all levels, workload demands, increased and complex student needs, negative interactions with parents and careers, and performance expectations" (p. 2). Longmuir et al.'s (2022) study, which included 5,497 teachers' responses to an anonymous online survey, states that "a quarter of teachers reported feeling unsafe in their workplaces" (p. 4). These post-pandemic findings suggest that the experience for teachers is worse than before and requires immediate intervention. The need for this intervention, so that teachers feel safe and supported, begins at the induction stage in schools.

A Caring Approach to Teacher Induction

I propose an approach to teacher induction that meets the relational needs of teachers that are currently not being met through insufficient and inadequate institution-led processes. Schools are generally approaching the teacher induction process as an opportunity to induct teachers into the institution of the school and the regulatory institutions that oversee the profession, such as VIT. The focus is on systems, processes, and accountability. The accounts of teachers who have experienced these induction processes suggest that they are creating work environments where people feel untrusted, observed, and measured.

In response, teachers are searching for mentors and groups that extend beyond their school context that will provide them with what they need, which is assistance with the development of their identity and agency, and ongoing support through dialogic discussions. There is extensive literature that supports these findings and advocates for supportive professional communities for teachers (e.g., Doecke, 2004; Doecke & Parr, 2011; Owen, 2020; Owen & Whitney, 2022; Parr et al., 2020; Pereira & Doecke, 2016; Smith & Wrigley, 2012; Whitney, 2008). The communities discussed in the literature are not about surveillance or reductive de-professionalizing forms of accountability. Rather, they focus on the relational and ethical work of teachers and are about nurturing and promoting the identity work that informs teachers' development and becoming. Although the needs of teachers have not changed from pre-pandemic times, the increased pressure and stress on teachers means that these needs are more acute.

Current teacher induction practices are developed from the perspective of the institution by school leaders. This means teacher induction is meeting the agenda of the school and the assumed needs of teachers. The result is teacher induction processes that are standardized, where all teachers are the "same … regardless of interests or aptitudes" (Noddings, 2012, p. 777). As Noddings (2012) writes, this has created an environment where "almost explicitly, the aim of education is to gain high test scores" (p. 777) and therefore teacher induction is about inducting teachers into this agenda.

A care approach to teacher induction that focuses on caring as relation would redirect schools to the explicit needs of teachers. Care as relation recognizes the responsibility individuals have for others and the relationship between the cared for and the carer (Noddings, 2012). The cared for and carer each have a responsibility towards each other. This responsibility is based on expressing needs and meeting these expressed needs. In a caring relation approach to teacher induction rather than there being institutionalized processes, carers, such as the leadership teams in schools and mentors, listen to and respond to the needs of those they are caring for, teachers entering the profession. These teachers also, in a caring relationship, have a responsibility to express their needs explicitly.

To enable this sharing of expressed needs and the meeting of these needs, Noddings (2012) outlines the key tenets of care—listening, dialogue, critical thinking, reflective response, and thoughtful connections to discipline and life. Each of these tenets was part of the structure of the learning communities the participants of my study were involved in and other examples in literature (Doecke, 2004; Doecke & Parr, 2011; Owen, 2020; Owen & Whitney, 2022; Parr et al., 2020; Pereira & Doecke, 2016; Smith & Wrigley, 2012; Whitney, 2008), though they did not often explicitly link to Noddings' (2012) framework. These tenets resulted in a sense of belonging, which provided a sense of place and security (Hobson, 2009). These tenets are currently missing from most teacher induction processes in schools and hence schools are not addressing the expressed needs of teachers that are based on the relational and affective work of teachers (Kostogriz, 2012).

Introducing these tenets into schools requires the development of learning communities that are not focused on accountability and standardized skill and knowledge development. Rather, they are communities where teachers bring an openness to discuss their views, values, and beliefs about education. An example of such a community is the English Education Praxis Group (Owen, 2020). The community consisted of 30 members but usually only 15 attend any meeting. The meetings were in person and involved three stages. Stage 1 was providing reading prior to the meeting. The readings were academic but the theme was selected by the group. Stage 2 was the beginning of the meeting, where teachers either read the reading (if they had not had time prior to the meeting) or wrote in response to the reading. Stage 3 was discussion. In this third stage, teachers shared their writing or their ideas and engaged in dialogic discussion with the group.

While this example comes from a learning community external to schools, it is a structure that I used in my school when I returned to classroom teaching after completing my doctorate. Colleagues asked me to run a Praxis group after reading about the English Education Praxis Group in my doctorate study and asking about my work. To ensure trust, I had one rule for participation: No teacher with authority could attend. This meant that heads of school, heads of department, and the leadership team of the school could not participate. The reasoning was that this ensured that the teachers did not feel observed and could openly discuss the structures of the school. The group ran for a year before I returned to higher education, demonstrating its effectiveness and teachers' willingness to participate, despite it not being official professional learning. These examples show the ability of such groups to occur externally and internally to schools.

The benefit of these communities is not just for the individual but the group. Doecke and Parr (2011) comment on the collective capacity of such communities, which extends care from the individual to collective caring. They enable teachers to "derive genuine satisfaction from feeling that their learning is recognised [sic] by those around them and that they are contributing to the greater good" (p. 14). This links to Noddings' (2012) care as relation, where there is a move to self-care as collective care (Owen & Whitney, 2022). Teachers involved in these communities feel they are part of a community where they can share, listen, and engage to co-construct meanings about themselves, their work, and the profession of teaching.

Care-based approaches to teacher induction in schools have the potential to support the development of agency, identity, and knowledge of beginning teachers. Such ongoing support would assist teachers in the challenging and constantly changing world of teaching and learning post-pandemic and into the future.

References

Allard, A., & Doecke, B. (2014). Professional knowledge and standards-based reforms: Learning from the experiences of early career teachers. *English Teaching: Practice & Critique, 13*(1), 39–54. http://education.waikato.ac.nz/research/files/etpc/files/2014v13n1art3.pdf

Australian Institute for Teaching and School Leadership. (2011). *Australian professional standards for teachers.* Author. https://www.aitsl.edu.au/docs/default-source/apstresources/australian_professional_standard_for_teachers_final.pdf

Bulfin, S., Diamond, F., McGraw, A., O'Mara, J., & Parr, G. (2023). *Sustaining the secondary English teaching profession/al in uncertain times: Interim report.* Victorian Association for the Teaching of English (VATE).

Delamont, S. (2014). *Key themes in the ethnography of education: Achievements and agendas.* SAGE.

Doecke, B. (2004). Professional identity and educational reform: Confronting my habitual practices as a teacher educator. *Teaching and Teacher Education, 20,* 203–215. 10.1016/j.tate.2003.12.001

Doecke, B., & Parr, G. (2011). The national mapping of teacher professional learning project: A multi-dimensional space? *English in Australia, 46*(2), 9–19.

Green, J., & Bloome, D. (2005). Ethnography and ethnographers of and in education: A situated perspective. In J. Flood, S. B. Heath & D. Lapp (Eds.), *Handbook of research on teaching literacy through the communicative and visual arts* (pp. 181–202). Lawrence Erlbaum.

Hammersley, M. (2006). Ethnography: Problems and prospects. *Ethnography and Education, 1,* 3–14. 10.1080/17457820500512697

Hobson, A. J. (2009). On being bottom of the pecking order: Beginner teachers' perceptions and experiences of support. *Teacher Development, 13,* 299–320. 10.1080/13664530903578256

Kostogriz, A. (2012). Accountability and the affective labour of teachers: A Marxist–Vygotskian perspective. *The Australian Educational Researcher, 39,* 397–412. 10.1007/s13384-012-0072-x

Kostogriz, A., & Doecke, B. (2011). Standards-based accountability: Reification, responsibility and the ethical subject. *Teaching Education, 22,* 397–412. 10.1080/10476210.2011.587870

Longmuir, F., Gallo Cordoba, B., Phillips, M., Allen, K. A. & Moharami, M. (2022). *Australian teachers' perceptions of their work in 2022.* Monash University. 10.26180/21212891

Noddings, N. (2012). The caring relation in teaching. *Oxford Review of Education, 38*(6), 771–781.

Owen, C., Enticott, E., Harlowe, J., Kolber, S., Rees, E., & Wood, A. (2021). Teaching during lockdown: English teachers' experiences in the time of COVID-19. *English in Australia, 56*(2), 7.

Owen, C. & Whitney, A. (2022). Learning communities as caring communities during COVID: Caring as relation that empowers teacher education. In M. Shoffner & A. W. Webb (Eds.), *Reconstructing care in teacher education after COVID-19: Caring enough to change* (pp. 236–246). Routledge.

Owen, C. C. (2020). *Becoming an English teacher: The shaping of everyday professional experiences in early career teaching* [Thesis, Monash University]. 10.26180/13210970.v1

Parr, G., Bulfin, S., Diamond, F., Wood, N., & Owen, C. (2020). The becoming of English teacher educators in Australia: A cross-generational reflexive inquiry. *Oxford Review of Education, 46,* 238–256. 10.1080/03054985.2019.1667319

Pereira, Í. S. P., & Doecke, B. (2016). Storytelling for ordinary, practical purposes (Walter Benjamin's 'The Storyteller'). *Pedagogy, Culture & Society, 24,* 537–549. 10.1080/14681366.2016.1210200

Selwyn, N., Nemorin, S., Bulfin, S., & Johnson, N. F. (2018). *Everyday schooling in the digital age: High school, high tech?* Routledge.

Shoffner, M., & Webb, A. (2022). Introduction: Care after COVID: Moving forward as caring teacher educators. In M. Shoffner & A. W. Webb (Eds.), *Reconstructing care in teacher education after COVID-19: Caring enough to change* (pp. 1–12). Routledge.

Smith, J., & Wrigley, S. (2012). What has writing ever done for us? The power of teachers writing groups. *English in Education, 46,* 70–84. 10.1111/j.1754-8845.2011.01116.x

Troman, G., & Jeffrey, B. (2004). Introduction. In G. Troman, B. Jeffrey & G. Walford (Eds.), *Identity, agency and social institutions in educational ethnography* (pp. ix–1). Elsevier.

Victorian Institute of Teaching [VIT]. (2023). *PRT guide: Moving from provisional to full registration.* Victoria, Australia.

Whitney, A. (2008). Teacher transformation in the National Writing Project. *Research in the Teaching of English, 43,* 144–187.

Woods, P. (1996). *Researching the art of teaching: Ethnography for educational use.* Routledge.

9

PROTOCOLS AS A MECHANISM OF CARE

Helping Novice Science Educators

Elizabeth W. Edmondson

Entry into the field of education always presents novice (i.e., first- and second-year) teachers with challenges, such as learning school policies, assuming responsibility for a classroom, communicating with parents, and becoming a part of a new community (Grillo & Kier, 2021; Ingersoll & Strong, 2011; Luft et al., 2015). During and after the COVID pandemic, teachers, both new and experienced, faced additional challenges, including learning recovery, student absenteeism, and student violence (Kuhfeld et al., 2022). These challenges are driving teachers out of the profession at higher rates than ever before (Barnum, 2023).

To sustain and retain our novice teachers, faculty and staff in teacher education programs must demonstrate a high level of care for these individuals and continue supporting them in their first years of teaching. New teachers need programs for mentoring, induction, and professional development to allow for continued knowledge and skills building and to increase their access to other supports (Luft et al., 2015; Navy et al., 2020). Supports such as these can reduce the attrition of early career teachers (Ingersoll & Strong, 2011; Ronfeldt & McQueen, 2017; Savka et al., 2013).

I interpret care as listening or providing options and ideas—via phone calls, text messages, or emails throughout the day—as well as providing resources to help teachers work through issues as they continue to grow in the profession. I do not see this role as providing all answers but one to help teachers develop agency and confidence in their ability to solve problems. This approach is supported by researchers like Noddings (2005) who describe care in education as teachers giving concerted attention to the needs of students, developing trusting relationships with them, and helping them learn skills to satisfy their own needs.

In this chapter, I focus on how the Virginia Commonwealth University (VCU) induction program, situated at an urban serving institution in Richmond, Virginia, nurtures a sense of care and support. I highlight two protocols used in the program, i.e., a set of steps to accomplish a procedure (Oxford University Press, 2023). This induction program, in its fourteenth year, is part of a Robert F. Noyce Scholarship Program Track 1 project supported by the National Science Foundation (NSF). Our induction sessions are facilitated by faculty or students in VCU's doctoral education program; our participants are graduates in their first and second years of teaching. As a requirement of the Noyce scholarship, graduates are hired

DOI: 10.4324/9781032707471-12

by districts that meet one of the requirements of a high-need school district, including 1) not less than 20% of children served are from low-income families, 2) eligible for funding under the Rural and Low-Income School Program, and 3) high teacher turnover or teaching out of field (NSF RFP Robert Noyce Grant, 2023). Most Noyce graduates are hired by schools that are recognized as high-need schools in these districts; not all schools within a high-need district must meet this definition.

Theoretical Framework

Three concepts framing this chapter are care, induction models, and protocol use. Care is the foundation of the VCU Noyce program, as we work to establish trust, set high expectations, and promote understanding of culturally responsive practices (see https://soe.vcu.edu/academics/). Induction models support graduates in their initial years of the teaching profession. Finally, the use of protocols as part of the VCU Noyce induction program allows for care to be given and received by the participants and facilitators.

Care

Noddings introduced the need for an ethics of care in the education field through *Caring: A Feminine Approach to Ethics and Moral Education* (1984). Forty years later, educators face many similar concerns and some new challenges today in relation to care. Noddings's notion of care focuses on looking at an "affective foundation of existence" (p. 3). Within this foundation, Noddings (2005) describes care as the needs of students being at the forefront for teachers. In order to consider student needs, teachers must build trusting relationships with their students and consider the skills students want to learn, which may be different from those expected by district and state entities.

Student attention, trust, and support continue to be the focus of many education programs today. Noddings (1984, 2005) points out that, with an ethics of care, there is an interaction between two individuals as one takes on the role of carer and one the cared-for; the relationship may be unequal, with the carer having responsibilities that are not expected of the cared-for. Both individuals must contribute to the relationship if it is to be established and later maintained (Noddings, 2012). Without the cared-for contributing to the relationship, there is no caring relationship (Noddings, 1984, 2010). Noddings (2005) identifies two types of needs: inferred and expressed. The inferred needs come from the carer and the expressed needs from the cared-for. Both types of needs can and should be addressed in the relationship.

For this chapter, the carers are the faculty members and other team members participating in the activities and supports as part of the induction protocol. The cared for are the new Noyce teachers who have worked with the faculty members throughout their Master of Teaching program, starting with advising, continuing through taking course work, and culminating with their first two years of teaching. To support our Noyce graduates in these settings, the VCU secondary teacher education program implements opportunities for candidates to develop a deep understanding of how to become culturally responsive educators (Gay, 2010; Ladson-Billings, 1995). One aspect of culturally responsive education is building relationships with students that demonstrate care and understanding of who they are and their prior experiences (Gay, 2010; Ladson-Billings, 1995). To build this understanding and mindset, we model the same throughout our program.

Role of Induction Support

Induction programs aid novice teachers in the transition from their education program to their role as full-time, stand-alone teachers responsible for a classroom (Ingersoll, 2012; Luft et al., 2011; McDonnough & Henschel, 2015). März and Keltchtermans (2020) highlight the importance of induction as a social process providing interactions with others, either within the school or with a cohort of new teachers outside of their school.

Induction programs frequently use professional learning community (PLC) models. PLCs allow for different affordances, as noted by Webb (2015), who compared PLCs conducted within a school versus models outside of the school day. García-Carrión et al. (2020) investigated a community-based induction model that involved families and the community in teachers' professional development, which they considered as important to the success of this approach.

Use of Protocols

In the 1990s, the School Reforms Initiative found that teacher discussions and collaborations needed support; using earlier prototypes, protocols for these types of interaction were designed (McDonald et al., 2013). Protocols provide a set of steps for participants and a facilitator. These steps help focus sharing and discussion within a group via constraints that serve as procedures or rules and routines for working together. When protocols were established in the 1990s, the goal was to help facilitate discussions and work toward equity (McDonald et al., 2013). Now, protocols have been useful for teachers to use during PLC time and professional development sessions to facilitate challenging conversations and lead to improvement in teacher practice (Easton, 2009). Protocols shared by McDonald et al. (2013) include providing all participants time to think, talk, and receive different types of feedback.

The VCU Induction Model

VCU's induction model brings together two cohorts of graduates for optional monthly meetings in year 1 and year 2 of their teaching. A trained facilitator, usually a graduate assistant or member of the grant team, leads the session and supports the presenter, one of the teachers, and the other teachers who serve as consultants by listening and asking questions. The principal investigator (and chapter author) and other grant investigators do not facilitate sessions so that they can be participants and members of the group during the protocols. These roles match those identified by the protocols in McDonald et al. (2013).

Prior to COVID and beginning again in the fall of 2022, the meetings commenced with the participants having the opportunity to eat together. Beginning in this way provided much-needed time to build community and to discuss other topics not addressed in the protocols. During COVID, this community-building was brokered through games and other check-in strategies. These approaches, as well as the protocols, allowed the facilitators to model care for the group.

Each fall, the first meeting is an opportunity to establish norms and to introduce or reintroduce the two key protocols: 1) Descriptive Consultancy and 2) Success Analysis and Reflective Questions (McDonald et al., 2013). There is also discussion of other supports that the group would like to implement for the year. These two protocols were chosen because of their documented effectiveness in educational settings (Bryk, 2010; Mindlich & Lieberman, 2012; Yau & Lawrence, 2014).

The final session each year is a focus group interview to learn from the participants whether their needs were met and how future sessions might support them. I am not present in this final session, as the principal investigator of the grant, although I do obtain a transcript of the interview with de-identified participant names. This is done for two reasons: to provide the participants with an opportunity to be open and honest, and as a piece of data for the external evaluator.

Protocols Used

The Descriptive Consultancy and the Success Analysis and Reflective Questions protocols (McDonald et al., 2013) are presented via Microsoft PowerPoint during the session to provide prompts for the participants to consider at each step. The Descriptive Consultancy Protocol (McDonald et al., 2013) is used first, after participants have re-established community through dinner. This protocol is described as an "open-minded exploration" (McDonald et al., 2013, p. 2) of dilemmas in practice. The participants assume the role of presenter (one person) or consultants (everyone else in attendance). The protocol allows for expanded and clarifying questions to be posed to learn more about the issue. Key to this protocol is the idea that participants do not impose "premature interpretive frames or press for deeper analysis" (McDonald et al., 2013, p. 2) before the dilemma or problem is thoroughly outlined.

This eight-step protocol (outlined below) allows and expects everyone to contribute as each step of the protocol is conducted, which usually takes approximately 50 minutes.

1 *Problem Presentation:* The selected presenter is given five minutes to outline their dilemma. No one is allowed to interrupt or ask questions during this time.
2 *Clarifying Questions:* The consultants are given five minutes to ask questions of the presenter. The presenter records questions to answer in the next block of time.
3 *Response:* The presenter is given five minutes to respond to each of the questions posed. The consultants listen and do not respond or ask new questions during this time.
4 *Reflecting Back:* During this time, the consultants consider what they have learned about the dilemma. With up to 10 minutes for this step, the consultants are prompted to ask additional questions within a frame of paraphrasing what they have heard from the presenter before asking for additional clarification.
5 *Response:* The presenter is now given five minutes to clarify anything heard during the paraphrasing and to respond to any new questions.
6 *Brainstorming:* The consultants are now given 10 minutes to provide suggestions for how to resolve the dilemma. This is the first opportunity to contribute suggestions for the presenter to consider.
7 *Response:* During this time, the presenter has five minutes to respond to ideas shared by the consultants that they believe they could implement to work through their dilemma.

8 *Debriefing:* During this final time slot of five minutes, the presenter shares how it felt to be in this role and what they gained from this opportunity. The consultants are also given time to reflect on their role and what they are taking away from this experience.

The second protocol each evening is a Success Analysis and Reflective Questions Protocol (McDonald et al., 2013). This protocol seeks to explore what made a lesson successful rather than what did not go well. This focus allows the participants to celebrate what they are doing well so that others may learn from their successes and it changes the tenor of the evening after looking at a dilemma or challenge. One of the participants volunteers to share a success for the next meeting. This allows them to bring any materials or examples they wish to share with the group.

This protocol follows six steps and takes 30 to 45 minutes:

1 *Sharing:* The presenter shares the lesson or strategy with the group by engaging the other participants in the strategy as much as possible. This usually lasts up to 15 minutes.
2 *Analysis and Discussion:* During this time, about five minutes, everyone discusses what made the lesson or strategy successful. Time is given for each person to share their perspective. They consider what the presenter did to facilitate the success and what other factors might have contributed to the success.
3 *Compilation:* The group continues to brainstorm and discuss the success by compiling the ideas on chart paper for another five minutes.
4 *Reporting Out:* The group takes five minutes to review what was compiled on the chart.
5 *Discussion:* The group has a discussion about the overall learning from this lesson or strategy and considers whether anything surprised anyone about the lesson or strategy. This lasts for five minutes.
6 *Debriefing:* The protocol is completed by the facilitator asking the group to discuss what they liked or disliked about the protocol. The facilitator will also ask what of the protocol could be used in other parts of their work.

Examples from the Induction Meetings

Induction meetings prior to COVID were face-to-face while meetings during COVID were via Zoom; post-COVID meetings have included both modalities. Each in-person meeting was video-recorded and transcribed; virtual meetings conducted using Zoom were recorded and transcribed by Zoom. An examination of the transcripts from the last six years of induction showcases how care exists for each protocol before, during, and after COVID. The examples in this chapter come from the session transcripts and the end-of-the-year focus group session.

Descriptive Consultancy Protocol

This example, from March 2023, reflects a common classroom management dilemma raised by participants before and after COVID. As the presenter, a participant shared that in their classes, students stay on their phones: "They just don't care. They just sit on their phone, all of class ... they don't even acknowledge my presence in the room until the bell rings." These same students have gone to their case workers or their counselors to say they do not understand: "They want tutoring from me after school." The teacher has tried to explain that students need to participate in class and, if they still "are misunderstanding and having trouble with the work, then I'm happy to help." Even during tests, this teacher has trouble: "Please get off your phone like we're trying to take a test, and she just won't get off." They believe that their next step is to call the parents but they have not had time.

After several rounds of clarifying questions, the consultants (i.e., the other teachers and grant leadership team members) made suggestions. These suggestions included trying to establish stronger class policies so that students hold each other accountable; using a clear shoe box or a shoe storage bag for phones, providing reward time on the phone if students finish all daily work, and calling or texting the parents during the class when the problem is occurring.

The teachers have raised many issues over the years of using the Descriptive Consultancy Protocol. During COVID, several issues remained much the same as they did prior to and after the pandemic. Examples of these issues are waiting until the end of the quarter to complete assignments, using inappropriate language, and honors students not performing to expectations. The biggest difference was that, during COVID, our schools were virtual for over a year. During this time, the participants talked frequently about the difficulty with engaging students and student accountability for completing assignments. Since the pandemic, the teachers have raised issues about attendance and students not having "grit" or persistence. One issue that has been raised several times is that students are cheating on assignments by using online resources to complete their homework. While some of these issues are not uncommon for novice teachers (Merk et al., 2015), it is interesting to note that an outcome of the pandemic is students finding additional ways to get around doing the work of learning the content addressed in school.

Success Analysis and Reflective Questions Protocol

The Success Analysis Protocol allows participants to showcase strategies or a particular lesson that they feel was received well by students and the learning goals were met. The amount of time for sharing in the protocol limits what participants have shared with the group in many cases; for example, a strategy is shared rather than a complete lesson. Four different categories of instructional strategies (e.g., engagement, content delivery, student sharing, and review strategies) have been shared before, during, and after the pandemic. Before the pandemic, engagement activities such as jot thoughts, line up, carousel feedback, and lock boxes were shared. Prior to the pandemic, anchor charts and student mini-posters were used as a review tool and for student sharing of thinking. Interestingly, but not surprising, the strategies shared during COVID were technology-based (VanDevelder et al., 2021), such as various ways to use Jamboard for engagement and review. Nearpod, Whiteboards, Google Earth, and ArcGIS StoryMaps were also shared as strategies to engage students in content during and after the pandemic. Since the pandemic, the strategies shared are a mixture of approaches using technology and more hands-on strategies. Lessons shared before and after the pandemic have also included short labs for chemistry and math and teaching scientific argumentation. Engagement of students, as well as content delivery modes, are approaches that these novice teachers have had success with and are willing to share with their colleagues, both prior to and after the pandemic.

Reflections on the Sessions and Protocols

During the final session each year, the participants engaged in a focus group protocol to share their feedback about the year and requests for the next year. These sessions were always conducted by someone on the team, not by the principal investigator/author, to allow for open and frank discussion. The participants shared that they appreciated the support and positive acknowledgement from peers during the protocols. They also appreciated that, when few were in attendance, the protocols were not formally followed and "just open conversation could occur" (2022).

Of interest is why they chose to attend the meetings. Comments reflected that "it is a place, outside of school, that I can get feedback and constructive criticism." This was important to them as they were just building their school networks and did not always feel the trust or care they needed from their school colleagues. They appreciated that, "while we teach different students in different classes and different age levels, some of the specific issues can be similar." They also liked "check[ing] in with people from my cohort," as they are all at different schools and some in different districts.

When asked about the structure of the protocols, the participants shared that school-based meetings were "not as collaborative as we are." One participant expressed their "favorite thing is the problem solving [protocol]. And, knowing that either, I have a problem or where somebody else has a problem that I'm probably also experiencing. Then talking through it and I still have my little sticky [note with suggestions]" from the group sharing. Another participant shared that "it was nice to have a structure for the meeting. It was helpful because you know exactly where this is going and you know what is coming next." One participant during COVID noted, "I really like the protocol, especially virtually ... I like being able to type the questions into the chat box, and then, as a presenter to see those questions." The protocol was not always helpful, however, as one participant shared: "It got like too kind of robotic ... " A final comment that highlights the value of the model was offered by this participant:

> I felt very listened to and heard. It was very helpful to come to hear other people's suggestions ... For me, it's been very helpful to have that structure of, like, this is when you listen, this is when you ask questions, and when you can share.

The participants shared reflections on a variety of topics during the end-of-the-year session. Their thoughts indicated that the protocols helped them feel a part of a caring group. While the protocols in some cases were limiting, overall, the participants felt heard and cared for during the sessions.

Implications

Care can be shown in many ways. Care for our preservice and new graduates is critical to their growth and retention in the profession (Noddings, 1984, 2005). This project found that, for novice teachers, protocols used during the induction sessions provide an important level of care from the university faculty and from their cohort. Protocols allow the participants and facilitators to take time to think before responding, to get at the deep issues, highlight the successes, and respect everyone in the group. The norms of the group are established at the beginning of each fall and are reviewed each month. This establishes the need to care about one another and to respect what everyone brings to the group (Noddings, 2005). These two protocols allow for attention to detail and thoughtfulness of questions and possible solutions. The protocols also slow the process so that dilemmas are well understood and the group does not move to the solution phase too quickly (McDonald et al., 2013). Slowing the process to solutions provides a sense of caring as all ideas are valued and important in the process. The protocols provide needed support and care for each participant as noted by participants earlier. Finally, the protocols are not difficult to incorporate into group interactions.

Many protocols exist and they have different purposes and outcomes (McDonald et al., 2013), but one common outcome of all the protocols is a level of care for one another that is not usually found in traditional group meetings. For novice teachers, the opportunity to build camaraderie in school or outside of school, to problem solve in a safe environment, and to celebrate everyone's success through shared lessons or strategies is critical to finding their place in their chosen profession. Providing these avenues works toward furthering their growth as teachers, as well.

For programs that use protocols within school interactions, the opportunity to develop a sense of "I am a member of this team and I am valued" is critical for retention in the school. For programs that use the protocols outside of the school, novice teachers have a safe place to explore problems and vent, as well as one of the few places where teachers can collaborate across multiple districts. These opportunities also work to support novice teachers and to retain them in the profession. These protocols can be used in many other settings, such as teacher preparation classes, used by teachers in the classroom to model care and respect for each other, and within and between university collaborators (Hargraves et al., 2020). Care is critical to the retention of our novice teachers, and these protocols can provide a mechanism for care and respect.

Acknowledgement

This paper was developed in part through the project VCU Noyce Track 1 Phase III with support from the National Science Foundation, Robert Noyce Award 1758385. The opinions expressed here are those solely of the author and do not reflect the opinions of the funding agency.

References

Barnum, M. (2023, March 6). 'I just found myself struggling to keep up': Number of teachers quitting hits new high. *USA Today*. https://www.usatoday.com/story/news/education/2023/03/06/more-teachers-quitting-than-usual-driven-stress-politics-data-shows/11390639002/

Bryk, A. S. (2010). Organizing schools for improvement. *Phi Delta Kappan*, 90(7), 23–30.

Easton, L. B. (2009). Protocols: A facilitator's best friend. *Tools for Schools. National Staff Development Council*, Feb/Mar.

García-Carrión, R., Padrós Cuxart, M., Alvarez, P., & Flecha, A. (2020). Teacher induction in schools as learning communities: Successful pathways to teachers' professional development in a diverse school serving students living in poverty. *Sustainability*, 12(17), 7146. 10.3390/su12177146

Gay, G. (2010). *Culturally responsive teaching: Theory, research, and practice*. Teachers College Press.

Grillo, M. & Kier, M. (2021). Why do they stay: An exploratory analysis of identities and commitment factors associated with teaching retention in high-need school contexts. *Teaching and Teacher Education*, 105, 103423.

Hargraves, R. H., Hofrenning, S. K., Bowers, J., Beisiegel, M., Piercey, V., & Young, E. S. (2020). Structured engagement for a multi-institutional collaborative to tackle challenges and share best practices. *Journal of Mathematics and Science: Collaborative Explorations, 16*(1), 43–57. https://scholarscompass.vcu.edu/jmsce_vamsc/vol16/iss1/5

Ingersoll, R. M. (2012). Beginning teacher induction. What the data tell us. *Phi Delta Kappan, 93*(8), 47–51.

Ingersoll, R. M., & Strong, M. (2011). The impact of induction and mentoring programs for beginning teachers: A critical review of the research. *Review of Educational Research, 81*(2), 201e233.

Kuhfeld, M., Soland, J., Lewis, K., & Morton, E. (2022, March 3). The pandemic has had devastating impacts on learning. What will it take to help students catch up? *Brookings Blog.* https://www.brookings.edu/articles/the-pandemic-has-had-devastating-impacts-on-learning-what-will-it-take-to-help-students-catch-up/

Ladson-Billings, G. (1995). Toward a theory of culturally relevant pedagogy. *American Educational Research Journal, 32*(3), 465–491.

Luft, J. A., Roehrig, G. H., & Patterson, N. C. (2003). Contrasting landscapes: A comparison of the impact of different induction programs on beginning secondary science teachers' practices, beliefs, and experiences. *Journal of Research in Science Teaching, 40*(1), 77–97.

Luft, J. A., Firestone, J. B., Wong, S. S., Ortega, I., Adams, K., & Bang, E. (2011). Beginning secondary science teacher induction: A two-year mixed methods study. *Journal of Research in Science Teaching, 48*(10), 1199–1224.

Luft, J. A., Dubois, S. L., Nixon, R. S., & Campbell, B. K. (2015). Supporting newly hired teachers of science: Attaining teacher professional standards. *Studies in Science Education, 51*(1), 1–48. 10.1080/03057267.2014.980559

März, V., & Kelchtermans, G. (2020). The networking teacher in action: A qualitative analysis of early career teachers' induction process. *Teaching and Teacher Education, 87*, 1–15. https://doi.org/10.1016/j.tate.2019.102933

McDonald, J. P., Mohr, N., Dichter, A., & McDonald, E. C. (2013). *The power of protocols.* Teachers College Press.

McDonnough, J. M., & Hanschel, M. (2015). Professional learning community-based induction: Creating support for new teachers of science. In J. A. Luft & S. L. Dubois (Eds.), *Newly hired teachers of science: A better beginning* (pp. 145–154). Sense Publishers.

Merk, H., Baird, T., Brandt, A., Giresen, K., Jackson, S., & Reid, J. (2015). Establishing professional practice through a new teacher support group. In J. A. Luft & S. L. Dubois (Eds.), *Newly hired teachers of science: A better beginning* (pp. 155–164). Sense Publishers.

Mindich, D., & Lieberman, A. (2012). *Building a learning community: A tale of two schools.* Stanford Center for Opportunity Policy in Education.

National Science Foundation. (2023). *Robert Noyce Teacher Scholarship Program.* https://www.nsf.gov/funding/pgm_summ.jsp?pims_id=5733&org=NSF

Navy, S., Nixon, R., Luft, J., & Jurkiewicz, M. (2020). Accessed or latent resources? Exploring new secondary science teachers' networks of resources. *Journal of Research in Science Teaching, 57*(2), 184–208.

Noddings, N. (1984). *Caring: A relational approach to ethics and moral education* (2nd ed.). University of California Press.

Noddings, N. (2005). Identifying and responding to needs in teacher education. *Cambridge Journal of Education, 35*(2), 147–159.

Noddings, N. (2010). *The maternal factor: Two paths to morality.* University of California Press.

Noddings, N. (2012). The caring relation in teaching. *Oxford Review of Education, 38*(6), 771–781.

Oxford University Press. (2023). *Oxford Languages.* Retrieved September 10, 2023, from https://www.google.com/search?q=protocol&rlz=1C1GCEA_enUS976US976&oq=protocol&aqs=chrome.0.69i59j69i64j69i61j69i64l3j69i61l2.2654j0j7&sourceid=chrome&ie=UTF-8.

Ronfeldt, M., & McQueen, K. (2017). Does new teacher induction really improve retention? *Journal of Teacher Education, 68*(4), 394–410. 10.1177/0022487117702583

Savka,Y., Southerland, S. A., Kittleson, J., & Hunter, T. (2013). Understanding the induction of a science teacher: The interaction of identity and context. *Research in Science Education, 43*, 1221–1244.

VanDevelder, M., Dossick, A., Kirk, S., & Edmondson, E. (2021). Technoheutagogy: A virtual learning walk with SEED. *Journal of Virginia Science Education*, *14*(1), 19–23.

Webb, A. (2015). Creating awareness of science teacher identity: The importance of who newly hired teachers of science are expected to be and who they become during induction. In J. A. Luft & S. L. Dubois (Eds.), *Newly hired teachers of science: A better beginning* (pp. 99–112). Sense Publishers.

Yau, J., & Lawrence, J. (2014, April). *School reform initiative scope of work*. School Reform Initiative. https://www.schoolreforminitiative.org/wp-content/uploads/2014/05/SRI-Impact-April-2014.pdf

10

"I AM TERRIFIED OF BEING ONE OF MY STUDENTS' BAD MEMORIES"

Stories of Teacher Induction through a Lens of Care

John Weaver, Shelbie Witte, and Nicole Skeen

Trends across the country paint a grim picture of the current state of the teacher shortage crisis. Even prior to the COVID-19 pandemic, Garcia and Weiss (2019) saw that "the teacher shortage is real, large and growing, and worse than we thought. When indicators of teacher quality (certification, relevant training, experience, etc.) are taken into account, the shortage is even more acute than currently estimated" (p. 1). Recent data show that the COVID-19 pandemic only exacerbated the problem. In 2022, more than half of all public schools were operating with vacancies, with many reporting that more than 10% of their positions were left unfilled (Schmitt & DeCourcy, 2022).

The challenge for schools does not end once teachers are hired. Both national and state-wide data continue to show a significant number of new teachers leave the profession early in their careers. Although the exact number is difficult to track, an estimated 30% to a staggering 50% of teachers leave teaching within their first five years (Darling-Hammond, 2003; Ingersoll & Strong, 2011). High teacher attrition negatively impacts students, schools, and communities, as research has demonstrated that teacher effectiveness increases significantly with years of experience. Although there is rapid growth in the first five years, teachers with 5-15 years of experience produce gains in student learning that represent one to two months of additional instruction over teachers with one to five years of experience (Kini & Podolsky, 2016). These findings strongly suggest that placing an emphasis on retaining teachers in the classroom has the potential to significantly and positively impact student learning.

Beyond the negative impact on students and schools, teacher attrition also creates a substantial financial cost for districts. Estimates by the Learning Policy Institute (2017) indicate that filling vacancies cost school districts more than $20,000 on average per teacher in recruitment, hiring, onboarding, and training costs, putting additional pressure on already stressed school budgets. According to Sutcher et al. (2019), the national price tag for replacement costs for teachers was estimated to be more than $8 billion dollars, a number that has continued to grow as the shortage worsens. The collective impact of these data tells us that, while high-quality preparation and recruitment are essential, effective retention support must be a key factor if we hope to mitigate the astonishing levels and impacts of

DOI: 10.4324/9781032707471-13

teacher attrition. We propose that in order for teacher retention support to truly be effective, it must be reimagined through a lens of care.

Within this article, the vignettes serve as illustrative anecdotes, weaving throughout the text to provide real-life context and examples for a deeper understanding of the ways care is centered in the learning of new teachers. Each vignette is presented as a composite narrative (Willis, 2019). As Willis (2019) describes, composite narratives include data from multiple sources to tell a single story. This approach was selected for two reasons. First, the stories shared in this chapter represent common experiences many teachers have expressed in our work. Second, composite narratives allow us to protect the anonymity of the teachers in our programs and ensure confidentiality, a critical component of the support we provide. Following each vignette, we offer related research, discuss the implementation of the principle, and share the feedback we have received from our teachers regarding the impact of our programs.

Reimagining Induction Support

One of the critical factors in improving the retention rates for early career educators is providing comprehensive induction programs (Sutcher et al., 2019). While many states and districts provide induction programs, support tends to be delivered through large group professional development trainings rather than one-on-one coaching and mentoring, both of which have been shown to be the most powerful components of induction (Darling-Hammond, 2003). While the support provided by schools and districts is critical, the limiting factors of time and resources often restrict the level of responsive support they are able to provide. The result is an unintentional void in new teacher support.

To address this identified void in teacher support and the looming teacher retention crisis, the Carolina Teacher Induction Program (CarolinaTIP) was founded in 2017 at the University of South Carolina and is led by the program's founding director, Nicole Skeen. The Retention of Innovative Educators (OK-Thrive) was launched in 2022 at Oklahoma State University and is led by John Weaver and Shelbie Witte. CarolinaTIP and OK-Thrive are innovative university-based induction programs that supplement local induction support and seek to provide novice teachers with individualized, responsive, teacher-focused support aimed at improving teacher retention by increasing self-efficacy, lowering stress, and improving job satisfaction. While adapting to the specific needs of teachers in Oklahoma, OK-Thrive is closely aligned with CarolinaTIP principles, practices, structures, and evaluation models. Alignment between the programs has allowed program leadership to identify what we believe are emerging universal and transferable elements of effective novice teacher support.

Through our collaborative work, we have identified three leading principles that have proven to be essential in providing comprehensive teacher support:

- Care as Creating Space to be Heard
- Care as Facilitating the Healthy Development of Teacher Identity
- Care as Guiding Teachers in Navigating Challenges

These principles, applied through a lens of care, are consistent with Shoffner and Webb's (2022) call to reimagine teacher induction in the wake of the COVID-19 pandemic.

Care as Creating Space to Be Heard

It is early September. After weeks of setting up a new classroom, exploring curriculum, meeting families, and getting to know students, a group of first-year teachers gather together for professional development. Whirling in a mix of shellshock, excitement, and exhaustion, the teachers take their seats.

The Induction Coach (referred to as Coach throughout), seeing the looks on their faces, gives the group a few minutes to talk with those around them and catch their breath. After taking care of some logistics, the session begins with Coach asking, "What would you like to get out of today?"

One teacher comments, "I am interested to hear what strategies other teachers are using." Another teacher mentions, "I am curious to hear whether others are struggling with the same things I am?" Yet another says "I feel like I am failing and just need all the help I can get!"

After several head nods, Sally seemed to put into words what everyone in the room was feeling: "I need to talk about the challenges I am having in my classroom without anyone assuming I hate my job"! Coach responds, "Would you be willing to elaborate a bit?"

Sally explained, "The last month has been hard, and some days have been really hard. I have tried talking to other teachers, but that usually leads to commiserating and I end up having to be the encourager. I have called home, but no one in my family is a teacher, any hint that things aren't going well results in an 'I told you so'. I have reached out to friends, they try to listen, but they don't understand what it is like working with kids all day. I am excited to be around a group of people who are in the trenches with me. Colleagues that recognize that me voicing a struggle doesn't mean I am in the wrong profession or do not love what I do".

Our first principle, *Care as Creating Space to Be Heard*, highlights the posture with which we approach new teacher support. Typically, teacher induction focuses on onboarding and training on policies, procedures, resources, curriculum, and schoolwide initiatives that will help teachers succeed in their specific district and school. While this kind of support is critical and something only the district/school can provide, teacher support applied through a lens of care means providing responsive support based on the needs of the individual teacher (Shoffner & Webb, 2022). In order to address the needs and concerns of teachers, our programs create a space where teachers feel safe to voice their questions, struggles, and insecurities.

What the Experts Say

The notion of creating space for one to be heard has a foundation in both the work on care in education and the field of coaching. According to Noddings (2012), "a carer is first of all attentive, and watches and listens" (p. 773). Although Noddings (2012) focused largely on describing a caring relationship between a teacher and their students, she suggested that a person who trusts that their thinking is respected is more likely to engage in dialogue. This allows the coach as carer to attend to "the expressed needs of the cared-for, not simply the needs assumed by the school as an institution and the curriculum as a prescribed course of study" (p. 773). However, students are not the only ones who need to feel heard. According to Lopez and Sidhu (2013), a survey of more than 150,000 people from a variety of fields indicated that teachers were the least likely to indicate their voice mattered at work.

In his book *Better Conversations*, Jim Knight lists six beliefs that lead to more effective conversations. Of those, two articulate key approaches that increase the likelihood someone feels heard. First, Knight (2016) suggests that both partners need to enter the conversation as equals. He explains that a "top-down" conversation will likely be unsuccessful because the person positioned as less-than will often resist ideas simply because they feel undervalued. Van Nieuwerburgh (2020) echoes this idea and suggests coaching must be approached as a collaborative partnership based on mutual respect. Second, Knight (2016) argues that for coaching to be effective, it must be approached from a nonjudgmental stance. He argues that a judgmental environment is an unsafe environment. However, when a coach approaches a conversation with humble curiosity, it encourages conversation partners to voice whatever is on their mind.

Why It Matters

Providing an unbiased space for teachers to voice their questions, challenges, frustrations, and successes is a pillar of our programs and can be seen throughout the structure of our programs and our teacher-focused coaching. Structurally, our induction programs are non-evaluative, emphasize confidentiality, and remain external from the schools with which we partner. These structural characteristics prevent the perception of judgment and ensure teachers see our coaches and program leaders as guides, collaborators, and partners who are there to support and encourage.

This principle is clearly demonstrated in the coaching approach we employ. Rather than predetermined topics or a set agenda, coaching conversations are designed to be responsive, just-in-time support that address the individual needs of the teacher. Coaches focus on topics introduced by the teacher and are trained to listen and accept without judgment or bias what the teacher is saying. The goal of the conversation is not always to arrive at a solution. Some of the most impactful coaching conversations are those that allow a teacher to clarify their thoughts and say aloud for the first time something they have been wrestling with internally.

Sally seemed to articulate what each new teacher in the room was feeling in that September professional development meeting. Her desire to share and have her concerns validated and corroborated, not only by her coach and program leaders but by nearly every teacher in the room, highlights how isolating and daunting it can be to be a new teacher.

Bolstered by feedback from our participating teachers, Sally emphasizes how creating space to be heard is an impactful and essential component of care in new teacher support: "Our group meetings allow me to talk and reflect with peers and colleagues who are in the same boat as me. I have ranted, cried, and laughed in our sessions and never once have I felt alone ..."

The impact of this principle does not come from providing solutions to problems but from allowing teachers to voice challenges and struggles without fear, judgment, or concern regarding how others in their building view them or their evaluation. This protected space reassures teachers they are not alone and that they are not failures because they are understandably struggling as they find their footing in the classroom.

Care as Facilitating the Healthy Development of Teacher Identity

"Could we close the door today?" Maria asked her coach as they entered her classroom, a hint of uncertainty in her voice. Until now, Maria had given the impression that her first few months as a teacher had gone smoothly.

"It seems like something is on your mind. Do you want to talk about it?" Coach asks.

"Classroom management … I have really struggled lately" Maria responds.

"What are you noticing?" Coach asks.

After discussing what she has been seeing from her students and what she has tried, Maria looks to be sure the door is closed and says, "I think the problem might be one of the other teachers on my team."

"How do you think another teacher is impacting your classroom management?" Coach questions.

Maria responds, "I have a few students that came with a reputation of being 'bad kids.' But, we got off to a GREAT start. I didn't lower the bar. I picked my battles carefully and tried not to worry about small things."

"What changed?" Coach asks.

Maria responds, "A few weeks ago, one of my students was having a really tough day. He was disruptive and I couldn't get him back on track so I asked another teacher for help. Since then, he has started checking in on me regularly."

"How has that impacted your classroom?" her Coach prods.

Maria responds, "I appreciate the support, but he gets on the students for things that don't bother me. He speaks to students differently than I do. Sometimes he will intervene when I am talking if he doesn't feel like they are responding appropriately. I know he is just trying to be helpful … but I don't think I want my classroom to be that strict."

"Do you have to manage your classroom like he does?" Coach inquires.

Maria reflected, "I guess I don't have to, but he is experienced and he's the mentor the district assigned to me for my first year. His class is almost always silent, so maybe his approach works."

"Would managing your classroom that way work for you?" Coach asks.

Maria chuckles, "I have been trying to make it work … but it just doesn't! It feels like the expectation … but it isn't how I want to manage my class … it isn't working for me and my students."

Novice teachers find themselves in a unique context. Although they may be walking into their own classroom for the first time, most will have spent hours a day for nearly two decades as a student. Many engage in teacher preparation programs where they create and observe carefully crafted lessons in their courses and work closely with veteran teachers during student teaching experiences. These experiences help shape a novice teacher's beliefs about teaching. *Care as Facilitating the Healthy Development of Teacher Identity* describes the importance of aiding novice teachers in reconciling these beliefs and discovering who *they* have the power and potential to be as teachers.

What the Experts Say

Although one's identity was initially considered to be a stable attribute unaffected by external factors, recent research has indicated identity development to be a dynamic, active, and social process that influences one's actions and judgments (Hong, 2010). Further, professional teaching identity is an important factor in teacher motivation (Hong, 2010) and commitment to the profession (Rots et al., 2010).

Although there is still much to learn about the development of a teacher's professional identity, Hong (2010) provides valuable insights. She found that the perceptions a new teacher brings into the initial years of their career play a central role in identity formation. Unfortunately, many early career teachers enter the profession with an idealized perception of who they are expected to be as a teacher and struggle to reconcile these perceptions while experiencing the challenges of their induction years. The tension created when teachers act in ways that are inconsistent with their emerging values and beliefs will likely lead to a lack of motivation and destabilize their identity as teachers (Hong, 2010). Without support, teachers who experience these tensions long-term are likely to make the decision to leave the profession (Borman & Dowling, 2008).

However, professional identity tensions (Pillen et al., 2013) do not have to be a source of frustration leading to an early career change. Instead, Cross Francis et al. (2018) suggest, "[w]hen teachers experience identity tensions, it can be potential sources of both challenges and professional growth" (p. 135). However, for this to occur, these tensions must be managed. Van Nieuwerburgh (2020) and de Haan (2008) echo this idea and note that critical moments in coaching often occur in the midst of uncertainty or discomfort rather than in the absence of it. With this in mind, effective coaching of novice teachers should focus, at least in part, on supporting teachers in reconciling their professional identity tensions (McIntyre & Hobson, 2016).

Why It Matters

The personal nature of identity development creates a need to design teacher support that is flexible and personalized to the individual teacher. For this reason, in whole group teacher sessions, we provide practical resources that address the universal struggles new teachers face but dedicate time for teachers to reflect individually on how these practical resources may benefit their own classroom. We explicitly affirm with teachers during each meeting that every teacher in the room is in a different context and has different strengths and leadership styles. With this in mind, resources and strategies are not presented in a prescriptive manner. Rather, teachers engage in dialogue with one another and are encouraged to explore and identify what may work for them and their students. Perhaps the most valuable time spent is providing teachers with opportunities to plan how they intend to implement positive change when they return to their classroom the next day. This has the most pronounced impact when followed up with individual coaching to support teacher-led implementation and promote continued reflection.

In a coaching context, we support identity development by always positioning the teacher as the decision-maker and expert while the coach acts as a thinking partner and conversation guide. We approach coaching conversations with the intention of tapping into what the teacher already knows about student learning, best practices, and their specific context and guide them in leveraging that knowledge to create their own solutions. Coaches are trained not to impose their preferences or tell teachers how they should resolve their challenges. Rather, coaches strive to help teachers derive a solution as a means of developing their unique strengths and identity.

112 John Weaver et al.

Maria finds herself in a state of disequilibrium. Comments like *"I don't think I want my classroom to be that strict"* demonstrate the tension she feels as she explores her teaching identity. Her attempt to reconcile what she wants her classroom management approach to be and the guidance she receives from her mentor causes stress and doubt regarding her self-efficacy in managing her classroom. She knows the advice she is receiving will not work for her but does not have the clarity or confidence to vocalize how she wants to move forward. Teachers consistently report how valuable it is to have time and space to discuss and think through issues in coaching conversations. As one teacher stated, *"My Coach asks questions that lead me to have realizations and form my own ideas for how to tackle everyday issues in the job. [My coach] helps me recognize my strengths as a teacher, which is difficult for me to do at times."* Another shared, *"The [coaching, whole group sessions, and non-evaluative support] I received assisted me in realizing the skills and unique mindset I bring to the education world."*

Left on her own, Maria may have eventually worked through this issue. However, as the comments above suggest, coaching can provide the structure that allows novice teachers to wrestle with who *they* are as a teacher and arrive at a solution that works in *their* classroom as they continue to refine *their* practice. Using coaching conversations to foster critical thinking and support novice teachers in making the best decision for them and their students not only promotes a healthy creation of teacher identity, but also has the capacity to increase self-efficacy and decrease stress.

Care as Guiding Teachers in Navigating Challenges

"Did you hear what happened yesterday?" Mitch asks his coach as he sits down at the table.

"Some, but I don't know any of the details. How are you?" Coach asks.

"I'm OK, but frustrated by the whole thing," Mitch responds.

"Would it be helpful to talk through it or is there something else on your mind?" Coach inquires.

"We can talk about it" Mitch responds as he begins to recount the events of the previous day. As too often happens, the school was alerted to a threat and out of an abundance of caution, the school was forced to go into lockdown.

"You mentioned being frustrated. What do you think is frustrating you?" Coach asks.

Mitch responds, "I understand why we needed to do it but I am upset that this is something we even have to deal with. What's really bothering is the responses I have gotten from people and the posts on social media."

"What are you seeing and hearing?" Coach asks.

"People just keep saying 'thank goodness it wasn't real' and have even criticized how we handled it. I guess I understand what they mean … of course I am thankful everything was OK, but those 45 minutes of sitting in a dark classroom with my students while none of us had any idea what was happening … it WAS real. And scary. And unnerving. People don't understand how hard that was."

Care as *Guiding Teachers in Navigating Challenges* highlights the parameters we use when identifying the focus of our teacher sessions and crafting our coaching approach. As Klein (2021) reports, the average teacher makes more than 1,500 decisions a day. This comes to approximately four decisions every minute of every school day. Many of the decisions teachers make fall in the realm of what one would expect: decisions about instruction or classroom management. However, sometimes the most challenging decisions teachers face are those that no amount of preparation would address. Teacher support through a lens of care means helping teachers navigate the challenges, both instructional and non-instructional, personal and professional, that impact them, their students, and their classroom.

What the Experts Say

In order to apply this core principle, it is necessary to distinguish between mentoring and coaching. Although frequently used interchangeably, these two relationships convey very different roles and responsibilities. Bresser and Wilson (2016) state that a mentor acts as an advisor or teacher who can share their knowledge with someone who is less experienced. This description closely resembles the support provided to new teachers when they are partnered with a veteran teacher. Working with a mentor, a novice benefits from receiving the knowledge and advice a more experienced teacher has gained over the years.

A coach, on the other hand, does not seek to share their knowledge or give advice but rather to encourage the critical thinking and creativity of the coachee. As van Nieuwerburgh and Love (2019) state, "a coach believes her coachee is an autonomous individual who, with time, reflection and encouragement can craft a way of taking forward the challenge or success she has brought to the coaching session" (p. 46). From this perspective, a coach does not need to have expertise in the topic at hand. A coach's expertise lies in their ability to promote the thinking and problem-solving capacity of the coachee, both critical elements in increasing a teacher's self-efficacy to navigate challenges on their own.

Why It Matters

Goodson (2004) reminds us that, every time a teacher walks through the door, there is the potential to confront a situation that is truly unexpected and for which there is no rule book.

In our work with teachers in pre-K to 12th grade, we witness a myriad of challenges new teachers encounter. While the specific challenges vary, we find there is typically a combination of contributing external and internal factors that increase stress and dampen job satisfaction. Helping teachers recognize and address these factors assists them in confronting underlying issues and navigating a path forward.

External factors often arise from the broader school environment. Some educators face a dearth of support from school administration, while others contend with toxic relationships amongst their adult colleagues. Troublingly, student tragedies, disruptions in support systems, and a lack of parental involvement can further compound their challenges. The specter of building lockdowns, violence, threats, and even political battles casts a shadow over their daily work. Additionally, the ever-evolving policies, initiatives, and expectations, such as those thrust upon schools during the COVID-19 pandemic, can prove bewildering and demanding.

Internal factors are deeply personal to each teacher. The struggle to balance the demands of work, particularly the elusive work-life equilibrium, weighs heavily on many. Internal battles include self-doubt and a lack of confidence, impacting their ability to excel in their roles. Personal life challenges, such as family illnesses, strained personal relationships, or financial concerns, can seep into their professional lives, adding to their burdens. Wellbeing issues, ranging from stress and anxiety to conflicts with colleagues, may become internal hurdles. Some educators may feel powerless, unable to voice their concerns or influence change in the face of relentless changes and challenges.

Through our whole group sessions, we help teachers navigate a diverse range of challenges by prompting them to identify what they can control, and conversely, what they cannot. We prompt teachers to name both the internal and external factors of each challenge and provide space for them to generate solutions for responding to the relevant factors as a means of facilitating positive change. For teachers who actively participate in this process, we tend to see an increased self-awareness, specifically in their ability to recognize and accept control over their own actions and reactions, as well as an improved ability to respond to and mitigate the impact of challenges over which they have no direct control.

Our coaches employ similar practices in individual coaching conversations to the ones we utilize in teacher sessions as they help teachers maneuver challenges. In addition to these practices, our coaches are trained to implement coaching processes based on Whitmore's GROW model (1992) and the subsequent GROWTH model (Campbell, 2016). Guiding teachers through the process of analyzing and widening their perception of reality, creating options for how they can resolve or navigate their perception of reality, and determining what action(s) they choose to employ are intentional coaching processes designed to strengthen novice teachers' capacity to navigate challenges by increasing their self-awareness, self-efficacy, autonomy, and hope.

In order to navigate a situation that had a significant impact on him, Mitch needed time to process his thoughts and reactions in a space removed from the judgment of others. Dedicated time to openly process their feelings and reactions to a challenge, as well as space to generate their own solutions for navigating a challenge, are components of our programs that teachers consistently tell us are the most impactful:

> [The program] provided a safe space for me to navigate my first year of teaching. The first year was difficult and tumultuous but I always felt like [the program] was there rooting for me and providing me with the support I required. My coach was always available and willing to talk and work through different situations with me …

In addition to creating a space where teachers feel safe displaying the vulnerability required for this level of introspection, the application of this principle requires time for teachers to reflect deeply, verbalize their reflections, identify their options, and analyze the possible solutions they have derived. These practices empower teachers to discover their agency and establish the core belief that they do have the capacity to create positive change.

Focusing on the Whole Teacher

Indicators such as classroom management, stress management, and burnout all impact the self-efficacy of a teacher (Zee & Koomen, 2016). The core principles described in this chapter are strategically designed to address these identified indicators of teacher attrition through the lens of care. When applied with the expressed intention to serve the whole teacher and in addition to crucial site-specific support, these core principles have the potential to mitigate the mass exodus of early-career teachers leaving the profession.

We recognize that the capacity to launch external and supplemental induction programs is not feasible in every area across the nation. We notice that the concept of care and teacher self-efficacy are rarely the primary focus of teacher professional development. We also know that, based on feedback from our participating teachers and program evaluation data, the application of these principles has been successful in increasing new teacher retention. We propose that reimagining new teacher support by intentionally incorporating principles centered on care, designed to increase self-awareness, broaden perspective, strengthen confidence, and, ultimately, bolster perseverance—within new or existing programs—has the potential to impact the longevity and long-term success for early-career educators as well as for the teaching profession.

References

Borman, G. D., & Dowling, N. M. (2008). Teacher attrition and retention: A meta-analytic and narrative review of the research. *Review of Educational Research, 78*(3), 367–409. 10.3102/0034 654308321455

Bresser, F., & Wilson, C. (2016). What is coaching? In J. Passmore (Ed.), *Excellence in coaching: The industry guide* (3rd ed., pp. 11–32). KoganPage.

Campbell, J. (2016). Framework for practitioners 2: The growth model. In C. van Nieuwerburgh (Ed.), *Coaching in professional contexts* (pp. 235–239). Sage.

Cross Francis, D., Hong, J., Liu, J., & Eker, A. (2018). "I'm not just a math teacher": Understanding the development of elementary teachers' mathematics teacher identity. In P. A. Schutz, J. Hong & D. Cross Francis (Eds.), *Research on teacher identity: Mapping challenges and innovations* (pp. 133–143). Springer.

Darling-Hammond, L. (2003). Keeping good teachers: Why it matters and what leaders can do. *Educational Leadership, 60*(8), 6–13.

de Haan, E. (2008). I struggle and emerge: Critical moments of experienced coaches. *Consulting Psychology Journal: Practice and Research, 60*(1), 106–131. 10.1037/1065-9293.60.1.106

Garcia, E., & Weiss, E. (2019). *The teacher shortage is real, large and growing, and worse than we thought.* Economic Policy Institute. https:// epi.org/163651

Goodson, F. T. (2004). *Teaching in the time of dogs.* National Writing Project.

Hong, J. Y. (2010). Pre-service and beginning teachers' professional identity and its relation to dropping out of the profession. *Teaching and Teacher Education, 26*(8), 1530–1543. 10.1016/ j.tate.2010.06.003

Ingersoll, R. M., & Strong, M. (2011). The impact of induction and mentoring programs for beginning teachers: A critical review of the research. *Review of Educational Research, 81*(2), 201–2033. 10.3102/0034654311403323

Kini, T., & Podolsky, A. (2016). *Does teaching experience increase teacher effectiveness? A review of the research.* Learning Policy Institute. https://files.eric.ed.gov/fulltext/ED606426.pdf

Klein, A. (2021, December 5). 1,500 decisions a day (at least!): How teachers cope with a dizzying array of questions. *Education Week.* https://www.edweek.org/teaching-learning/1-500-decisions-a-day-at-least-how-teachers-cope-with-a-dizzying-array-of-questions/2021/12

Knight, J. (2016). *Better conversations: Coach yourself and each other to be more credible, caring, and connected.* Corwin.

Lopez, S. J., & Sidhu, P. (2013, August 1). *In U.S., newer teachers most likely to be engaged at work.* Gallup. https://news.gallup.com/poll/163745/newer-teachers-likely-engaged-work.aspx

Learning Policy Institute (2017, September 13). *What's the cost of teacher turnover?* https:// learningpolicyinstitute.org/product/the-cost-of-teacher-turnover

McIntyre, J., & Hobson, A. J. (2016). Supporting beginning teacher identity development: External mentors and the third space. *Research Papers in Education, 31*(2), 133–158. 10.1080/02671522 .2015.1015438

Noddings, N. (2012). The caring relation in teaching. *Oxford Review of Education, 38*(6), 771–781. 10.1080/03054985.2012.745047

Pillen, M., Beijaard, D., & den Brok, P. (2013). Professional identity tensions of beginning teachers. *Teachers and Teaching: Theory and Practice, 19*(6), 660–678. 10.1080/13540602.2013.827455

Rots, I., Aelterman, A., Devos, G., & Vlerick, P. (2010). Teacher education and the choice to enter the teaching profession: A prospective study. *Teaching and Teacher Education, 26*(8), 1619–1629. 10.1016/j.tate.2010.06.013

Schmitt, J., & deCourcy, K. (2022). *The pandemic has exacerbated a long-standing national shortage of teachers.* Economic Policy Institute. https://www.epi.org/publication/shortage-of-teachers/

Shoffner, M., & Webb, A. W. (Eds.). (2022). *Reconstructing care in teacher education after COVID-19: Caring enough to change.* Routledge.

Sutcher, L., Darling-Hammond, L., & Carver-Thomas, D. (2019). Understanding teacher shortages: An analysis of teacher supply and demand in the United States. *Education Policy Analysis Archives, 27*(35), 1–40.

van Nieuwerburgh, C. (2020). *An introduction to coaching skills: A practical guide* (3rd ed.). Sage.

van Nieuwerburgh, C., & Love, D. (2019). *Advanced coaching practice: Inspiring change in others.* Sage.

Whitemore, J. (1992). *Coaching for performance: A practical guide to growing your own skills.* Nicholas Brealey.

Willis, R. (2019). The use of composite narratives to present interview findings. *Qualitative Research, 19*(4), 471–480. 10.1177/1468794118787711

Zee, M., & Koomen, H. M. Y. (2016). Teacher self-efficacy and its effects on classroom processes, student academic adjustment, and teacher well-being: A synthesis of 40 years of research. *Review of Educational Research, 86*(4), 981–1015. 10.3102/0034654315626801

PART III

PARTNERSHIPS AND COMMUNITY AS SITES OF CARE

11

UNDERSTANDING AND RESPONDING TO THE NEW TEACHER EXPERIENCE

One TEP's Commitment to Connections of Care

Megan Guise, Sarah Hegg, Jesse Sanford, Tanya Flushman, and Nancy Stauch

"On Thursday before I even got into my classroom, here is what happened: One student asked me to eat grasshoppers with him. One student asked me if he could set up ping pong in my door. One student showed me a PowerPoint about how KFC is killing you. LOL. There is no other job where this would be normal, but it is my normal." (First-Year Science & English Language Development Teacher)

The experience of a new teacher (NT) is multi-faceted and includes challenges and successes, some common and others unique to each NT. Teacher education programs (TEPs), together with districts, have a responsibility to prepare and support NTs for the job of teaching. The NT quoted to begin the chapter approaches a diverse group of students with care and intentionality. It is in this same way that our TEP approaches NT support, understanding that the reality of the NT role demands innovation and holistic care.

In response to the demands of this first year of teaching, many states and school districts offer NT induction programs. These programs provide a range of NT support with one to two years of programming that typically include veteran teacher mentoring and general professional development. There is a movement toward innovative induction models that prioritize care in addition to meeting the state requirements of clearing a credential. Similarly, we believe the education of teachers requires a caring community and sustained support into and beyond the first year of teaching.

In this chapter, we share our six-year journey partnering with PK-12 districts and NTs to re-envision teacher education. We describe our experience implementing holistic support through district and alumni NT learning communities (NTLCs) and share interview data to show the impact of these communities. We also outline the research we conducted on the experiences of NTs, and from our findings, provide implications for creating a more humane experience for beginning teachers.

A Framework of Care

For some time, researchers have closely examined the role of care in teaching (Lavy & Naama-Ghanayim, 2020; Mercado, 1993; Noddings, 1984, 1992; Owens & Ennis, 2005;

DOI: 10.4324/9781032707471-15

Tarlow, 1996). Care can be defined as "those emotions, actions and reflections that result from a teacher's desire to motivate, help or inspire their students" (O'Connor, 2008, p. 117). Researchers (e.g., Levin & Rock, 2003; Noddings, 1984) put caring at the center of schooling and the educational system while arguing that student-teacher relationships (both caregiver and being cared for) are foundational to learning (Noddings, 1992).

These relationships are not hierarchical but rather interconnected in a way that requires the relationship itself to be centered. These relationships beget moments of care, where the caregiver gives attention to the cared for, allowing them to be moved by their needs and feelings (Noddings, 2003). Empathy and perspective-taking are essential as "the one-caring does not give the cared-for what she would want were she in his situation but attempts to feel what the cared-for feels in order to discern what he himself would want" (Goldstein, 1999, p. 657). Each situation is contextualized and nuanced but the relationship itself is always at the center. When relationships are positioned as core to our humanity and how we identify ourselves, care is a necessary requirement for educators (Noddings, 1984) and arguably essential pedagogical content knowledge for teachers (Owens & Ennis, 2005).

As teachers of teachers, we believe in the centrality of taking care to build relationships with our preservice teachers and these relationships do not end when they graduate from our TEP. We see the work of teacher education as collaborative and built on relationships between many vested partners (e.g., TEP faculty, district mentors). We believe a focus on care in teacher education can be reinforced by an emphasis on, and development of, social-emotional competencies in NTs. Researchers highlight the importance of teachers developing skills such as emotional regulation, self-awareness, and relationship-building (Mansfield et al., 2016; Morgan, 2011; Schonert-Reichl et al., 2015). These competencies enrich the work experience for NTs, helping them establish positive classroom cultures, manage student behavior effectively, and develop strong relationships with students and colleagues that are a critical part of the induction process.

Literature Review

Effective teacher induction and support are essential for ensuring success, job satisfaction, and retention (Ingersoll, 2001; Ingersoll & Strong, 2011). However, many teachers feel unprepared for the challenges of teaching, which can lead to high turnover and low morale. Therefore, it is crucial to understand the connections between TEPs and the PK-12 classroom. Both formal and informal approaches to teacher induction must be explored to provide the best, most appropriate support for NTs. The COVID pandemic further highlighted the need for teacher induction to adapt to current contexts and for social-emotional competencies to be nourished and developed.

Researchers have called for induction programs that provide localized, teacher-specific professional development (Darling-Hammond, 2009; Espinoza et al., 2018). Personalized professional development and learning experiences that address the specific needs, strengths, and goals of individual teachers become possible with differentiated induction support that honors the unique lived experiences of individuals while leveraging the assets they bring to the table (Fry, 2007; Teehan, 2017). Differentiated induction support based on teacher needs and interests and offerings of ongoing professional development can lead to increased job satisfaction and retention (Stewart & Jansky, 2022; Teehan, 2017).

Research on improving induction programs has also highlighted the importance of building robust communities for new teachers to foster feelings of belonging (Stewart & Jansky, 2022). Intentional relationship-building opportunities with fellow teachers, including structured occasions and spaces for teachers to interact and collaborate, help to impart trust, mutual respect, and a sense of belonging among colleagues (Kardos & Johnson, 2007; Keese et al., 2022; Ingersoll & Strong, 2011). Focusing on relationships is further supported by Noddings (2003) who envisions effective teaching situations where colleagues work together, acting as a part of a greater community where members simultaneously care for each other and strive for continual improvement.

In addition to NT-specific professional development and creating communities of care for NTs, Espinoza et al. (2018) identified high-quality induction elements such as non-evaluative systems of support and lengthened induction programs lasting two to four years. Other innovations include supplementing induction programs with reduced teaching assignments and extra planning time (Keese et al., 2022), as well as modeling and encouraging reflective practices (Genor, 2005). In their research to develop a reflection framework, Genor (2005) presents teacher reflection as essential for NTs to navigate teaching challenges and problematize questions about teaching and student learning. Ingersoll and Smith (2004) have found that these innovative models have positively impacted teacher retention.

The research highlighted above identifies foundational principles of effective induction programs in the face of ongoing change. Supports that are consistent and high-quality, such as sustained collaborative experiences with other teachers and differentiated professional development, prove to be most effective. These supports focus on more than just preparedness for the norm but, rather, wrap-around care that acknowledges and appreciates the unique challenges that teachers face. These approaches are intended to be implemented with care and compassion, honoring NTs as individuals, nurturing their unique areas of need, and further honing their strengths, just as they would do for the students that they serve. This research guided our TEP as we embarked on the creation and implementation of our own innovative support models.

Our Context

We are a small TEP in rural California, offering credentials in elementary, secondary, and mild/moderate special education, graduating approximately 130 NTs annually. Preservice teachers complete a one-year post-baccalaureate credential program consisting of three to four quarters of coursework and a yearlong clinical practice. Approximately 40–60% of TEP graduates secure full-time employment in a local district. In our smaller TEP, faculty serve not only as course instructors but also as academic advisors and clinical practice supervisors. Our faculty/staff build relationships with the preservice teachers during their TEP and, as owners of these programs, have the authority to implement course and policy/process changes. In this way, faculty act with care in ways that are timely and responsive to the needs of NTs.

The authors of this chapter include three TEP faculty (Megan, Tanya, and Nancy), one staff member (Sarah), and one district induction mentor (Jesse). Having both university and district personnel involved in this work allowed us to consider ways to strengthen the partnership between our TEP and PK-12 districts and envision wrap-around support.

Initial Inquiries

Our journey to better understand and support the NT experience has been ongoing for several years and was shaped by many factors, including faculty investment in alumni success, local district attrition, ongoing research, and grant funding. Our efforts began in earnest with the award of two large grants that required TEPs to engage with induction alongside districts. These fiscal resources were leveraged throughout our journey and provided the means for expanding our TEP role to include better care and support for NTs.

Initial inquiry efforts included conducting empathy interviews (i.e., interviews that elicited the stories and feelings of constituents to uncover a deeper understanding of their lived experiences) and collecting data on alumni employment and attrition trends. Drawing on improvement science frameworks (Bennett et al., 2022), we conducted interviews with TEP program coordinators, faculty, and staff. Interviews were used to better understand the informal support individuals and programs offered to care for our NTs. These supports were not systematic or expansive but organic and teacher-specific (e.g., emails, informal gatherings).

In addition to TEP interviews, we interviewed a district principal and NTs. Data informed our first efforts to support NTs with a separate community—the new teacher learning community (NTLC)—that augmented district induction and addressed local attrition. We focused on NT transition as a conduit for retention while also creating a feedback loop for our TEP's continuous improvement. We posited that if our TEP could maintain contact with alumni during the first few years of teaching, providing holistic care via already-established relationships, we had the potential to mitigate transitional challenges.

New Teacher Learning Communities

One key component of our holistic care for NTs includes the NTLCs: communities established to support teachers as they navigate their first years of teaching. For six years, we have facilitated ten different cohorts of NTs engaged in two different types of NTLCs, including district-specific (i.e., NTs within one district) and TEP-specific (i.e., program alumni across multiple districts). Over 200 NTs participated in these opportunities, and district-specific NTLCs occurred in four different districts. Although the type of NTLC differed and processes evolved over time based on continuous improvement, the intent was always to provide a safe, collaborative, and caring space for NTs to share and discuss common issues. Throughout the years, many supports remained the same, including in-person and virtual sessions focused on community building, teacher-driven content, and problems of practice; informal check-ins between community sessions; online space for sharing resources; co-teaching opportunities with TEP faculty; and social activities.

Prior to the first district NTLC, the team developed, in coordination with district mentors, a tentative scope and sequence for the year to supplement the district's induction program. Participation was voluntary and incentivized by both the district and TEP; the district provided hourly pay for NT attendance and our TEP provided a stipend for NTs who attended a majority of sessions. NTLC sessions were jointly planned and implemented; data collected informed small and iterative changes.

A typical NTLC session consisted of NTs informally interacting with members and facilitators. NTs engaged in either a problem of practice (PoP) protocol—an inquiry-based protocol where teachers identified a problem and group members shared interpretations and solutions—or content provided by the TEP facilitators. This content was determined in advance via a survey of NTs. Some material was directly connected to furthering teaching practice (e.g., how to support emergent bilinguals), while at other times, the material had a social and emotional learning focus (e.g., communication skills). Periodically, sessions concluded with survey distribution to capture participant feedback and inform future sessions.

One guiding principle for the district NTLC was creating a sense of belonging and a space that affirmed NTs since research shows the importance of relationship building among colleagues (Fry, 2007; Noddings, 2003). The community was intended to foster feelings of affirmation and care in part through meeting others going through similar experiences. In addition, we believed that having someone check in on their well-being would help NTs to feel cared for both professionally and personally. The design of the community did not include administrators, induction mentors, or district faculty in supervisory roles. This design was deliberate and allowed for vulnerability while fostering belonging. The first years of teaching can be very isolating (Kardos & Johnson, 2007) and the NTLC created a place across schools within the same district for NTs to network. NTs commented on the sense of belonging in interviews: "The NTLC created the ability to connect specifically with other new teachers and to give us our own little community ... For me, especially those connections were important because I felt like it gives me somebody ... I know I'm not alone." Additionally, the NTLC included TEP faculty; some participants each year were alumni of our institution, and involving program faculty in the NTLC allowed alumni to continue TEP relationships.

Problem solving was a second NTLC principle that showed care for NTs. Faculty and district partners were intentional in selecting activities and content that allowed NTs to engage in problem solving in a non-evaluative community of support (Espinoza et al., 2018). We believed that fostering effective decision-making skills through problem solving would allow NTs to best navigate their first years of teaching and provide a way to practically care for participants by developing social-emotional competencies (Mansfield et al., 2016; Schonert-Reichl et al., 2015).

As mentioned above, NTs engaged in PoP inquiry cycles and rich discussions with peers. NTs appreciated the practical applications and identification of real strategies to address their problems. When referring to the PoP activity, one NT said,

> I felt like anytime someone posed a problem or something that's going on in their classroom they wanted support with, everyone had really good ideas. It was very comfortable to share what we needed support in, and a lot of people were able to really help with that. I did also feel like this was a really positive experience.

By engaging in PoP, NTs had access to resources offered by peers and facilitators that could be used to address problems in their classrooms.

A third principle of care included latitude for NT agency. We posited that by allowing the voices of NTs to guide NTLC norms, content, and structures, NTs might have increased self-efficacy that could transfer to their classrooms. We wanted to honor the voices of NTs and allow their successes, concerns, and questions to guide sessions and create space for differentiated, localized professional development (Darling-Hammond et al., 2009;

Espinoza et al., 2018). Specific ways that we created space for agency included establishing community norms and revisiting these norms throughout sessions. NTs brought the problem that mattered most to them and had structured time to receive feedback. Sessions that included professional development were guided by NT input in advance. Reflecting on the agency afforded to NTs, one participant remarked,

> I think they [NTLC facilitators] really made sure that we understood that this community was guided by us. They ask at every single meeting what do we want to talk about at the next meeting? What would be beneficial? What do we not need? We would write it on sticky notes every time. I think that was really powerful just knowing that we actually ... got to steer it in whatever direction we needed to be guided in.

Building off the district-specific NTLCs and in response to the COVID pandemic, our TEP for the past three years has also facilitated an alumni NTLC. For the 2020–21 academic year, preservice teachers enrolled in our yearlong program had 100% of their program courses and 75% of their clinical practice online due to the pandemic. Recognizing the unique challenges for this cohort, having had limited in-person time in PK-12 classrooms, we facilitated a virtual NTLC during their first year of employed teaching that included a two-day virtual summer institute with a focus on techniques for building community and establishing classroom procedures, a panel presentation of veteran teachers, and a guided book discussion. The summer institute was followed by three participant-driven virtual sessions held throughout the year. We continue to offer the summer institute and yearlong NTLC to TEP alumni for their first year of teaching. The online teaching skills developed during the pandemic helped us to see a new possibility of extending our connection to our program alumni by using video conferencing to engage with alumni teaching outside of our local districts.

While co-facilitating the NTLC with local districts, our TEP conducted research on the NTLC's impact, informing future iterations and providing feedback to TEP faculty, shaping course and clinical practice reforms. In implementing the NTLCs, we recognized the importance of better understanding the experiences of NTs. Most recently, our current research has examined the experiences of NTs, following a subset of program alumni to learn about first-year teaching successes and challenges.

Understanding the New Teacher Experience through Research

Our journey to support NTs is informed by our ongoing effort to research the NT experience. For the duration of the 2022–23 academic year, we followed the first-year teaching journeys of 21 secondary teachers. At the start of the academic year, we invited recent alumni who were teaching full-time to participate in this research in which, every week, they completed an online teaching reflection. The reflection contained both open-ended questions (e.g., What was your most memorable moment this week?) and Likert scale questions (e.g., statements about work/home life balance and level of success on a variety of teaching skills). We also conducted semi-structured interviews during the middle and end of the first year. Through this research, we aimed to better understand the journey of NTs, gain insight into the emotions experienced and the social and emotional skills utilized, and learn more about how TEPs and districts can enact change to better prepare and continue to support NTs.

A total of 23 NTs participated in this research, with two NTs withdrawing from the study mid-year. The 21 remaining participants consisted of four agriculture teachers, six English, two mathematics, eight science, and one social studies. Twelve of the NTs taught at a high school, eight at a middle school, and one at a combined middle/high school. Schools included both public and private.

To capture individual stories, we took a case study approach (Yin, 2009). Each researcher read and coded all reflections from four to five NTs, coding for NT successes, challenges, and references to retention. For successes and challenges, secondary codes included identifying the aspect of teaching that was successful or challenging (e.g., school site/district context, student learning, classroom environment). Each researcher also wrote a synthesis memo for each month of that NT's experience. In addition, the faculty lead read all reflections, writing a weekly analytic memo noting trends across all participants.

We valued the time of the NTs and their willingness to be vulnerable and share their experiences and approached the design and facilitation of this research from this place of care. Accordingly, the NTs enrolled in this study were compensated for their time, receiving stipends for the completion of their weekly reflections and for each semi-structured interview. In addition to compensation, we also provided care via weekly communication. At the end of each week, the faculty lead sent a reminder email to complete the online reflection. Included in this email was a brief description and access to "This Week's Resource." Often this resource connected to a challenge the NTs faced the previous week (e.g., a "Reframing Classroom Management" framework from Learning for Justice [2022] to support NTs in building community and responding to student behavior). We view resource sharing as a way to support the professional development of NTs and to be responsive to their needs, which research has shown to be an effective model for induction (Darling-Hammond et al., 2009).

Another form of care this research afforded was the opportunity to reach out individually to the NTs to offer support or celebrate successes. The faculty lead read the reflections each week and reached out with an individualized email for any NT who shared a challenge that was a cause for concern. For example, during Week 4, one NT shared the following:

This week, the school received a tip about what they thought was a social media threat naming me. I was removed from the classroom while they investigated and eventually determined that the threat was not directed to me … It was a very scary situation.

The faculty lead reached out to ensure the NT felt supported and had notified appropriate supervisors. The faculty lead also emailed NTs to congratulate them on successes shared in a reflection. This individualized communication resulted in some NTs asking to meet for coffee or emailing for curriculum ideas. In the reflections, some NTs spoke directly to the faculty lead, showing an awareness that their reflections were read and their experiences mattered, perhaps reducing feelings of isolation (Kardos & Johnson, 2007). We recognize that these types of "interventions" may have impacted the data collected but, as a research team, we felt it was essential to support NTs in instances like these since our primary intention was to enact this research with a concern for NT wellbeing.

Data also showed that creating space for reflection can be viewed as a form of care. When asked why they decided to participate in this study, one NT explained, "Because I kind of wanted to journal my experience" and another stated, "Reflecting, in general, helps me kind of keep track … and reflect upon my practices when I feel like I don't always have time for … It kind of forces that to happen, which is really important." A third NT explained, "Because reflecting and learning from your mistakes is just a huge part of your first year of teaching … So I think it's just a great tool to make sure that I'm reflecting on what I'm doing." We make the argument that this reflection is a form of self-care that aids teachers in navigating the ups and downs of an undoubtedly formidable first year.

The greatest care we can show is honoring the stories of these NTs and using these data to support efforts to re-conceptualize induction models. Inspired by *Street Data: A Next-Generation Model for Equity, Pedagogy, and School Transformation* (Safir & Dugan, 2021), we designed this study to capture "qualitative and experiential data that emerges at eye level" (p. 2) and is "a next-generation paradigm that roots equity, pedagogy, and school transformation in what matters most: human experience" (p. 12). In centering NT stories in the reading and coding of reflections, we were afforded an opportunity to critically examine our TEP and thought-partner with other communities invested in induction reform. At the local level, we have developed a collaborative, composed of grant leadership faculty/staff, PK-12 district liaisons, clinical practice supervisors, and an external grant evaluator. We meet twice a month to engage in professional development and have shared a de-identified case study and quantitative data on all 21 participants. These conversations grounded in NT experiences have led to actionable changes in the NTLC content described previously. At the state level, we have also shared a case study from this research with the Continuous Improvement Collective, a working group of California State University (CSU) faculty/staff using continuous improvement to reform TEPs and induction. This resulted in a collaboration with the CSU Educator Quality Center to support their creation of NT listening sessions. Through these ongoing conversations grounded in the lived experiences of NTs, we envision implications for future NT support.

Implications

Engaging in this care-centered inquiry provided many distinct learning opportunities for participants and researchers. We cannot overstate how meaningful and significant it is to center NT experience and voice when working to improve PK-12 schooling more broadly and increase retention and job satisfaction for teachers more specifically. By focusing on the NT perspective, we are provided with a unique view of schools/schooling that makes transparent the complex highs and lows of teaching. For example, we witness the emotional high of an NT when receiving an end-of-the-year gift from a student who had extremely challenging behavior, often causing the NT to doubt her choice to teach. We saw this same teacher spend the first few months of the school year focused on classroom management due to the very real socio-emotional needs of students in post-COVID classrooms but, when able to engage in concerted study of her own practice, this NT was surprised by how much her instructional practice made a difference in student learning. Living in and navigating these tremendous shifts is the work of being an NT.

What, then, does this work tell us about how NTs and TEPs can use this understanding to improve the experience of teaching? This same teacher, by all measures, had a typical, yet successful, year. We hypothesize that her ability to care for herself on this journey allowed her to navigate it more smoothly. This self-care included involving herself in outside extracurricular activities and time with friends and family. Perhaps even more importantly, she gave herself permission to maintain a more stable and balanced perspective, despite the highs and lows of her week. She recognized those peaks and valleys as inherently part of the work over which she had little control. The mindset she brought to the work could make the biggest difference in her experience and the experience of her students. Learning from stories like this, we hope to support NTs to mitigate the ups and downs of a challenging profession and to be productive and happy in the profession.

The work of TEPs and districts is to both honor and affirm these experiences as they are the work of teaching in 2023. The most helpful conversation is one where we conceptualize teacher education and induction as a continuity of care. When the experiences of NTs are affirmed and they can take a caring perspective that honors their need for balance, they may have a better chance of weathering those first few challenging years. It also may help them lay a foundation for a longer, more successful career. In this chapter, we have outlined the spectrum of care we provided for a cohort of NTs. We recognize our grant funding and unit structure helped support this work but we do strongly believe TEPs and districts can provide similar support at other levels with a care-centered focus.

An important first step for TEPs is to reframe the way we think about the duration of our programs. NTs require support from mentors well into their first few years of teaching and faculty from TEPs are well-positioned to help them navigate the ups and downs from a place of caring. After all, faculty no longer hold any evaluative role in their lives and can be a guide for NTs without fear of judgment. The weekly reflective practice with faculty oversight that we implemented is one way to do this but there are many others. For example, a faculty member can hold a book circle of newly graduated teachers, host informal community meetings at a coffee shop, or develop an alumni network engaging in professional learning.

While in the program, courses and clinical practice can be framed to realistically expose preservice teachers to the work of teaching while also helping them to view it in a balanced manner. This may include engaging in critical discussion with scenarios that ask preservice teachers to reflect and analyze "typical" days of NTs. Critical conversations could help preservice teachers prioritize and balance their efforts, thoughts, and emotions as they consider the extreme highs and lows of any given day in the classroom. For many reasons, it is not possible for a TEP through coursework and clinical practice to expose preservice teachers to the vastly different situations they may encounter as a teacher (Kardos & Johnson, 2007). However, there is something disingenuous about preparing someone to do a job that you know they are not entirely prepared for and then letting them go off on their own. This exposure comes in the first year and the time to be of help, the time to help them navigate, is then, not necessarily in the TEP. This makes an even stronger case for sustained contact and care into the first year of teaching.

We agree with Keese et al. (2022) that PK-12 districts and TEP leaders should invest heavily in induction. TEPs and districts would be well-served to spend time developing strong partnerships to provide a comprehensive continuum of care, signaling to all that training and developing teachers is a collective effort requiring a village of caring professionals. This could be done through fostering partnership agreements between TEPs and districts, developing advisory groups that include members from both TEPs and districts, and leveraging district personnel and resources to create NTLCs led by TEP faculty.

To approach this work from a more comprehensive and organized place of caring takes resources. In our case, grant funding allowed us to compensate the NTs for their valuable time and to pay faculty engaged in this extra-duty work to conduct the research and support NTs in real time. However, given the nation's pressing issues with teacher recruitment and retention, state and federal governments would be well-served to consider allocating more funds to TEPs and districts to support NTs (Espinoza et al., 2018). TEPs and districts would also be wise to think of creative ways to partner and pool funds so that NTs do not feel cast adrift or as if they are receiving disjointed care in the first few years.

Our research afforded us the unique opportunity to witness the NT experience in a comprehensive way. When one NT was asked in an interview to provide three words to describe her first year, she replied,

> Tumultuous, taxing, rewarding … Just yesterday, I had one of my students … [an] "I hate science" kind of student, give me this note at the end of class, which says, "Best teacher ever." And so that means a lot … And that shows that I'm doing something right. I don't know what, but I'm doing something right. So yeah, I would say tumultuous, taxing, and rewarding at the same time.

We believe innovative induction supports play an important role in supporting NTs to navigate the diversity of the first-year teacher experience. While traditional TEPs can lay the groundwork for what NTs may encounter, our continued presence and support play an important role in helping NTs problem-solve through the tumultuous times, talk through the taxing ones, and reflect with NTs as they feel rewarded in their work.

References

Bennett, B., Grunow, A., & Park, S. (2022). *Improvement science at your fingertips: A resource guide for coaches of improvement*. ISC LLC.

Darling-Hammond, L., Wei, R. C., Andree, A., Richardson, N., & Orphanos, S. (2009). *Professional learning in the learning profession: A status report on teacher development in the United States and abroad*. National Staff Development Council. https://edpolicy.stanford.edu/sites/default/files/publications/professional-learning-learning-profession-status-report-teacher-development-us-and-abroad_0.pdf

Espinoza, D., Saunders, R., Kini, T., & Darling-Hammond, L. (2018). *Taking the long view: State efforts to solve teacher shortages by strengthening the profession*. Learning Policy Institute.

Fry, S. W. (2007). First-year teachers and induction support: Ups, downs, and in-betweens. *Qualitative Report, 12*(2), 216–237.

Genor, M. (2005). A social reconstructionist framework for reflection: The "problematizing" of teaching. *Issues in Teacher Education, 14*(2), 45–62.

Goldstein, L. S. (1999). The relational zone: The role of caring relationships in the co-construction of mind. *American Educational Research Journal, 36*(3), 647–673.

Ingersoll, R. M. (2001). Teacher turnover and teacher shortages: An organizational analysis. *American Educational Research Journal, 38*(3), 499–534.

Ingersoll, R. M., & Smith, T. M. (2004). Do teacher induction and mentoring matter? *NAASP Bulletin, 88*(638), 28–40.

Ingersoll, R. M., & Strong, M. (2011). The impact of induction and mentoring programs for beginning teachers: A critical review of the research. *Review of Educational Research, 81*(2), 201–233.

Kardos, S. M., & Johnson, S. M. (2007). On their own and presumed expert: New teachers' experience with their colleagues. *Teachers College Record, 109*(9), 2083–2106.

Keese, J., Waxman, H., Asadi, L., & Graham, M. (2022). Retention intention: Modeling the relationships between structures of preparation and support and novice teacher decisions to stay. *Teaching and Teacher Education, 110*, 103594.

Lavy, S., & Naama-Ghanayim, E. (2020). Why care about caring? Linking teachers' caring and sense of meaning at work with students' self-esteem, well-being, and school engagement. *Teaching and Teacher Education, 91*, 1–48.

Learning for Justice (2022). Reframing classroom management: A toolkit for educators. https://www. learningforjustice.org/sites/default/files/2022-04/LFJ-Reframing-Classroom-Management-Handout-Single-PDFs-2022-04192022.pdf

Levin, B. B., & Rock, T. C. (2003). The effects of collaborative action research on preservice and experienced teacher partners in professional development schools. *Journal of Teacher Education, 54*(2), 135–149.

Mansfield, C. F., Beltman, S., Broadley, T., & Weatherby-Fell, N. (2016). Building resilience in teacher education: An evidenced informed framework. *Teaching and Teacher Education, 54*, 77–87.

Mercado, C. I. (1993). Caring as empowerment: School collaboration and community agency. *Urban Review, 25*(1), 79–104.

Morgan, M. (2011). Resilience and recurring adverse events: Testing an assets-based model of beginning teachers' experiences. *The Irish Journal of Psychology, 32*(3-4), 92–104.

Noddings, N. (1984). *Caring: A feminine approach to ethics & moral education.* University of California Press.

Noddings, N. (1992). *The challenge to care in schools: An alternative approach to education.* Teachers College Press.

Noddings, N. (2003). *Caring: A feminine approach to ethics and moral education.* University of California Press.

O'Connor, K. (2008). You choose to care: Teachers, emotions and professional identity. *Teaching and Teacher Education, 24*(1), 117–126.

Owens, L. M., & Ennis, C. D. (2005). The ethic of care in teaching: An overview of supportive literature. *Quest, 57*, 392–425.

Safir, S., & Duggan, J. (2021). *Street data: A next-generation model for equity, pedagogy, and school transformation.* Corwin.

Schonert-Reichl, K. A., Hanson-Peterson, J. L., & Hymel, S. (2015). SEL and preservice teacher education. In J. A. Durlak, C. E. Domitrovich, R. P. Weissberg, & T. P. Gullotta (Eds.), *Handbook of social and emotional learning: Research and practice* (pp. 406–421). The Guilford Press.

Stewart, T. T., & Jansky, T. A. (2022). Novice teachers and embracing struggle: Dialogue and reflection in professional development. *Teaching and Teacher Education: Leadership and Professional Development, 1*, 1–9.

Tarlow, B. (1996). Caring: A negotiated process that varies. In S. Gordon, P. Benner, & N. Noddings (Eds.), *Caregiving: Readings in knowledge, practice, ethics, and politics* (pp. 56–82). University of Pennsylvania.

Teehan, T. M. (2017). *Improving induction of new preschool to 12th grade teachers through differentiated induction activities tailored to individual teacher's needs.* Rowan University.

Yin, R. K. (2009). *Case study research: Design and methods.* SAGE.

12

"I AM LUCKY TO BE SURROUNDED BY SO MUCH TALENT"

Growing a Professional Learning Community for Early Career Teacher Mentors

Jessica Murdter-Atkinson, Elizabeth Colquitt Ries, Beth Maloch, LeAnne Hernandez, Kerry Alexander, Audrey Stein Wright, and Melissa Mosley Wetzel

In the United States, public education has reached a crossroads. Fewer teachers are entering the workforce and nearly 50% leave the profession within the first five to seven years (Carver-Thomas & Darling-Hammond, 2017). Preparing and retaining high-quality teachers is an important, pressing issue. Induction programs for early career teachers (ECTs) are a promising approach to increasing teacher retention and student success outcomes (Ingersoll & Strong, 2011). This support is particularly helpful in light of the pandemic, which disrupted the clinical experiences of preservice teachers and created continued and varied challenges for teaching and learning in schools (Darling-Hammond & Hyler, 2020). In addition, a growing number of alternatively certified teachers entering the workforce also need support (National Center for Education Statistics, 2022; Texas Education Agency, 2022). Induction and mentoring programs, such as the one described in this chapter, can support ECTs as they enter the field of education (Baumgartner & Webb, 2022; Ingersoll & Strong, 2011; Maloch et al., 2022). The examples shared in this chapter are part of a larger, four-year qualitative study that considers induction program implementation to better understand the experiences and perspectives of ECTs and mentors.

Induction Program Background

In response to ongoing concerns regarding teacher shortages and turnover in our state, induction support for new teachers has long been an interest of our teacher education program and college. In the fall of 2019, we began designing an innovative induction program that would be a robust response to the needs in schools related to teacher turnover. Amid this broader and large-scale design work, COVID-19 struck. The pandemic significantly impacted our student teachers' preparation routes and experiences as they no longer had opportunities to teach students in person while receiving ongoing mentoring and coaching.

At the time, we were engaged in a long-term collaborative partnership with a neighboring school district. This central Texas school district served roughly 75,000 students during the

DOI: 10.4324/9781032707471-16

2020–2021 school year. Of the students enrolled, approximately 55% identified as Latino; 30% White; 6.9% Black; 4.3% Asian; 3.4% two or more races/ethnicities; and 0.1% Indian/Alaska Native and 0.1% Hawaiian/Pacific Islander. Through this partnership, we heard first-hand about the acute and urgent needs emerging, including their hiring of hundreds of first-year teachers with inadequate opportunities to engage in supervised in-person student teaching. We secured funding through local donors and philanthropic foundations and planned closely with district personnel to design the induction program. All Texas school districts are required by law to have an induction program and our partner district already had induction support built in. We were cautious not to conflict with the supports they had in place. To avoid overlapping with each other, we decided that our program would support ECTs at 14 elementary schools experiencing higher-than-usual turnover and the district would provide comparable support to middle schools.

Researcher Positionality

Within our research team, each of us has experience as a classroom teacher, with three of the research team members formerly teachers in our partnership district. In our work as teacher educators, we are committed to preparing knowledgeable, humanizing, and resilient teachers. We all identify as white cisgender women and are aware of the limitations of our perspectives, especially in regard to honoring the diverse voices and positionalities of our participants. For this study, we each took on various research roles, including (but not limited to) principal investigator, co-investigators, and participant-observer. Each member of the research team engaged in data analysis, both individually and collectively. We iteratively examined how our identities, roles, and perspectives influenced our data analysis and analytic writing throughout the process.

Structure of the Induction Program

The overarching goal of Texas Education START (Supporting Thriving and Advancing Resiliency in Teaching) was to support ECTs in their first three years of teaching. START aimed to increase new teacher self-efficacy, provide targeted support in social-emotional wellness, literacy, and building classroom community, and foster communication and collaboration between teachers, administration, district, and university faculty.

A committee of university faculty and district stakeholders met to hire a team of teacher leaders. Upon hiring, the program built a community of TLs and encouraged them to respond to ECTs in authentic and caring ways, given the unprecedented circumstances emerging from the pandemic. Rather than ask TLs to mentor the ECTs using a specific model, the induction program encouraged the TLs to draw on their diverse identities and expertise. This gave the community richness and enabled TLs to engage in humanizing approaches to mentoring (Maloch et al., 2022). Each TL was appointed for 10–20 hours per week and was assigned two schools in which to provide support, with the freedom to respond to ECTs as needed or requested. Due to varied COVID-19 protocols on campuses, some TLs began building relationships virtually with campus leaders and individual ECTs. As campuses opened to visitors in the fall of 2021, however, TLs engaged with ECTs in person.

Growing TLs through Weekly Center Hours

Weekly Center Hours occurred virtually for one hour. The program director and TLs voluntarily gathered for program updates, professional learning opportunities, and informal check-ins. Check-ins entailed mentors sharing stories from the field, including ECTs' experiences, processing what the TLs encountered, and problem-solving as a community. Over time, Center Hours evolved into a ritual space where mentors could ask questions, seek others' expertise, display vulnerability, and gather and extend resources. This communal space allowed mentors to feel confident returning to the field and addressing the immediate needs and concerns of the ECTs they worked alongside. As the program developed, our research showed that Center Hours became an integral feature of the induction program as it offered a safe and structured ritual space where mentors could enact care.

One recurring feature of the weekly Center Hours included professional learning experiences arranged by the program director. Invited speakers provided learning on topics such as culturally responsive teaching (Ladson-Billings, 1995), the science of teaching reading (Pearson, 2004), justice-focused coaching (Wetzel et al., 2023), restorative practices (Passarella, 2017), and special education supports and frameworks. Professional development included workshop-style experiences such as quick writing, role-playing, direct engagement with observational data, and small group reflection. These learning experiences were directly related to themes generated in TL discussions and were planned purposefully to center issues of justice and local inequities. In this way, the weekly Center Hours could evoke and complement tensions arising in praxis and foster shared dialogue on coaching across contexts.

A Communal and Collective Space

According to Noddings (1995), establishing a foundation of care is essential to our work as educators. Intentionally listening contributes to caring, reciprocal relationships (DeCoursey, 2022; Noddings, 1995; Salmerón et al., 2021). For example, in a caring relationship or encounter, the one caring (or the carer) is attentive and the cared-for recognizes the caring and responds (Noddings, 1995). With this in mind, we read through our data sources and looked for places where the TLs demonstrated close listening or relational care with their ECTs to determine and respond to their immediate needs. Additionally, we found places where TLs demonstrated this with each other, primarily during Center Hours. Ahead, we offer several stories and vignettes to illuminate how Center Hours was an essential space for TLs to come together in the community to explore and understand the complexity of their shared mentoring roles.

Methodology

This chapter's findings emerged from a larger qualitative research study using case study methodologies to examine seven TLs' mentoring and coaching approaches and perspectives (Wetzel et al., 2023). From this data set, we selected and reviewed 18 hours of Center Hours transcripts to identify examples of how TLs cared for one another and their ECTs. After culling the data [n = 10] to illustrative events, we engaged in a thematic analysis (Terry et al., 2017) to code for discursive language functions relating to instantiations of collective care as a social practice. Examples included *advocating for or with, demonstrating care,* and *drawing*

Growing a Professional Learning Community for ECT Mentors 133

TABLE 12.1 Participants' Identities and Background/Experience

TL	Self-Reported Identities	Background/Experience
Jacqueline	Asian-American	5 years of experience in middle school ELA; instructional coach
Louise	African-American	Retired elementary music teacher; 32 years of experience; heavily involved in district initiatives; active in local ministry
Lisa	White	Retired; 2nd career teacher; 6 years of elementary experience; alternatively certified; district math content specialist and curriculum writer
Susie	White	10 years of elementary experience; taught both public and private; cooperating teacher; teacher coach; district science and ELA curriculum writer and technology leader
Madison	White	7 years of elementary teaching experience; former instructional coach; ELA district curriculum coordinator; Assistant Principal
Kristina	Latina	5 years of elementary DL teaching experience; cooperating teacher; DEI coach; PhD in Educational Leadership and Curriculum & Instruction
June	White	Former special education teacher; Reading Interventionist; State Literacy Liaison; self-employed education consultant

Note. This table was reproduced and adapted from another empirical study using the same data corpus in Wetzel et al., 2023.

on experience (non-exhaustive list). From this list of initial codes, the research team collapsed themes into patterns of participation, as delineated in the findings section below.

Participants

The TLs' diverse identities, backgrounds, and professional experiences (see Table 12.1) informed how they built relationships and supported ECTs. Jacqueline and Susie (all names are pseudonyms) had former mentoring experience and their approaches to mentoring ECTs reflected this. Lisa, a passionate and recently retired teacher, approached ECTs as more of a co-teacher, often working with small groups of students. A former administrator, Anne, used leadership experience to build rapport with principals as an entry point to mentoring. Louise's background as a grief counselor allowed her to provide ECTs and her colleagues comfort and counsel in times of distress. Lastly, Kristina displayed a transparent equity-focused approach to building relationships to support ECTs. Despite varying approaches, TLs shared commonalities in their mentoring. All TLs routinely checked in with their ECTs regarding their mental wellness, advocating for them to take care of themselves first to serve students better. TLs guided their ECTs through difficult conversations and situations with administration, parents, and district personnel. They also leaned on each other for communal support. In Center Hours, they collectively wrestled with, made sense of, and problem-solved how to best support and empower ECTs as they considered their shared responsibility in improving ECTs' experiences.

Developing a Community of Care

In this next section, we share how a community of care was developed and enacted during Center Hours. We first detail how TLs used Center Hours to share reflections from the field,

134 Jessica Murdter-Atkinson et al.

leverage and seek expertise, and advocate with and for ECTs. Then we highlight how TLs exhibited responsive and humanizing care for students, ECTs, and each other.

Sharing Reflections

Every Friday morning, starting at 9:00 a.m., TLs joined the Microsoft Teams video conferencing platform. The program director typically opened the conversation by asking everyone, "How's it going?" Over the next hour, the ritual process of "check-ins" ensued, whereby TLs recapped their professional and personal week. They shared progress updates in their work with ECTs, including discussions around relationship building, coaching and mentoring strategies, and navigating interactions with administrators. The TLs often shared their reflections through narrative storytelling, including detailed descriptions of interactions and events, discussing how they navigated the everyday realities of their respective campuses. They also described how they responded to challenges that arose, sharing the ups and downs of both their own and ECTs' experiences in the field.

Leveraging Expertise to Support ECTs

As mentioned, one of the unique qualities of this community was the diverse expertise each TL showed through their stories. Lisa had the opportunity to write a math curriculum for the school district and she often talked about coaching around math during Center Hours. Louise led professional development sessions for the district on classroom management; many of her stories centered on the organizational and behavioral supports she provided her ECTs.

The Texas Education START director, Carrie, paid close attention to these stories and noticed that each TL brought certain knowledge(s) and expertise to the conversation. To build leadership capacity among the TLs, Carrie strategically asked each TL to facilitate a brief professional development session during Center Hours related to their areas of interest. During this time, TLs explored specific topics, including how to deconstruct a special education IEP, positive behavior support strategies, and restorative justice circles. By sharing and expanding each other's stories, they collectively leveraged resources and support in response to ECTs' needs. In the following example, Carrie invited a TL, Jacqueline, to share an encounter she had with an ECT:

Carrie: Jacqueline, did you want to talk about your teacher?

Jacqueline: There's a first-grade teacher at Daniel Elementary (pseudonym) who has a nice system for her station work, and I asked if she's interested in working with novice teachers … she has a management system that uses the BUILD acronym. It's a nice system if teachers don't have one. She's willing to talk with teachers and do a little session.

Jacqueline then turned the conversation over to the others, asking them how to best structure the professional learning opportunity. The TLs responded,

Kristina: Definitely interested, yes, in person … All in.

Jacqueline: Definitely after school. The teacher is hesitant but willing.

| Lisa: | I wonder if there are funds available to incentivize attendance. |
| Jacqueline: | I thought about a train-the-trainer model, too, depending on the numbers. Maybe we can all go to the teacher's room, ask questions, and turn that over to the teachers. That may be more efficient. |

Carrie, the director, opened the conversation by asking Jacqueline to share something about one of her ECTs. In her turn, Jacqueline highlighted the ECT's celebration (i.e., finding a successful classroom management system) and attempted to lift up her ECT as a potential instructional leader. She then asked her colleagues if their ECTs might be interested in learning more about this system. In subsequent turns, the TLs' talk built. Not only did they express interest in participating, they also brainstormed ways to make the professional learning opportunity more accessible. Jacqueline gathered feedback and ideas in this conversation, informing her next coaching moves. Through ritual check-ins and sharing stories about their work with ECTs, the TLs shared their expertise. In turn, they gathered ideas and resources that they could take back into the field.

Advocating With and For ECTs

During the 2021–22 school year, ECTs faced unprecedented challenges, largely related to the COVID-19 pandemic, including rapidly changing teaching assignments, classroom rosters, and available teaching materials. They navigated through these challenges with their TLs. At times, the TLs took on advocacy roles as they analyzed systemic inequities and sought to improve them. For example, one of the ECTs Louise worked with started her first year of teaching after the school year began. Because of her late start date, Human Resources did not process her new employment paperwork in time for her to receive payment. This ECT was not compensated, and her teaching assignment changed multiple times throughout the fall. She started as an in-person fifth-grade teacher but was moved to second grade and then to virtual kindergarten a few weeks later. By the spring, the ECT was ready to resign. Louise brought these inequities to the larger group of TLs during Center Hours:

> We met several times, you know. The first thing I tried to do was talk her into staying. We talked about the pros and cons. You know, I had to learn to speak, you know, talk to her husband before she made any major decisions ... I pulled a bunch of legal things and then some. We looked through all the TEA guidelines because I wanted her to know there was a chance this wasn't going to go exactly the way she had planned ... They call it, you know, abandonment. So we drafted up her resignation letter and made sure everything was covered.

In this excerpt, Louise shared her humanizing choice in her role as TL to ensure the ECT would not receive sanctions on her teaching certification for abandonment of contract. Initially, Louise encouraged the ECT to consider multiple perspectives, including her husband's. Eventually, Louise acknowledged that the ECT had been placed in an unsustainable, demoralizing situation and assisted the ECT in resigning. Louise's choice to research the state education agency policy and draft a resignation letter with the ECT showed us how she centered the present and future well-being of the teacher. As such, the teacher did not face legal consequences for her mid-year resignation.

As the above conversation continued, several TLs asked Louise questions related to the policy as well as the contents of the resignation letter. They, too, had ECTs who seriously considered resignation. Toward the end of the discussion, Louise offered to email a copy of the letter. By sharing the sample resignation letter with other TLs, Louise advocated for other ECTs who experienced poor working conditions. While one of the goals of the Texas Education START program is to increase teacher retention, Louise demonstrated that sometimes the most authentically caring thing to do is to follow the ECT's lead in finding a different path forward. Louise prioritized the ECT's needs as opposed to the needs of the school or district. As external to the district, the TLs were afforded the ability to not adhere to the same influences or pressures that a mentor who works for the district might. Many of the ECTs in our induction program reported that one of the things they appreciated most about their TLs was their positioning outside of the district structures.

Enacting Care for Students, Teachers, and One Another

During many Center Hours discussions, we recognized the ways that TLs enacted care by intentionally listening and offering genuine validation and support (Baumgartner & Webb, 2022). Care was expressed for ECTs, their students, and the TLs themselves. Over time, the TLs began to refer to Center Hours as therapeutic, collectively celebrating their successes and engaging with their challenges. We offer two stories demonstrating TLs' care for elementary students, the ECTs, and each other.

Care for Students and Teachers

Through their weekly check-ins, TLs' stories often included descriptions of how they responded to students and ECTs. They all established relationships of trust at their campuses that enabled responding in meaningful and humanizing ways. We offer a story demonstrating how one TL and the community of TLs enacted care for an ECT and her students in a time of grief.

In the spring of 2022, Susie came to Center Hours to share that a student had passed away. She reflected,

> There was a tragic event at one of my campuses this week ... It feels like chaos there. I've tried to spend a lot of time up there this week because I feel like they've had a huge lack of support. Rather than have licensed counselors to tell the students, the district gave the teacher a script ... Other teachers on that campus see how poorly it was handled. Our plan is to fix up an old garden in honor [of the child]. June got a book for [the teacher], and we've been trying to do little check-ins and class meetings. The resources you shared, Louise, have been helpful, too.

What followed was an outpouring of support and care for Susie, the ECT with whom she worked, and the students who were experiencing immense heartbreak. Additionally, TLs came together to offer Susie potential next steps on how she could continue to provide care and support for the school community despite the district's hollow response.

Susie:	The hardest part of it is how to answer the students' questions … No one has come in to support the teacher.
Kristina:	As a parent, I don't think [young children] understand to the extent that adults do. I would keep doing what you're doing. It is above your ability to support her when she is retraumatized, and I think you should refer her to the employee assistance program. It's hard to navigate the system but work with her admin team to see who to contact in HR on behalf of [the teacher]. She needs a mental health counselor.
Madison:	I think at that age, grief is cyclical. As time moves forward, children will need more support, not less. I like Kristina's idea of advocating for support for [the teacher].
Louise:	You may want to suggest that she reach back out.
Susie:	June recommended that they write about (her) in centers. It's such a hard line because we are trying to protect them, but also, they lost someone they love.
Lisa:	I see that Louise reached out to you. I can also tell from your voice that you are traumatized, too. So, I think you should reach out to Louise for support for yourself.

Susie perceived the district's actions as missteps in caring for the humans directly impacted by the event. In the ensuing conversation, colleagues asked additional questions to understand the response better, offering condolence and advice for Susie to ensure the students and the ECT were cared for responsively. Care was central to this emotional conversation because the TLs prioritized *people* and their social and emotional needs in their time of loss.

Care With and For Each Other

The TLs consistently displayed care and concern for each other. During Center Hours, "How are you doing?" led to TLs sharing personal updates (e.g., sick children) and coming together as a community in response to circumstances that were impacting them as humans as well as in response to situations that occurred in local and global contexts. For instance, when Lisa underwent medical care that put limits on her work, June, a literacy content specialist for the program, stepped up and supported Lisa and her ECTs and campuses directly. These two TLs worked together to continue providing support by meeting with ECTs and campus leaders until Lisa could fully return to work. Although Lisa had to "hold back" (e.g., not helping ECTs set up their classrooms), she was appreciative of June's assistance and was extremely excited to return to interacting and coaching in person as she regained health.

A second example occurred in late spring of 2022 after the intentional act of gun violence at Robb Elementary School in Uvalde, Texas. The Center Hours meeting following this event was heavy, dark, and emotional as this senseless tragedy hit hard on many levels. Madison, a faculty member, began the meeting by acknowledging the lost lives and how this community might be experiencing this news similarly and differently. She opened the space by saying, "Before we do check-ins, maybe we take a few minutes to write, draw, pray, or scream to reflect on how you're coming in today." We offer a snapshot of those reflections:

Kristina:	I've been an emotional mess. I feel like I can't control myself.
June:	I felt like Kristina earlier this week … then my sadness turned to rage, so I'm seeing what avenues to pursue to make a difference. I feel you, Kristina, here with you.
Kristina:	Being a parent has hit me harder. Feeling close to home, knowing people in the community … Trauma after trauma this week.

Lisa had recently returned to her role as a TL and offered brief updates on her campuses before quickly shifting the conversation back to the tragedy, noting that she was trying to compartmentalize what had happened. She shared that she'd been experiencing nightmares and wished to share a written reflection with the group:

> I'm going to take this time to tell you all how much I appreciate being a part of this [group]. You always made me feel relevant, and I'm so grateful for the outpouring of support and beautiful, elegant ways. The cards, emails, texts, and comforting words during center time meant so much to me. Work continues to be a vital part of my recovery.

Lisa continued with specific acknowledgments to different team members, noting how everyone supported her recovery. Here she tied together the care she felt during her illness with the support she felt as the community dealt with their collective feelings regarding the tragedy. She concluded by thanking everyone for their kindness. Throughout Lisa's reflection, TLs were visibly wiping tears from their eyes. Carrie acknowledged that this community of TLs created a space where everyone was "ready to care, ready to be vulnerable, ready to be open."

This Center Hours story specifically stands out for many reasons. Through their exchanges, the TLs displayed many emotions as educators and some as parents. Their reflections illuminated feelings of unease, anxiety, and anger, as well as how teachers across campuses were feeling and experiencing the aftermath. This Center Hours were also hopeful and full of gratitude. The TLs displayed their vulnerability by discussing their raw and honest emotions, which can only happen when care is established as the norm.

Envisioning the Future

Authentic caring centers on reciprocal relationships built on trust and vulnerability (Salmerón et al., 2021). Amid the pandemic, we learned much about the role of mentors in providing care to ECTs as they worked together to navigate multiple challenges. During Center Hours meetings, we observed that the TLs shared stories, advocated for change, and gathered input for additional ways to support their ECTs.

While we initially envisioned an induction and mentoring program that would have a strong *instructional* focus, early on, we found that many ECTs were in crisis. TLs noted that many ECTs needed support in meeting their immediate and most basic needs (i.e., safety, routines and procedures, assurance, acceptance, and normalizing their struggles). With the support of the mentoring community, the TLs adjusted and adapted mentoring and coaching moves in the moment to meet their needs best. Through their coaching and mentoring work, the TLs built meaningful relationships with their ECTs, engaged in intentional listening, and modeled vulnerability—all facets of a program rooted in notions of care (DeCoursey, 2022; Noddings, 1995; Salmerón et al., 2021). This work highlights the importance of fostering caring, responsive, induction support.

The rituals established here created opportunities for TLs to deepen their capacities for mentoring ECTs as they expanded their perspectives, enhanced their critical lenses, and responded to inequities faced by ECTs. Center Hours was a safe space for deconstructing encounters and constructing responses. Of utmost importance, though, Center Hours became a community where TLs connected and demonstrated care for each other. Our learnings from these interactions speak to the significance of creating and sustaining caring communities of coaches that know each other beyond mentorship, but also as people and teachers they may rely upon—not just for expertise but for validation, love, and understanding (Noddings, 1995, 2012).

As we think forward to the program's future and potential expansion, we carry these learnings with us as we advocate for induction support that prioritizes the well-being of ECTs *and* their mentors. Building professional communities of mentors for ECTs requires ongoing professional learning, financial support, and the establishment of reciprocal relationships among stakeholders. Perhaps most significantly, our work demonstrates why mentors who endeavor to advance responsive and humanizing coaching and mentoring need a collective space where they, too, can engage in rituals of care and support.

References

Baumgartner, J., & Webb, A. W. (2022). Lessons learned: Approaching care for preservice and novice teachers after COVID-19. In M. Shoffner & A. W. Webb (Eds.), *Reconstructing care in teacher education after COVID-19: Caring enough to change* (pp.138–148). Routledge. 10.4324/9781 003244875

Carver-Thomas, D., & Darling-Hammond, L. (2017). Teacher turnover: Why it matters and what we can do about it. *Learning Policy Institute*. https://learningpolicyinstitute.org/product/teacher-turnover-report

Darling-Hammond, L., & Hyler, M. E. (2020). Preparing educators for the time of COVID ... and beyond. *European Journal of Teacher Education*, *43*(4), 457–465. 10.1080/02619768.2020.181 6961

DeCoursey, K. (2022). Attending to the expressed needs of preservice and novice teachers post-covid. In M. Shoffner & A. W. Webb (Eds)., *Reconstructing care in teacher education after COVID-19: Caring enough to change* (pp. 169–178). Routledge. 10.4324/9781003244875

Ingersoll, R. M., & Strong, M. (2011). The impact of induction and mentoring programs for beginning teachers: A critical review of the research. *Review of Educational Research*, *82*, 201–233. 10.3102/0034654311403323

Ladson-Billings, G. (1995). Toward a theory of culturally relevant pedagogy. *American Education Research Journal, 32* (3), 465–491.

Maloch, B., Mosley Wetzel, M., Tily, S., Daly, A., Murdter-Atkinson, J., & Krafka, C. (2022). Mentoring in a university-based induction program. *The Teacher Educator, 57*(4), 431–451. 10.1 080/08878730.2022.2107131

National Center for Education Statistics (2022). *Characteristics of Public School Teachers Who Completed Alternative Route to Certification Programs. Condition of Education.* U.S. Department of Education, Institute of Education Sciences. Retrieved April 16, 2024, from https://nces.ed.gov/programs/coe/indicator/tlc.

Noddings, N. (1995). Care [1984]. In Held, V. (Ed.), *Justice and care: Essential readings in feminist ethics*, (pp. 7–30). Routledge.

Noddings, N. (2012). The caring relation in teaching. *Oxford Review of Education, 38*(6), 771–781. 10.1080/03054985.2012.745047

Passarella, A. (2017). *Restorative practices in schools.* Johns Hopkins Institute for Education Policy.

Pearson, P. D. (2004). The reading wars. *Educational Policy, 18*(1), 216–252. 10.1177/0895904 803260041

Salmerón, C., Batista-Morales, N., & Valenzuela, A. (2021). Translanguaging pedagogy as an enactment of authentic cariño and an antidote to subtractive schooling. *Association of Mexican American Educators Journal, 15*(3), 30–46. 10.24974/amae.15.3.444

Terry, G., Hayfield, N., Clarke, V., & Braun, V. (2017). Thematic analysis. In C. Willig & W. S. Rogers (Eds.), *The SAGE handbook of qualitative research in psychology*, (pp. 17–37). Sage.

Texas Education Agency (2022). *Employed teacher attrition and new hires 2007-2008 through 2021-2022.* Public Education Information Management System (PEIMS). https://tea.texas.gov/sites/default/files/employed-teacher-attrition-and-new-hires-2022.pdf

Wetzel, M. M., Holyoke, E., Alexander, K. H., Dunham, H., & Collins, C. (2023). *Coaching in communities: Pursuing justice, teacher learning, and transformation.* Harvard Education Press.

13

REFLECTIONS ON CARING FOR EARLY CAREER TEACHERS IN TIMES OF CHALLENGE

Angela W. Webb, Robbie Higdon, and Jennifer Gibson

On the heels of the COVID-19 pandemic, much of the country faces a teacher shortage (Jones, 2023), with shortages more prominent in high-need schools (Negussie, 2022). While the demands and tumult of pandemic life and pandemic teaching—coupled with concurrent sociopolitical issues affecting today's classrooms—likely exacerbated the issue, teacher shortages have been a chronic problem plaguing schools across the country for more than a decade (ABC News, 2022). More specifically, the alarm was sounded about science and mathematics teacher shortages four decades ago with the publication of *A Nation at Risk* (National Commission on Excellence in Education, 1983), and troubles hiring and retaining fully qualified science and mathematics teachers persist (National Academy of Sciences et al., 2007).

Against this backdrop, a variety of initiatives and programs exist to curb the tide of science and mathematics teacher shortages. The Robert Noyce Teacher Scholarship Program, funded by the National Science Foundation (n.d.), is one such program that "seeks to encourage talented science, technology, engineering, and mathematics (STEM) majors and professionals to become K-12 mathematics and science … teachers" (Synopsis section) through direct support during teacher education and induction. Specific to induction, our university's Robert Noyce Teacher Scholarship Program (from here forward, Noyce Program) strives to support Noyce scholars' continued development as effective and ambitious teachers at the start of their teaching careers through mentoring and other professional engagement structures, such as professional learning communities (PLCs).

Contextualizing Care

Our Noyce Program's project team, of which the chapter authors are an integral part, facilitates three distinct professional learning opportunities for program graduates during their initial years in the classroom: (1) a summer Induction Academy, (2) professional mentorship, and (3) a PLC. Additionally, before their final year in the teacher education program, they participate in August Experience, which we consider a pre-induction program and often reference during the Induction Academy.

DOI: 10.4324/9781032707471-17

August Experience and the Induction Academy

Teacher learning is never complete; it continues and deepens over time along a professional learning continuum that extends the career trajectory (Feiman-Nemser, 2001). Yet "both teacher preparation and induction are deeply interconnected processes of becoming (Deleuze and Guattari, 1987) that supersede liminal boundaries and encompass a range of subjectivities and skills" (Wallace et al., 2021, p. 1). From this perspective, we view August Experience alongside the Induction Academy when describing our formal induction program.

Our scholars engage in August Experience before the start of their final academic year in teacher education. During this experience, they partner with science and mathematics teachers at the local high school to observe and assist with the last teacher workday and the first day of school. Through this experience, scholars become aware of ways to develop and implement first-day plans focused on establishing expectations and building a collaborative learning community (Brooks, 1985; Webb, 2022a; Wong & Wong, 2018). During the summer after graduation from teacher education and before starting their first year of teaching, scholars participate in the four-day virtual Induction Academy. During Induction Academy, reflections from August Experience are used to support discussions and work sessions about

- mapping curriculum scope and sequence for essential and enduring understanding,
- designing the learning environment to promote equity and inclusion,
- facilitating disciplinary discourse and promoting sensemaking, and
- engaging mentors and colleagues.

This virtual experience also forms the foundation for the PLC events that are held throughout the upcoming academic year.

Professional Mentorship

Over the past two decades, induction and mentoring programs have become increasingly common because of the role that they play in teacher performance (Ingersoll, & Strong, 2011; Smith & Ingersoll, 2004) and teaching practice (Wong & Luft, 2015). Specifically, there is a link between ECTs' participation in induction programs and their retention; the strength of the effect depends on the number and types of support that beginning teachers receive (Smith & Ingersoll, 2004).

To support our Noyce scholars during their induction, we provide a professional mentor for each scholar during their first two years in the classroom. These mentors are recruited from local school divisions and have taught in the same content area and/or grade level as the mentee/early career teacher (ECT). Mentoring and induction quality are important, and matching teachers with mentors in the same subject area provides more benefits (DeAngelis et al., 2013). We also acknowledge the importance of pairing the mentee with a professional mentor who is not employed within the same school division and has no supervisory relationship with the mentee. By having someone from outside their organizational structure, we hope that the ECTs will feel more comfortable sharing thoughts and concerns that could be perceived as signs of weakness or failure.

These professional mentors provide multiple types of support including disciplinary mentoring, facilitating reflective dialogue, and structure within a professional learning community. Within this mentoring model, the ECTs build long-term relationships with their mentors. Mentors are asked to meet with their mentee—either virtually or in-person—at least once every two weeks during the first year and decide together the frequency of their meetings during the second year. The professional mentors provide content-focused and pedagogical support and engage scholars in reflective dialogues regarding their areas of strength and growth. This long-term partnership has allowed the mentors to build trusting and supportive relationships with their mentees.

Professional Learning Community

We believe that a program where ECTs have a well-defined community for support will help those teachers become more reflective practitioners and persist in the field. Our Noyce Program's PLC offers such a context and includes ECTs and their professional mentors along with our Noyce project team. Keeping with the notion that PLCs involve "a group of teachers sharing and critically interrogating their practice in an ongoing, reflective, collaborative, inclusive, learning-orientated, growth-promoting way (Mitchell & Sackey, 2000; Toole & Louis, 2002)" (Stoll & Louis, 2007, p. 2), the topics selected for our virtual PLC meetings are informed by various inputs, such as ECTs' interests and concerns, mentor discussions and feedback, and classroom observations. We plan these PLC events to serve as professional development for the ECTs while also maintaining the community they built as Noyce scholars during teacher education. A focus on reflection and continued growth is highlighted in every meeting.

We also use GroupMe, a group messaging app, to maintain communication and connection (see Webb, 2022b). Through this app, our ECTs can reach out to us and other Noyce alumni about their concerns and share and receive resources, thus reducing feelings of isolation. Additionally, we can provide just-in-time support to these teachers in between our scheduled PLC meetings or their mentorship meetings.

Care

The importance of relationships and an ethics of care lies at the heart of these supports. Our institution's Noyce Program scholarships were awarded in the fall of 2019. These scholarships carried specific commitments: The scholars committed to teaching for two years in a high-need school district for each year of scholarship they received. In turn, our Noyce project team committed to supporting scholars' professional learning as they completed their teacher education program and during the first two years of their teaching careers. Then, the pandemic hit … and we needed to make significant changes in our support for our scholars. During and after this transition, we realized a key component for supporting ECTs was care.

Care is complex, relational, and non-neutral—complex, in part, because it is relational and non-neutral. Care can be understood to include

> everything that we do to maintain, continue and repair "our world" so that we can live in it as well as possible. That world includes our bodies, our selves, and our environment, all of which we seek to interweave in a complex, life-sustaining web. (Tronto, 1993, p. 103 cited in de la Bellacasa, 2017)

At the core, then, "to care and be cared for are fundamental human needs" (Noddings, 1992, p. xi). Because care is interwoven into a complex, life-sustaining web, care takes many forms (Noddings, 1984, 1992), and what counts as caring is not universal. Rather, perceptions and expectations of care mediate and muddle how care is given and received. Simply put, the carer cannot know what may be perceived as caring without listening to someone (i.e., the cared-for) and understanding their needs (Noddings, 2012). Yet instead of listening authentically, "perhaps too much of what we do as helpers, teachers, and liberators is based on assumed needs. We fail to engage the other in genuine dialogue and, simply because we assess certain needs as legitimate and important, we assume that others also have these needs" (Noddings, 2019, p. 140). For instance, we plan and provide induction support based on large-scale research studies or what we thought we needed, ourselves, as new teachers at the expense of listening to current ECTs as they talk about and make sense of their lived experiences in a specific, situated context. Care should "[emphasize] receptivity, relatedness, and responsiveness" (Isenbarger & Zembylas, 2006, p. 122), which is impossible without listening to those we purport to care for.

It is from this perspective that we come to care about and for (Noddings, 2012) our Noyce program graduates as they enter the teaching profession—a brave new world that has been shaped by the ever-present pandemic, continuing societal unrest, and increasing deprofessionalization of and distrust in teachers.

Our Individual Perspectives on Caring for New Teachers

Angela

As a former high school science teacher and current science teacher educator, I work with Noyce scholars through our PLCs and induction experiences, including the pre-induction August Experience and summer Induction Academy.

Like teacher candidates in other teacher education programs, our Noyce scholars join us from a variety of backgrounds, with unique experiences and values around teaching and learning, and a range of hopes and questions related to their chosen profession. Our scholars pursue teacher licensure through either undergraduate or graduate teacher education pathways, and upon graduation, secure jobs in a variety of school contexts. So, when it comes to planning our PLCs for ECTs, we cannot take a one-size-fits-all approach. Instead, we must be responsive to teachers' interests, questions, and concerns.

In practice, caring about and responding to ECTs' expressed needs (see Noddings, 2005a, 2005b) looks like

- asking ECTs to respond to questionnaires about topics of interest or concern to them, pre-populating some ideas based on research, past experience, or informal conversations with graduates, and holding space for them to submit new ideas we (the Noyce team) hadn't yet considered;
- responding to questions or concerns as they come up in informal means of support like our GroupMe channels (see Webb, 2022b); and
- holding space in the planned topics of our PLC meetings to include topics of pressing relevance and concern to our ECTs, as communicated by the teachers themselves or through their professional mentors.

For example,

- A brief questionnaire given to Noyce scholars at the start of the school year indicated that the ECTs were concerned with responding to students' needs in high-need schools. A PLC was planned with panel speakers that included a science teacher leader from our local high school (a high-need school by the NSF's definition) and a faculty member who specializes in behavior analysis and has prior experience as a special education teacher in a high-need school district.
- In spring 2020, then-student teachers expressed concern for their well-being and self-care in our GroupMe channel. Resources were shared in GroupMe and a PLC was planned to support teachers in developing a proactive self-care plan.
- When professional mentors shared that our ECTs seemed to have trouble setting and maintaining boundaries, we planned a PLC with panel speakers that included third- and fourth-year teachers from our institution's teacher education programs and a former high school physics educator who serves as a coordinator in the university's Science and Math Learning Center.

Conversations of care and support are iterative among the moving pieces of our Noyce Program, as our support mechanisms work in tandem to support ECTs. Multiple avenues for learning about ECTs' needs and concerns are used to inform induction experiences and PLC topics. Although August Experience was initially planned based on our knowledge that none of the scholars' practicum experiences allow them to see the start of a school year, specifics of the experience have been shaped over the years by scholars' questions. In the current iteration of August Experience, scholars starting the last year of their teacher education program observe and work with multiple teachers at the local high school. They see several approaches to and perspectives on how the initial days of the school year could be, including establishing the learning community and setting expectations, and then debriefing their experience with Noyce team members (see Webb, 2022b).

Between August Experience and other field experiences, our program graduates have a front row seat to many teacher interactions. They also encounter varying dynamics within the departmental cultures they join as ECTs. Some of these are supportive, others are discouraging, and ECTs need to know how to respond to and cope with all sorts of collegial relationships. Observing this need among our scholars, we added a study of the article, "Find Your Marigold: The One Essential Rule for New Teachers" (Gonzalez, 2013), to the Induction Academy. We encourage scholars to think about who their marigolds (i.e., colleagues who support and encourage) and walnut trees (i.e., colleagues who discourage or overwhelm) are and how they can identify and nurture relationships with marigolds while limiting the negative effects of walnut trees. These candid conversations about navigating professional relationships can support ECTs' boundary setting and self-care.

Robbie

For this work with these ECTs, I have called upon my experiences as a former middle school science teacher, instructional coach, and administrator to enable me to step into the roles of cheerleader, instructional collaborator, and confidant as needed. This need became even more prudent for our scholars who completed much of their teacher education program during the pandemic. These teachers were robbed of the opportunity to practice their craft in the same instructional environment for which they would eventually be hired. Their preparation and practice occurred primarily in a virtual and/or hybrid space while their first teaching position was an in-person learning environment filled with students who needed to re-establish their norms for learning. Therefore, I developed a mentoring program as part of our Noyce program for the ECTs to provide them with a safe space as well as a "sounding board" to share their feelings, frustrations, doubts, and dreams.

As beginning practitioners, ECTs are implementing practices while having extreme pressures on their cognitive demands. Therefore, they often continue to utilize practices that are ineffective or unsuccessful without being able to assess the effectiveness of those practices (Downey et al., 2004; Schön, 1983). Having a professional mentor can assist these ECTs in identifying how their existing ideas and beliefs may be influenced by their perceptions about their competence, efficacy, and performance. Engaging in continuous learning throughout one's career promotes effective teaching and learning (Loucks-Horsley et al., 2010). Any form of instructional practice can involve an intricate sequence of planning, acting, observing, and reflecting as well as continually making decisions about classroom interactions that are constantly changing. Therefore, having a professional mentor can facilitate a process of ongoing reflection that can enable the ECT to frame their perceptions more appropriately while being challenged to accommodate new conceptions about their instructional practice.

The professional mentors who work with our Noyce Program help the ECTs identify points of conflict or strife that could be contributing to mental and physical stress. As one professional mentor stated, "Learning occurs between the comfortable and uncomfortable" (J. Sullivan, personal communication, July 19, 2023). We perceive that our professional mentors provide the needed support for ECTs to continue to push themselves into the uncomfortable so that they are continually reflecting and refining their practice. Downey et al. (2004) estimate that teachers make over 1,000 decisions in a school day. With current demands to differentiate and promote the academic growth of every child, teachers have become even more pressured to make informed decisions regarding instructional practice. In the rapidly changing environment of the classroom, teachers often depend on beliefs in making decisions about practice (Fletcher & Luft, 2011) rather than implementing a step-by-step problem solving process. The professional mentors help ECTs put things into a more realistic perspective. Teacher mindset matters: If ECTs believe they can persist, they most likely will (Wong & Luft, 2015).

Jenny

As a current math teacher educator and member of our Noyce faculty team, I draw from my previous positions as a high school math teacher and division K-12 math supervisor to inform my work with our Noyce scholars and ECTs. I help facilitate our Noyce PLCs and summer induction academy, as well as mentor Noyce graduates in their first years of teaching.

Through my role as mentor, I have discovered that the social-emotional needs of our ECTs mirror the increased post-pandemic social-emotional needs of the middle and high school students they serve. As one would expect, check-in sessions with my mentees consist of discussions about content and pedagogy, determining the best methods for teaching specific topics, and managing classroom behaviors. However, most of my sessions comprise affirmation, consolation, and strategy development for self-care. I offer a shoulder on which to cry, an attentive ear, and a caring and understanding heart. I provide on-call advice through emerging difficulties with students, parents, or faculty and offer short affirming texts and emails throughout the year to support the ECTs. I spend much of our time together listening to stories of classroom hardships, confirming that they have approached an issue in a mature and productive manner, or offering a new perspective. I serve as a cheerleader, assuring them that, though the first years are tough, they are also rewarding, and the ECTs can and will survive them.

The bulk of my mentee conversations involve naming at least one success and one challenge of the past two weeks and one goal for the next week, which usually stems from the identified challenge. We celebrate the success and develop together a strategy for mitigating the negative experience or at least the significance thereof. In this way, we begin and end in a positive manner but still acknowledge and address the hardship. They feel heard and safe. Since I am neither an employee in their division nor an evaluator, I pose no threat, and my confidence can be trusted. As a result, they are open and honest about their concerns. We acknowledge how situations that seem insurmountable in the moment can be manageable with time, patience, or distance. We talk through ways to let go of things over which they have no control. This "letting go" has proven to be the most difficult, yet essential, component to the success and retention of my mentees. They must learn to make peace with what they cannot change, work to improve the things they can change, and find joy in small daily successes.

One of those aspects over which the ECTs have little control is the initial reception they receive from their department. Some of my mentees were embraced by their department and given abundant support. However, other mentees found themselves in departments in which the culture was not one of care and positivity. The departmental conversations were dominated by jaded or passive-aggressive personalities. The veteran teachers sequestered themselves in their classrooms, lacked a collaborative approach, or focused solely on the daily challenges of teaching. The ECTs in these departments felt isolated and unsupported, both emotionally and pedagogically. In response, they relied heavily on the emotional support of others with whom they connected and on their mentor. They craved positive conversations with colleagues who loved the profession, cared about their success in the classroom, and enjoyed talking with the ECTs about their concerns, hardships, and plans—particularly when they'd had a challenging interaction with a student or parent or when they wanted advice about unfamiliar content. In our mentor meetings, we discuss strategies for steering the direction of some of the department conversations and ways to excuse themselves from the conversations that become overly negative. Distinguishing relationships that will uplift them in their first years from those that may not be beneficial is part of my self-care discussions with each of my mentees.

Because of the dedication of teachers to their students' wellness and academic progress, my mentees often seek the advice and involvement of their counseling department and administrators. In the wake of the pandemic, counselors and administrators are facing unprecedented demands of their time and services, and like many of us, struggle to meet those demands. The ECTs often felt, rightly or wrongly, that they were not receiving the appropriate support from their counselors and principals. Many of our conversations center around defining fair expectations of their counseling and administrative teams. The ECTs sometimes have a narrow view of their students' needs, based solely on their interactions with the student, and must acknowledge the perspectives, expertise, and experience that others may have with the student that informed their individual responses. In cases where the ECTs' expectations are fair and are not being met, we discuss how to request the support they desire in productive ways, to listen, and to frame the situation in a more holistic student-centered manner. If and when this comprehensive approach is unsuccessful, we talk through other strategies and resources.

In all of my interactions with my mentees, my goal is to help them be successful, reflective practitioners who find joy in teaching despite the many challenges. The care we as mentors provide and the self-care strategies we help ECTs develop are key components to meeting this goal.

Connections and Quandaries

Our experiences supporting and caring for ECTs highlight three commonalities regardless of our specific roles with our institution's Noyce Program: 1) Committed listening and powerful questioning go hand in hand, 2) ECTs will need strategies to engage in self-care, and 3) fostering the reflective practice of ECTs takes intentional support.

Listening carefully while suspending assumptions is crucial for being responsive to ECTs' needs and concerns. Although several of our Noyce project team are former teachers, we recognize that today's classrooms are shaped by forces we did not experience—and, frankly, could not have fathomed. Assuming what our program graduates need as they enter the profession would be inappropriate and unwise, considering our goal to support better beginnings for those newest to the profession (see Luft & Dubois, 2015). Simply put, to care for our ECTs, we must respond to their expressed needs (see Noddings, 2005a, 2005b)—needs that we become aware of through committed listening and powerful questioning. Committed listening is

the ability to focus completely on what the other person is saying or not saying ... [by being] fully present for the agenda of the other person, attending to both the verbal and nonverbal cues ... [and allowing] the person to openly and authentically work on real issues and concerns. (Kee et al., 2010, pp. 61–62)

Coupled with committed listening, powerful questions are asked without an agenda, allowing the carer to better understand the cared-for's perspective, and help the cared-for clarify their thinking (Kee et al., 2010).

The need for and importance of self-care is the norm for teachers in today's classrooms. Yet, in attending to the expressed needs of ECTs, we find they have many questions about self-care, work/life balance, and managing expectations. This is unsurprising, as ECTs tend to conflate self-care with self-soothing strategies (Webb & Baumgartner, 2023) and may need focused support to move from recognizing the importance of self-care to using a comprehensive, individualized self-care approach (Cook-Cottone & Guyker, 2018; Webb & Baumgartner, 2023; White & Kern, 2018). Although teachers, like others in caring professions, may be inclined to put others before themselves, the pandemic and other societal factors are forcing us to reframe our expectations of caring for teachers, including how teachers care for themselves. An explicit focus on self-care strategies should take a more prominent place in teacher education and induction, as ECTs can expect to engage in self-care in order to fully and authentically show up in all aspects of their personal and professional lives.

To grow in their professional practice, ECTs must be reflective and, through reflection, they must intentionally engage with diverse ideas, experiences, and people to challenge their thinking and develop their actions. Meaningful reflection is also dependent on critically interrogating the self, which requires the ECT to remain open-minded with others and responsive to feedback, while acknowledging mistakes and seeking to grow as a teacher and learner (Shoffner, 2008, 2009, 2011). This is not always easy and sometimes is avoided in favor of comfortable recollections of teaching, yet reflection is an essential skill that can be nurtured. However, engaging in reflective practice—whether it be about one's instructional practice, the learning environment one fosters in the classroom, or one's self-care plan—tends to be among the first things abandoned when ECTs enter 'survival mode' during the rough and tumble of their first years in the profession. As important as reflection is, ECTs may drop it from their daily routines to find the time to accomplish basic tasks. Thus, ECTs should be aided in cultivating and engaging in reflective practices. Professional mentors and PLCs can be integral supports in this process.

Unspoken, yet ever-present, quandaries related to university-based induction support, such as our Noyce Program provides scholars, are time and reach. No one who supports ECTs through our program works with these teachers as their full-time job. We all balance other demands of scholarship, teaching, and professional service on our time. Similarly, those in schools who support ECTs (e.g., mentors, coaches, administrators) also carry many responsibilities. How can we best be responsive to the needs of ECTs, fulfill our professional and personal responsibilities, and not shortchange our own well-being while facing the finite resource of time? Further, our Noyce Program supports only our scholars during their initial years in the classroom. These teachers are a fraction of those who graduate from our university's teacher education programs. We know that all ECTs deserve support for better beginnings in the profession. How can we broaden the reach of our induction supports to make this a reality?

Moving Onward

This brings us to recommendations for moving onward to champion and support better beginnings for all ECTs. National longitudinal data from 1987–2018 document that approximately 40–50% of those who entered the teaching profession left within five years (Ingersoll et al., 2022). It stands to reason, then, that existing models of teacher induction were not working pre-pandemic, and they are certainly insufficient now. As ECTs navigate enduring pandemic effects, escalating social and political unrest, and growing distrust of teachers and schooling, their holistic lived experiences must be foregrounded in considerations of how best to support them.

Those of us who work with ECTs to navigate today's teaching landscape are also experiencing its unique challenges and opportunities for the first time. Thus, centering ECTs' successes, questions, and needs is vital to helping them thrive in the classroom. As we have echoed numerous times, authentic, committed listening and powerful questioning (Kee et al., 2010) must be integral aspects of mentoring relationships and PLCs to ensure we are responding to the expressed—rather than assumed—needs of ECTs. That said, being an effective teacher does not always translate into being a good mentor. Mentors should also be

150 Angela W. Webb et al.

supported to develop committed listening and powerful questioning skills and learn how to promote ECTs' reflective practice. Engaging mentors in PLCs centered on problems of practice may be a way to address this learning need.

We need also to expand the community of those championing ECTs. This is not the work of schools and school divisions alone. As we've discussed here, teacher educators (and teacher education programs) have a role and responsibility, too, in promoting the success of those newest to the profession. Teacher education programs can collaborate with local school divisions to support all ECTs through PLCs, book studies, professional development workshops, or faculty-in-residence programs. Teacher education programs can also network with their specific program graduates, regardless of teaching location, through social media and virtual meet-ups and offer support through virtual workshops and web-based just-in-time resources. These, of course, are not exhaustive possibilities and what is within the scope of a teacher education program depends on human and financial resources. Finally, we need to attempt to sway public perceptions of teachers and teaching and elect pro-education/educator school board members and politicians to enact beneficial policies and pass favorable laws. Achieving better beginnings for ECTs will take a necessary groundswell. After all, caring for those who care for our children is too important to leave to chance.

Acknowledgments

This material is based upon work supported by the National Science Foundation under Grant No. 1758433. Any opinions, findings, and conclusions or recommendations expressed in this material are those of the author and do not necessarily reflect the views of the National Science Foundation.

References

ABC News (2022, August 11). US has 300,000 teacher, school staff vacancies, NEA President Rebecca Pringle says. ABC News. https://abcnews.go.com/US/us-300000-teacher-school-staff-vacancies-nea-president/story?id=88242614

Brooks, D. M. (1985). The first day of school. *Educational Leadership*, 42(8), 76–78.

Cook-Cottone, C. P., & Guyker, W. M. (2018). The development and validation of the Mindful Self-Care Scale (MSCS): An assessment of practices that support positive embodiment. *Mindfulness, 9*, 161–175. 10.1007/s12671-017-0759-1

DeAngelis, K. J., Wall, A. F., & Che, J. (2013). The impact of preservice preparation and early career support on novice teachers' career intentions and decisions. *Journal of Teacher Education, 64* (4), 338–355.

de la Bellacasa, M. P. (2017). *Matters of care: Speculative ethics in more than human worlds [eBook edition]*. University of Minnesota Press.

Downey, C. J., Steffy, B. E., English, F. W., Frase, L. E., & Poston, Jr., W. K. (2004). *The three-minute classroom walk-through: Changing school supervisory practice one teacher at a time*. Corwin Press.

Feiman-Nemser, S. (2001). From preparation to practice: Designing a continuum to strengthen and sustain teaching. *Teachers College Record, 103*(6), 1013–1055. 10.1111/0161-4681.00141

Fletcher, S. S., & Luft, J. A. (2011). Early career secondary science teachers: A longitudinal study of beliefs in relation to field experiences. *Science Education, 95*(6), 1124–1146. doi:10.1002/sce.20450

Gonzalez, J. (2013, August 29). *Find your marigold: The one essential rule for new teachers*. https://www.cultofpedagogy.com/marigolds/

Ingersoll, R., & Strong, M. (2011). The impact of induction and mentoring programs for beginning teachers: A critical review of the research. *Review of Educational Research, 81*(2), 201–233.

Ingersoll, R. M., Merrill, E., Stuckey, D., Collins, G., & Harrison, B. (2022). Five trends shaping the teaching force. *State Education Standard*, *22*(3), 6.

Isenbarger, L., & Zembylas, M. (2006). The emotional labour of caring in teaching. *Teaching and Teacher Education*, *22*(1), 120–134. 10.1016/j.tate.2005.07.002

Jones, A., II. (2023, February 11). Most of the US is dealing with a teaching shortage, but the data isn't so simple. ABC News. https://abcnews.go.com/US/map-shows-us-states-dealing-teaching-shortage-data/story?id=96752632#:~:text=More%20than%20three%2Dquarters%20of,of%20the%20COVID%2D19%20pandemic

Kee, K. M., Anderson, K. A., Dearing, V. S., Harris, E., & Shuster, F. A. (2010). *RESULTS coaching: The new essential for school leaders*. Corwin Press.

Loucks-Horsley, S., Stiles, K. S., Mundry, S., Love, N., & Hewson, P. W. (2010). *Designing professional development for teachers of science and mathematics (3rd ed.)*. Thousand Oaks, CA: Corwin Press.

Luft, J. A., & Dubois, S. L. (Eds.) (2015). *Newly hired teachers of science: A better beginning*. Springer.

Negussie, T. (2022, December 7). Teacher vacancies more pronounced in high-poverty, high-minority schools since COVID. ABC News. https://abcnews.go.com/US/teacher-vacancies-pronounced-high-poverty-high-minority-schools/story?id=94579185

National Academy of Sciences, National Academy of Engineering, & Institute of Medicine. (2007). *Rising above the gathering storm: Energizing and employing America for a brighter economic future*. The National Academies Press. 10.17226/11463

National Commission on Excellence in Education. (1983). *A nation at risk: the imperative for educational reform: A report to the Nation and the Secretary of Education, United States Department of Education*. The National Commission on Excellence in Education.

National Science Foundation. (n.d.). *Robert Noyce Teacher Scholarship Program*. https://www.nsf.gov/funding/pgm_summ.jsp?pims_id=5733&org=NSF

Noddings, N. (1984). *Caring: A feminine approach to ethics and moral education*. University of California Press.

Noddings, N. (1992). *The challenge to care in schools: An alternative approach to education*. Teachers College Press.

Noddings, N. (2005a, May). *The challenge to care in schools (2nd ed.)*. Teachers College Press. https://www.tcpress.com/the-challenge-to-care-in-schools-2nd-edition-9780807746097

Noddings, N. (2005b, June). Identifying and responding to needs in education. *Cambridge Journal of Education*, *35*(2), 147–159. 10.1080/03057640500146757

Noddings, N. (2012). The caring relation in teaching. *Oxford Review of Education*, *38*(6), 771–781. 10.1080/03054985.2012.745047

Noddings, N. (2019). Concepts of care in teacher education. In J. Lampert (Ed.), *The Oxford encyclopedia of global perspectives on teacher education* (pp. 139–150). Oxford University Press. 10.1093/acrefore/9780190264093.013.371

Schön, D. A. (1983). *The reflective practitioner*. New York: Basic Books, Inc.

Shoffner, M. (2008). Informal reflection in pre-service teacher reflection. *Reflective Practice*, *9*(2), 123–134.

Shoffner, M. (2009). The place of the personal: Exploring the affective domain through reflection in teacher preparation. *Teaching and Teacher Education*, *25*(6), 783–789.

Shoffner, M. (2011). Considering the first year: Reflection as a means to address beginning teachers' concerns. *Teachers and Teaching: Theory and Practice*, *17*(4), 417–433.

Smith, T. M., & Ingersoll, R. M. (2004). What are the effects of induction and mentoring on beginning teacher turnover? *American Educational Research Journal.*, *41*(3), 681–714.

Stoll, L., & Louis, K. S. (2007). Professional learning communities: Elaborating new approaches. In L. Stoll & K. S. Louis (Eds.), *Professional learning communities: Divergence, depth and dilemmas* (pp. 1–13). Open University Press.

Wallace, M. F. G., Rust, J., & Jolly, E. (2021). 'It's all there.': Entanglements of teacher preparation and induction. *Professional Development in Education*, *47*(2-3), 406–420. 10.1080/19415257.2021.1887921

Webb, A. W. (2022a). *JMU Noyce scholarship program: A peek behind the curtain*. College of Education. https://www.jmu.edu/news/coe/2022/2022-09-09.shtml

Webb, A. W. (2022b). Messaging apps and pandemic induction: Supporting newly hired teachers in our current times. *VASCD Journal*, *19*, 46–61.

Webb, A. W., & Baumgartner, J. J. (2023). So much new to learn and so much unknown: Novice teachers' experiences during COVID-19. *Journal of Educational Research and Practice*, *13*(1), 237–250. 10.5590/JERAP.2023.13.1.17

White, M., & Kern, M. (2018). Positive education: Learning and teaching for wellbeing and academic mastery. *International Journal of Wellbeing*, 8(1), 1–17. https://doi.org/10.5502/ijw.v8i1.588

Wong, H. K., & Wong, R. T. (2018). *The first days of school: How to be an effective teacher*. Harry K. Wong Publications, Inc.

Wong, S. S. & Luft, J. A. (2015). Secondary science teachers' beliefs and persistence: A longitudinal mixed-methods study. *Journal Science Teacher Education*, *26*(7), 619–645.

14

WRITING AS HEALING

Reflections from Veteran Teachers as a Way to Understand Needs for Teacher Induction

Kristen Hawley Turner and Kara B. Douma

I was there the day after we lost a student. I remember hearing about this loss and feeling disbelief. After all, she was only a teenager. At that moment, we were just about to start the lesson. The class I was working with did not know this student. Professionally, I carried on with the day as planned. Thoughts of the student - their smile, their warm spirit, their willingness to put others before themself, their love of life, and their family - drifted through my mind. As soon as quiet surfaced in my classroom, I would remember again, and again, and again. A child, a teenager with so much that could have been, was gone. A life cut short. (Kara)

   I was there the day after we lost a student. I remember the moment I learned Pam had died. I was ten minutes from home, thirty-five minutes from school, when my cell phone rang. It was my supervisor calling to tell me Pam had collapsed on the track at our school. She would not be coming back, ever again. The feeling of loss and disbelief consumed me. After all, she was only a teenager. Thoughts of her smile, her warm spirit, her willingness to put others first, her love of life, and her family consumed me as hot tears streamed down my face. The next day I listened with my first period class as the principal shared the news with the school over the announcements. I watched the tears roll down the faces of my students. I felt their loss that she, a teenager with so much life ahead that could have been, was gone. A life cut short. (Kristen)

As teachers for over two decades, we have experienced trauma. Sometimes trauma lived within us, as depicted in Kara's anecdote above. We held it silently, away from our students. Other times, as Kristen shared, trauma engulfed the school community. We lived it alongside our students, carrying our own pain even while we tried to help them deal with theirs. As our vignettes show, however, there are parallels in the traumas we experienced, and we know we are not alone. Teachers experience trauma, grief, anxiety, and stress all the time, and they must continue on, day after day.

In March 2020, teachers and students experienced trauma when, overnight, schools shut down and remote learning began. As the world grappled with the impact and unknowns of COVID-19, educators soldiered on. Knowing that teachers needed support in this unprecedented moment, within a week of the pandemic shutdown, Kristen, Director of Teacher Education at a small university in New Jersey, launched regular online meetings for the Master of Arts in Teaching (MAT) candidates who were in their final semester of student

DOI: 10.4324/9781032707471-18

teaching. Knowing that all teachers were struggling at that moment, she invited novice and veteran teachers from the university's network to attend as well. This act of care for teachers in crisis ultimately resulted in spaces of care that offered a place for teachers of all experience levels to process what was happening and to find comfort in the community of educators that came together.

Perhaps because of the mixture of participants in these calls, questions about "what to do next" began to foreground the discussion. How would we help students who had lost their spring sports season or musical performances? How would we support those who had lost loved ones? These questions of re-entry turned to reflections from the more veteran teachers who had experienced major community traumas throughout their careers. September 11. Superstorm Sandy. Death of a student to gun violence.

The list of moments of trauma grew, and as it did, the group began to wonder how teachers processed traumatic situations alongside their students. How did they manage their own emotional turmoil while also shepherding their charges through fear, anguish, and a rebalancing of life forces? How did they, ultimately, care for themselves and their students? Kara, an English supervisor in a local school district who had joined the National Writing Project (NWP) site at Kristen's university that summer, was asking similar questions about the teachers under her guidance. With the idea of grappling together, Kara and Kristen invited other NWP educators to join a writing group, where veteran teachers wrote about their experiences, shared their writing, and processed the feelings associated with both past and current moments of trauma in their teaching. The process revealed that thinking about care across a teacher's career is important. The writing community we created provided support for those who participated; adapting the structure might be a way to provide care to novice teachers as they deal with the stressors of the profession.

Writing and Healing

The connection between writing and healing has been an ongoing topic across disciplinary fields for decades. A pioneer researcher in this area, Pennebaker (1997) documented that writing and reading it aloud could help individuals take control of their emotions. By the third edition of his groundbreaking book, Pennebaker and Smyth (2016) summarized years of research that indicated writing about traumatic events allowed individuals to gain insight that might provide a form of care that could help them to heal. Improvements in health across studies were both physical and mental. Even more recently, a clinical study by Glass et al. (2019) found that a "writing intervention including expressive, transactional, poetic, affirmative, legacy, and mindful writing prompts increases resilience, and decreases depressive symptoms, perceived stress, and rumination" (p. 240). Writing as a way to heal, then, has empirical backing.

Researchers have also investigated why this connection exists, especially when writing about trauma and stressors "temporarily increased people's feelings of distress" (Pennebaker & Smyth, 2016, p. 60). Lepore and Smyth (2002) edited a collection of essays that suggested expressive writing might help with issues of self-regulation, working memory, and biological factors related to stress (e.g., high blood pressure). It may be that writing "helps to quiet the mind" (Pennebaker & Smyth, 2016, p. 193), since overwhelming stress can lead humans to seek out activities that "adopt low-level thinking strategies" (p. 190), a state that can lead to deeper anxiety, depression, or insomnia. As Pennebaker and Smyth (2016) explained,

> We are often surprisingly ignorant of our needs, motivations, and conflicts. When out of control, anxious, or upset, we naturally change our thinking style. Although low-level thinking can reduce our pain, it can also narrow our thinking to such an extent that we fail to see that something is the matter. We can then become the central feature of our self-constructed paradox: if we naturally escape from the knowledge that something is wrong, how can we ever know about it? How can we ever hope to control our problems or change our lives? (pp. 193–194)

Put another way, if humans do not recognize that they need care, they may not heal.

Desalvo (1999) suggested that "writing regularly fosters resilience … because as we write we become observers" and are able to "reframe the problems in our life" (p. 73). However, not all writing has the same impact nor does writing impact all people in the same way. DeSalvo (1999) contended that linking "detailed descriptions of what happened with feelings'' (p. 25) is important. Simply venting in writing does not have the same healing impact. Lepore and Smyth (2002) noted that for some people, "focusing on positive aspects of a stressor" (p. 8) may be more helpful than writing about negative experiences.

Pennebaker's earliest experiments indicated that writing for 15 minutes per day over a period of four days could have a positive impact on health and well-being, and that talking—or sharing writing in a social network—was helpful to "maintain a stable view of their world and of themselves" (Pennebaker & Smyth, 2016, p. 246). Whitney (2020) brought these ideas to teacher-writing, sharing practices that might help teachers to "heal… understand … set intentions" and meditate (pp. 5–6). Through participation in writing groups as a novice teacher, Whitney expressed that writing "cured" her "shame" (p. 2). It was through writing and sharing that she processed her experiences in the classroom:

> When I wrote about my experiences in the classroom, those experiences became a story, and I could see them as a reader. With more of an outside perspective, I could see myself as a character. And I could see themes in the story, and I could sometimes see very clearly that whatever I was writing about wasn't my fault. I could be much more compassionate toward this me-on-paper than I could be to myself off paper. (p. 2)

Whitney's reflection serves to bring the connection between writing and healing into the conversation of teacher care.

Teachers Writing through Trauma: How We Worked

In the heart of pandemic teaching and with an intention to create space for teachers to write through the traumas they were and/or had been experiencing, we created an invitation to members of the Drew Writing Project titled "Writing and Healing":

> The last 20+ years have presented many traumas to us as teachers. We have survived - and thrived. Join us as we write about traumatic moments and discuss how we moved our students through them.

Over the course of the project, 17 educators engaged. They included veteran elementary, middle, and high school classroom teachers, as well as supervisors and teacher educators.

We scheduled three Saturday mornings over a one-month period for the group to gather synchronously on Zoom. There was no end time, only a start time. Writing and sharing lasted at least 60 minutes, and though some teachers participated in all three sessions, others came in and out according to their schedules. Following practices we adopted through our work with the NWP, we offered a prompt at each writing session but we did not limit writing to that prompt. We wrote independently during the first two sessions and shared writing without feedback or judgment as a community.

Considering the community traumas that many of the teachers had shared in the support meetings Kristen held earlier in the pandemic, we prompted teachers to write about the immediacy of a trauma that impacted them and their students. The first prompt was "I was there the day after …". We invited the teachers present at that meeting to continue writing on their own, aiming to share a full piece at the author's chair scheduled for the conclusion of our month together. We sent a similar invitation to those who had expressed interest in the group but could not attend that first session, offering them the prompt for the day.

The second meeting began with the prompt "Looking back now …" in order to ask teachers to connect the stories to their feelings through deep reflection. At this meeting, we moved into smaller workshop groups where authors could ask for specific feedback to help them move their pieces forward toward publication. Using a writer's memo approach used as part of our NWP work, the authors asked group members for specific feedback, read the piece or a portion of it aloud, and listened to the conversation of group members, allowing these responses to guide their next steps.

Teachers Writing Trauma

Several teachers focused on moments they experienced during the pandemic, their writing becoming a way to process emotions they were currently feeling. The following excerpts demonstrate the blend of storytelling and reflection that DeSalvo (1999) suggested could support their care and healing.

Ivelisse

I was there the day after a Louisville grand jury indicted Brett Hankison on wanton endangerment charges for firing bullets that landed in Breonna Taylors' neighbor's apartment, the day that he was not indicted for the bullets that landed in 26 yr old Taylor's body, the bullets that ended her life. I was there, and I felt pain but not shock. I felt disgust but not disbelief.

I was there, in online classes throughout the day, plowing through lessons, meeting with students to review essays, conferring with administration to plan PDs. In between classes and throughout the evening, I made meals for my children, folded laundry, and tweaked lesson plans. I processed the anger and indignation that day and the next and all throughout the weekend without ever having neglected a single personal or professional responsibility—or so I thought.

Ivelisse went on to describe a mundane Sunday that included lesson planning and household tasks, like preparing lunch, and how "shame struck me very abruptly." She recognized, through her writing, that in a solitary moment on a Sunday in her kitchen, she thought of her students:

I had not acknowledged their grief, which especially for my many Black students, was infinitely deeper than my own. How were they coping with their trauma? Their wounds, so frequently and violently reopened in the past year since the senseless murders of Ahmaud Arbery, Breonna Taylor, and George Floyd, were not hard to miss; but in this case, I had indeed overlooked them.

Ivelisse grappled in her writing—and in sharing it with the writing community—about that moment and how she moved forward. In response to the second prompt, she wrote,

When I look back now, I wonder, Why is it that time doesn't stop in our schools and classrooms when Black and Brown communities are traumatized? Why doesn't the system provide ongoing supports to students and colleagues who experience persistent racial trauma and grief? Is it because we don't feel the impact ourselves? Have we become desensitized to senseless violence against Black and Brown bodies? Or are we just unphased when it happens with impunity? When we proceed with business as usual, and ask our students to do the same, we deny them community support. We isolate them in their own grief … . Our PIBOC students and colleagues endure chronic race-driven stress and violence. Yet the system doesn't invest in readily available grief counseling. And instead of coming together, school communities are often divided on how to "handle" racial trauma in classes.

It wasn't easy for me to admit to my school children on Monday that I messed up. I told them the truth: I was angry and disappointed, but I packed the pain away, like I usually do. I apologized for unfairly expecting them to do the same. I also acknowledged that our pain was not equivalent.

As they had frequently done since the COVID-19 pandemic began, the students gave me grace. They opened up. "Miss, I can't believe it happened again!" "The wall, Miss! He was convicted for destroying a wall," they wrote in the chat. I let them be angry and hurt. I did not try to moderate their feelings—and I didn't make them stay in the class if they weren't ready to talk. Some of my Black students expressed weariness about our recidivistic system; my few White students offered support. Most of the kids were grateful for the time and space to talk. But this isn't a happy ending. And I don't congratulate myself for recovering after a mistake I should not have made.

Iveliesse processed several layers of pain in her writing – the pain she felt as Latinx in a country that did not seem to value Black and Brown lives and the pain she packed away as a teacher of Black and Brown students who did not address their trauma. Her writing also revealed that there was likely more care she needed to find to fully heal from this moment, something she had in common with Jade, another member of the writing community.

Jade

I was there the day after the pandemic closed the schools. It was scary and almost exciting. All of this unknown. Frightening but also unprecedented. Appreciative of the sudden, unexpected

time with my own children. Wracked with guilt and anxiety and working harder than ever trying to recreate lessons in brand new ways for my struggling students so that they could continue learning. Fearful of the possible impending doom that was my worst fear, had been my worst fear since childhood.

Jade processed the stress, grief, and overall trauma of the pandemic during the meetings of our writing community. She went on to write about the effort it took to move to "emergency teaching," that it

was hard trying to be funny and witty for the kids, creating an avenue for them to come together, bring some normalcy to their world. Trying to be professional and do my best work, trying to be the best mother to two toddlers, and mourning my grandfather, who was taken by Covid.

She recognized that she was drowning: "There never seemed to be a time for me to think, to breathe. I was drowning in anxiety, but smiling and baking and crafting and teaching and video chatting." Her writing blended her fears and struggles with her hopes for a different education system moving forward, one she had been working to impact through her graduate program.

As Jade continued to grapple with the trauma she had been experiencing for the better part of a year, she reflected,

When I look back, I realize the gravity of it all, the toll it took, and the toll it is still taking. So much has changed since then, but it is not over. Lives have been lost, but the ones who remain have lost parts of their lives. What we have endured has affected us in ways we have yet to know the true magnitude. We are all suffering to some degree. No one was left untouched. But the world could unite from this pain. It is easier to focus on the tragedy, but I have seen many positives shine through, for families, for the environment, and for society. It is necessary for our survival to focus on this and to keep going. The weight of the pandemic sits on the shoulders of us all, young and old. I hear it, and see it in the faces of my children, my parents, my colleagues, my students. This feeling of helplessness is debilitating. I'm hoping it will end and I know it will end, but right now it feels as though it's coming at me from all angles. This total lack of control is daunting. And as time goes on, I will look back at this trauma. But will it be just a memory? Something has altered the course of our lives.

Like Jade and Ivelisse, everyone in the group took time to write their stories and to reflect on them. Sharing their writing became part of the catharsis. The author's chair proved to be an emotional day as everyone shared their pieces, some in progress and others fully drafted. As authors shared very personal stories that touched upon raw feelings, they became understandably emotional. The listeners did, too. Pain turned to healing, at least the beginning of a healing process, as we shared, cried, and ultimately understood collectively the power of what had happened in the Zoom room and through the writing process.

Teachers Processing Trauma: What We Learned

We started the writing group with an invitation to join together to write about moments of trauma. We hoped that we could help each other understand how we were impacted by stress, grief, and anxiety and also how we carried on, leading our students and continuing our professional lives. While writing in isolation can be cathartic, much can also be achieved in a trusted writing community. Looking back over time and hearing others' stories was empowering for the teachers in our writing group. It helped us to understand that we were not alone, and in many ways decreased levels of perceived stress. Each teacher who shared an experience gave the others insight into how to deal with their own feelings. For individuals, returning to the writing to flesh out the underlying emotions and ultimate outcomes helped to process the event, whether it was well in the past or more contemporary in the teacher's life. While Ivelisse and Jade dealt with relatively recent traumas, Bill looked back 20 years to an event that had a great impact on him as a teacher.

Bill wrote about the Columbine massacre of 1999. His piece, "After Columbine, Student Voices Shattered the Silence," began with a reflection on the responses of a district building administrator and the local police, which was "silence," in juxtaposition with that of teachers and students. Bill described his journalism class in part of his essay:

On the day after the massacre, I allowed my students to share their thoughts, fears, and questions for a good bit of class, but we all felt some comfort in falling back into the normal classroom routines soon after.

In my journalism classroom, however, Columbine was not a distraction from the class: it was the biggest national news event these students had seen, and it was relevant to every person who spent every day in our building. Although school shootings had occurred nationally prior to Columbine, there was something enormous and evil about this event, beyond the non-stop coverage on CNN. My journalists realized that this WAS a big story, though I'm not sure any of us fully understood then what a "tipping point" for school safety Columbine would be. We did not foresee the security vestibules, "zero tolerance policies," and lock-down drills, now commonplace. We were too focused on putting out a newspaper as soon as possible ... .

The bulk of the paper ... consisted of our "Students Speak Out" section, which we used occasionally to broaden the array of student voices beyond my small staff. We invited all students to share their reflections upon Columbine, and we received far more than we had space to publish. Re-reading their words now, almost 22 years later, the emotions--ranging from fear to anger to bewilderment--are part of the history of the moment.

Bill went on to chronicle the one-year anniversary when his journalism "staff wanted to create a memorial issue." They "carefully researched and reported" on the anniversary and intended to distribute the paper. In the middle of a class, however, Bill was "informed that the issue had been pulled by the administration" because "there was concern that the content would upset students and cause problems." Bill advocated for his students to be able to share their voices and reflected, two decades later,

While these stories are all part of the sad local history around a national tragedy, I still cannot accept the motives behind these actions: both one day and one year after Columbine, my school chose to be silent AND to silence ... out of concern about upsetting our students. The broader truth is that when students experience trauma, we have to let their voices be heard. We have to let them grieve and rant and question, and we must listen hard ... [because] voices silenced and darkness hidden are the roots of the problem, certainly not the solution.

In *The Source of Self-Regard,* Toni Morrison (2019) wrote,

> Writers who construct meaning in the face of chaos must be nurtured, protected … The thought that leads me to contemplate with dread the erasure of other voices, of unwritten novels, poems whispered or swallowed … that thought is a nightmare. As though a whole universe is being described in invisible ink. (pp. viii–ix)

Imagine an absence of writing, as Bill described, the "voices silenced and darkness hidden" in times of trauma. Humans need to express their stories, grapple with their feelings, and develop reflective understandings of their experiences. With space for reflection and the community to listen, individuals move forward in time by making sense of the world through language. Following Columbine, Bill took the opportunity to invite students to process what they were experiencing through writing. In writing the story and reflecting on it, Bill joined the rest of the community in processing his own feelings with the benefit of years of experiences beyond that moment.

A Model for Teacher Induction

The teachers who participated in the writing community were all veterans. Some grappled with events in the distant past and considered how they shaped them as individuals and educators. Others wrote through events that permeated their current lives. All found community with each other, and in sharing, they empathized, encouraged, and helped each other heal.

We believe novice teachers would benefit from similar opportunities. According to a National Education Association (GBAO, 2022) survey of members, over 90% indicated stress and burnout were serious issues. New teachers need ways to process this stress, which may include traumatic events (like the ones described by our writing community) or more mundane aspects of the job. Writing about their experiences has the potential to mitigate some of the effects of job-related stress.

Forcing teachers to write and share could be traumatic in and of itself; therefore, any writing community should always be voluntary. Additionally, there are a few key elements to consider when implementing this kind of community within a school setting or as part of an external organization's support efforts:

Group Composition: The group can be composed of any educator interested in writing and potentially sharing as a community. There are no necessary departmental or grade level separations. Inviting veteran teachers to join novice teachers in writing allows for a broad range of experiences and perspectives. Attention to issues of power should be paid; supervisors and administrators might help to organize the group initially but participating might limit the honesty with which novice teachers are willing to write and share.

Scheduling: The group needs a time during the day in which teachers are already committed to being present. Being considerate of teachers' high-demand schedule is a priority to decrease stress and boost morale. Ideally the writing community would meet at least once every other week.

Flexibility: The group should be invitational in nature so that teachers can flexibly enter and exit as they deem appropriate. It needs to be their choice to join, leave at times, and know that there is always an open invitation to return.

Space: The space for the group's meeting can be in-person or virtual. It is important for each participant to feel comfortable in the space and for it to provide an opportunity for quiet reflection and collegial conversation. Because sharing can be emotional, the space should also provide privacy for the group members.

Agendas: Meetings should follow a structure of writing and sharing with prompts that invite a range of responses. Rather than focusing on stresses or traumas, prompts should lead writers down paths that describe immediate experiences or links from past to present. For example,

- What I thought I knew …
- What I now realize …
- Yesterday I experienced …
- Today I wonder …

Over time, agendas can include prompts to look back at earlier writing, to construct narratives to be shared in author's chair, or to engage in peer feedback.

Sharing and Feedback: Sharing writing is personal, and therefore, it should always be optional. Sharing can come in two forms: (1) informal with no response and (2) purposeful with solicited response. In every meeting where teachers write together, invitations to share informally can be offered. Responses to writers should refrain from judgment, good or bad. A simple phrase like "thank you for sharing" or "I connect with you" provides the author with community support without fear of judgment. If agendas include opportunities for feedback on the writing, the author should direct the nature of the feedback. A writer's memo allows the author to ask the readers to comment on particular aspects of writing. Writers can also limit reader response. For example, they may not want feedback on areas where they feel particularly vulnerable. Readers should keep their comments focused on the feedback the author has solicited.

Novice teachers who are invited into a writing community that is structured with attention to these elements may have the opportunity to work through job-related stressors, healing themselves as part of a community of educators who understand their situations. It is important to note that sharing expressive writing may increase negative feelings in the moment on both the part of the writer and the readers, who hold the burden of listening to others' traumas (Pennebaker & Smyth, 2016); however, building a community that is centered on trust and mutual support can have a positive impact in just a few sessions (Pennebaker & Smyth, 2016), and fostering that community over time may provide one way to offer care to novice teachers.

Conclusion: An Invitation to Write

Gary was an English language arts department head who participated in our writing group. Through our sessions, as well as some additional sessions with NWP writing circles, he wrote about being a school leader during the pandemic and the importance of joy and laughter. His piece "When to Smile, to Laugh Again" wove together prose and poetry that reflected the tension between his "oftentimes jovial, quirky, and sentimental disposition" and the trauma of the moment. As he contemplated, "When I struggle with this, it seems that I write."

Writing is a way to process pain, to work through trauma, and to heal. It is a form of care that might be useful to novice teachers as they face many situations where they need to work through negative experiences and reconcile the emotional stress that accompanies them. Gary ended his piece with an invitation to write, an invitation we similarly offer readers of this chapter:

> I'd like to leave you with an invitation to write. Moreover, find some other people who want to give this a try as well. Each of the three poems that I remixed into this piece were initially shared with and for my teacher colleagues: a quick read in a department meeting, a guest classroom reading in a writing class, a posting on our department Google Classroom stream … . It seems that writing and sharing my writing helped me find my smile (an endearing and empathetic grin, not a smirk!) in a way that gave me space to explore my ideas with a collegial audience in mind. It helps to have friends and colleagues on the ready.

A trusted writing community offers a form of group care, a remedy to the ills that lead teachers to burnout and stress. Moving from the worries of our minds to the sharing of our stories gives teachers the opportunity to renew and restore the self. It is a healthy practice to embrace across schools, especially at a time when there is a call for a *return to normal* that can never be. Whether personal, professional, local, or beyond, stress impacts teachers. The benefits of establishing a reliable writing community serve as a perpetual healing tool to navigate through these storms and thrive in a demanding profession. Offering this form of care to novice teachers may help to move them to process the first few, difficult years and to develop practices of self-care through writing that can sustain them through moments of stress and trauma throughout their careers.

Acknowledgments

We would like to thank all the participants in our writing community, and especially Ivelisse Ramos, Bill Connolly, Jade Feliciano, and Gary Pankiewicz, whose writing is included as part of this chapter.

References

DeSalvo, L. (1999). *Writing as a way of healing: How telling our stories transforms our lives.* Beacon Press.

GBAO. (2022). Poll results: Stress and burnout pose threat of educator shortages. *National Education Association.* https://www.nea.org/sites/default/files/2022-02/NEA%20Member%20COVID-19%20Survey%20Summary.pdf

Glass, O., Dreusickea, M., Evansa, J., Becharda, E., & Woleverb, R. Q. (2019). Expressive writing to improve resilience to trauma: A clinical feasibility trial. *Complementary Therapies in Clinical Practice, 34,* 240–246. 10.1016/j.ctcp.2018.12.005

Lepore, S. J., & Smyth, J. M. (2002). The writing cure: An overview. In S. J. Lepore & J. M. Smyth (Eds.), *The writing cure: How expressive writing promotes health and emotional well-being.* (pp. 3–14). American Psychological Association. https://doi.org/10.1037/10451-014

Morrison, T. (2019). *The source of self-regard: Selected essays, speeches and meditations.* A. Knopf.

Pennebaker, J. W. (1997). *Opening up: The healing power of expressing emotions.* Guilford Press.

Pennebaker, J. W. & Smyth, J. M. (2016). *Opening up by writing it down: How expressive writing improves health and eases emotional pain (3rd ed.).* Guilford Press.

Whitney, A. (2020). Teachers writing, healing, and resisting. *Teaching/Writing: The Journal of Writing Teacher Education, 9*(2), 1–10. https://scholarworks.wmich.edu/wte/vol9/iss2/2

INVITATIONS FOR CARING INDUCTION

Angela W. Webb and Melanie Shoffner

New teacher induction should be a moment of celebration for those stepping into their chosen profession. Given the statistics addressing teacher attrition during this career stage (Ingersoll et al., 2022), however, it is easier to dismiss the celebratory beginning to focus on the pessimistic future. To do so does not champion better beginnings for early career teachers—to do so does not demonstrate care.

The authors in this volume care about new teachers. In their chapters, they call on us—as mentors, as colleagues, as administrators, as teacher educators—to consider the lived experiences of early career teachers from fresh perspectives in order to reconsider contexts of caring and responsive induction support. The conclusions and recommendations offered in this volume invite us to reimagine teacher induction as a space offering support and care for early career teachers in response to today's educational context and beyond.

Invitation 1: Connection and Continuity

Teacher education and teacher induction are not disparate phases of teachers' professional lives. We should strive for continuity.

The completion of teacher education and professional certification does not close one book for teachers in order to open a new, blank book as teachers step into the classroom. There is no clear-cut summation of what was taught and learned in teacher education for early career teachers; the lived experience of beginning to teach moves seamlessly to both implicit and explicit professional learning during the induction years. As Feiman-Nemser (2001) clarifies, teacher induction is only one stop along the continuum of teacher learning.

Professional learning continues as teachers learn their profession. As early career teachers develop their contextualized knowledge of students and schools, curriculum and instruction, they revisit, apply, modify, and sometimes question what they learned in teacher education to enact meaningful teaching and reflective practices, foster positive and productive learning communities, and establish a professional identity (Feiman-Nemser, 2001). This organic, authentic continuity between teacher education and teacher induction should be reflected in

DOI: 10.4324/9781032707471-19

the ways early career teachers are supported and cared for during their initial years in the profession but, too often, these phases of teachers' professional lives are disconnected.

In practice, induction support intentionally developed for early career teachers should "take into account the preparation new teachers bring and the realities they encounter" (Feiman-Nemser, 2001, p. 1027). Mentors, coaches, administrators, professional developers, university-based teacher educators: None of the people charged with supporting induction should view beginning teachers as empty buckets waiting to be filled with the information and knowledge that we deem necessary. Such a deficit perspective neglects—in fact, intentionally dismisses—the experiences, knowledge, and skills early career teachers bring with them into the profession (see Darling-Hammond & Hyler, 2020). Moreover, such an approach lacks the care so necessary for those entering the profession.

Continuity between teacher education and teacher induction is a matter of care and it is accomplished, in part, through the extension of teacher education into the early career years. As chapters in this book explain, this continuity can be informal—through the continuation of mentoring relationships developed during coursework or practicum—or formal—through specifically designed induction programs or partnerships. Teacher education programs can follow their graduates to gauge how they perceive the support and care received during teacher education and how they carry these understandings forward into the care and self-care practices they enact during their first years in the classroom. Importantly, by doing so, teacher education programs can draw on their graduates' early career teaching experiences to authentically inform programmatic elements in teacher education.

Invitation 2: Centering the New Teacher

Support activities should be meaningful to early career teachers. Anything less is not authentically caring.

Just as early career teachers are expected to care for their students by listening and responding to their expressed needs (Noddings, 2005, 2012), so we must seek and value early career teachers' experiences and perspectives in ways that enable care for their expressed needs. Our own past teaching experiences in K-12 classrooms inform our assumptions about today's early career teachers' needs, yet most of us did not complete our teacher education programs and enter the profession during comparable times. We cannot claim to support early career teachers if we ignore their input to dictate how they are supported and in which areas that support focuses.

Whereas sweeping policies around teacher induction may be well-intentioned, such policies should not be enacted without considering their holistic effects on early career teachers. Looking to early career teachers' lived experiences helps identify successes, tension points, and shortcomings of both formal and informal induction. If policies and practices constrain worthwhile support for early career teachers, those policies and practices must be critiqued and transformed in order to respond to teachers' expressed needs.

To curb the tide of attrition and champion better beginnings in the classroom for early career teachers, induction support activities must be purposeful and meaningful to those they purport to help; otherwise, those activities are simply busywork, creating an additional burden on teachers' time and cognitive resources. Any agenda for teacher induction should be set by the interests, questions, and needs of the early career teachers we profess to support. As chapters in this book make clear, we can become aware of early career teachers' needs through conversation, observation, interviews, and questionnaires; reflective dialogue with those who mentor or coach early career teachers can also shed light on their experiences, successes, and needs.

Additionally, those of us who educate preservice teachers and support and mentor early career teachers must listen and respond to their expressed needs (Noddings, 2005, 2012), authentically listening in a committed manner to what they do—and don't—tell us and asking powerful questions to best illuminate and meet their needs (see Kee et al., 2010). Committed listening encompasses being fully attentive, focusing on what is and isn't said, and being interested in and open to the other person's agenda (Kee et al., 2010). In doing so, we must avoid unproductive listening tendencies such as judgment and criticism, autobiographical listening (i.e., listening for connections between the speaker's story and our own personal experiences), inquisitive listening (i.e., becoming curious and inquiring about a non-essential or non-relevant detail), and solution listening (i.e., listening in order to jump in with solutions to the problem) (Kee et al., 2010). If we approach teacher induction from *our* vantage point, we can easily fall into these unproductive listening patterns, shifting focus away from early career teachers, their experiences, and their needs.

Invitation 3: Caring Networks of Support

A network of support should be developed that offers complementary—not disjointed—support and care for early career teachers.

Authentic and committed listening to early career teachers reveals that no one person, program, or structure thoroughly addresses the breadth and depth of teachers' needs during induction. Rather, a mosaic (see Chapman, 2018) or constellation (see Elon University, n.d.) of supportive, developmental relationships is necessary.

For example, Chapman (2018) describes how the Thrive Mosaic developmental framework supports the success of marginalized STEM scholars through six types of partners. Associates are mutual accountability partners who help set realistic goals and evaluate progress and strategies toward achieving those goals. Advocates are familiar with the scholar's work, successes, and goals in order to promote access to opportunities, while Connectors link the scholar to otherwise unknown or inaccessible professional networks. Mentors attend to the scholar's overall career progress or a specific area of professional development, as opposed to Coaches, who identify the scholar's strengths in order to offer counsel on expanding strengths and minimizing areas of weakness. Lastly, Target Training partners help the scholar build a specific, often time-sensitive skill.

Beyond mentor or coach, the people that early career teachers develop relationships with often do not bear these titles officially; peers, colleagues, supervisors, administrators, faculty, and friends fill these roles nonetheless. Yet, conversations around teacher induction are dominated by a focus on new teachers and their mentors or coaches. If we broaden our consideration of who helps and advocates for early career teachers, we may well see an underutilized or untapped network of "multiple meaningful relationships ... [that] provide multifaceted support and guidance, acknowledg[ing] the complex realities of developmental relationships and the continuum along which mentoring occurs" (Elon University, n.d., para. 1).

Whatever the supportive, developmental relationships and networks, however, we must remain mindful of how various components work together. We should intentionally craft these networks for early career teachers to be complementary, not disjointed or contradictory. As chapters in this book highlight, one approach to this is supplementing local, site-specific (e.g., school division or school building) goals and needs for new teacher induction with responsive, teacher-centered, non-evaluative relationships and support. These latter components of wrap-around support can occur through university-based teacher induction programs or partnerships between school divisions and teacher education programs. The priorities of those in the mosaic (Chapman, 2018) or constellation (Elon University, n.d.) of developmental and relational support should be squarely on the needs of the early career teachers they support.

Accepting the Invite

Today's teaching landscape—continuously (re)shaped by the COVID-19 pandemic, social and political unrest, and distrust in teachers and schools—means teachers are caring for their students, one another, and themselves in more ways—different ways—than in years before. How are those newest to the profession experiencing and navigating this reality? How are beginning teachers being cared for so they can survive and thrive in the profession and, in turn, care for their students? These questions form the crux of this edited collection.

To those outside of education, an obvious goal for teacher induction efforts is the retention of early career teachers. Teacher retention is indeed an issue in education but those of us with experience in and passion for working with beginning teachers—like the authors in this book—know that the motivation for induction work is much deeper. Through our work, we champion better beginnings for early career teachers: beginnings that support the development of their teacher identity, the enactment of their instructional skills, and the realization of their teaching beliefs to the benefit of their students, their profession, and themselves—and care is essential to such beginnings.

We hope readers accept the invitations offered across the chapters of this book and join us in (re)centering care for early career teachers during teacher induction. Those newest to the profession *and* their students deserve nothing less.

References

Chapman, R. N. (2018). The Thrive Mosaic developmental framework: A systems activist approach to marginalized STEM scholar success. *American Behavioral Scientist, 62*(5), 600–611. 10.1177/0002764218768859

Darling-Hammond, L., & Hyler, M. E. (2020). Preparing educators for the time of COVID ... and beyond. *European Journal of Teacher Education, 43*(4), 457–465. 10.1080/02619768.2020.1816961

Elon University. (n.d.) *Mentoring constellations.* https://www.elon.edu/u/mentoring-relation-ships/ace-report/mentoring-constellations/

Feiman-Nemser, S. (2001). From preparation to practice: Designing a continuum to strengthen and sustain teaching. *Teachers College Record, 103*(6), 1013–1055. 10.1111/0161-4681.00141

Ingersoll, R. M., Merrill, E., Stuckey, D., Collins, G., & Harrison, B. (2022). Five trends shaping the teaching force. *State Education Standard, 22*(3), 6.

Kee, K. M., Anderson, K. A., Dearing, V. S., Harris, E., & Shuster, F. A. (2010). *RESULTS coaching: The new essential for school leaders.* Corwin Press.

Noddings, N. (2005). *The challenge to care in schools: An alternative approach to education.* Teachers College Press.

Noddings, N. (2012). The caring relation in teaching. *Oxford Review of Education, 38*(6), 771–781.

INDEX

acceptance 51, 66, 138
accountability 26–27, 53, 71, 86, 88–89, 92–93, 101, 166
achievement 3, 36, 38, 79–80, 81, 83
administration 14, 16, 31, 39–40, 44, 48–49, 70, 72, 113, 123, 131, 133–134, 137, 147, 149, 156, 159, 160, 164–166
advice 51, 80, 112–113, 137, 147
advocate 30, 51, 70, 71–74, 132–139, 159, 166
affective 34, 41, 43, 46, 50, 87, 89, 93, 97
agency 12, 18, 92, 94, 96, 114, 123–124
aspiration 68, 70, 74
attrition 53–55, 60, 96, 106–107, 114, 122, 164–165
Australia 86–87, 90, 92

balance, work-life 11–12, 15–16, 19, 35, 80, 113, 124, 127, 148–149
Bambino, D. 81
Barek, H. 22
Baumgartner, J. 35
Beach, C. 78
becoming a teacher 50, 67, 79, 87–88, 92, 97, 141–143
beginning 24, 44, 47–48, 56, 60, 70, 78–79, 81–82, 86, 93, 98, 103, 158, 164, 167; better beginnings 148–150, 164–165, 167
beginning teachers 32, 35, 37–38, 40–41, 53–62, 65–66, 77, 86, 94, 119, 142, 165, 167
behavior: student 12, 14, 18, 25, 28, 30–32, 36, 39–40, 46, 48, 55–58, 70, 73, 82, 86, 120, 125–126, 134, 146; teacher 66, 74
belonging, sense of 43–46, 50–51, 53, 66, 70, 76, 93, 121, 123
bias 70, 109

boundaries 14–15, 17, 19, 26–27, 35, 59, 82, 145
Brackett, M. 45
brave, being 39, 46, 51, 91
Bresser, F. 113
Bullough, R. V. 84
burnout 11–12, 19, 35, 114, 160, 162

Career Advancement and Development for Recruits and Experienced Teachers (CADRE) 54–57, 59–60
California 121, 126
California State University (CSU) 126
candidates; *see* teacher candidates
care 22–23, 25–31, 35, 39, 41, 45–46, 51, 53–54, 57, 59–61, 66–74, 76–77, 82–85, 92–93, 96, 102–103, 107–109, 114, 119–123, 125–128, 132–134, 136–139, 143–145, 147, 150, 154–155, 162, 164–165, 167; authentic care 66–67, 74, 131, 138, 144, 165–166; cared-for 92, 97, 108, 120, 132, 144, 148; carer 4, 92–93, 97, 108, 144, 148; caring communities 52, 74–75, 94, 139; ethic of care 54, 65, 68, 73, 97, 143; self-care 11–19, 91, 93, 126–127, 145, 147–149, 162
Carolina Teacher Induction Program (TIP) 107
case study 13, 17, 23, 36, 125–126, 132
challenges 3, 13, 15–18, 30–31, 35–36, 38, 47, 54, 57, 60–61, 65–66, 69, 73–74, 77, 81, 96–97, 109, 111, 113–114, 120–122, 124–125, 130, 134–136, 138, 147–148
coach/ing 3–5, 54–55, 57–58, 60–61, 70, 108–114, 132, 134–135, 138–139, 145, 149, 165–166; *see also* mentor
Columbine 159–160

communication 48, 55, 70–71, 74, 123, 125, 131

community 43–47, 49–51, 68, 70–71, 74, 92–93, 98, 119, 121–126, 131–134, 136–139, 154, 156–162; communities of practice 43, 45, 51, 70, 121–122, 124–125, 139, 142, 161; learning communities 2, 40, 66, 90, 93–93, 98, 119, 112–143, 164

competence 12, 36, 38, 53, 120, 123, 146

confidence 15, 43, 45, 56, 59, 73, 80, 96, 112–113, 115, 132, 147

connection 30, 45, 51, 53, 65–68, 70, 81, 83–84, 87, 93, 123–124, 154–155

COVID/COVID-19 1, 13, 19, 23, 31, 34–35, 37, 40, 47, 53, 65, 74, 83, 86, 90–91, 96, 98, 100–102, 106–107, 113, 120, 124, 126, 130–131, 135, 141, 153, 157–158, 167

critical thinking 87, 93, 112–113

Cross Francis, D. 111

Danielson Framework 25–26, 28–29

de Haan, E. 111

Desalvo, L. 155–156

Development: teacher 59, 69, 74, 81, 84, 86–88, 92–94, 110–111, 141, 166–167; professional 3, 31, 40–41, 53–55, 96, 98, 107–109, 115, 119–121, 123–126, 134, 143, 150; student 36, 39, 67, 79

Dias-Lacy, S. L. 28, 31

Dishena, R. 55

Doecke, B. 93

doubt 2, 112, 113, 146

Downey, C. J. 146

Dunn, M. B. 34

Eadie, P. 53, 61

early career teacher (ECT) 1–4, 44, 86–87, 89–90, 96, 107, 111, 114–115, 130–139, 142, 142–150, 164–167

education: early childhood education 30; elementary education 23–24, 30, 121; English/English language art/ELA education 23, 43–44, 46, 50, 89–90, 93; higher education 1, 86–89, 91, 93; mathematics education 65–68, 74; science education 23; special education 23, 121, 132, 134, 145; teacher education 1–2, 19, 22–23, 26, 29, 31–32, 35, 37, 40–41, 43, 48, 51, 53, 70, 76, 96–98, 119–120, 127, 141–145, 148–150, 164–167

educator 50–51, 54, 60–61, 65–66, 69–70, 72, 74, 76, 83–84, 97, 107, 113–115, 120, 138, 150, 153–154, 156, 160–161; early childhood educator 53; teacher educator 3, 22, 31, 34, 43, 46–47, 83, 88, 131–132, 144–146, 156, 164–165; *see also* teacher

efficacy/self-efficacy 12, 53, 56, 83–84, 107, 112–115, 123, 131, 146

elementary school 131; fifth-grade 135; first-grade 134; fourth-grade 26

Elon University 166–167

emotion 4, 11–17, 19, 27, 31, 34–36, 38–41, 45–49, 51, 60–61, 71, 73–74, 81, 87, 120, 123–124, 126–127, 137–138, 147, 154, 156, 158–159, 161; anger 39–40, 138, 156–157, 159; anxiety 12, 113, 138, 153, 155, 158–159; compassion 3, 12, 17, 121; discomfort 38, 48, 111; empathy 34, 59, 68, 74, 120, 122; enjoyment 19, 44, 54, 56, 59, 90, 147; exhaustion 50, 53, 108; failure 46, 72, 109, 142; fear 38–40, 46, 49, 59, 68, 83, 109, 127, 154, 158–159, 161; grateful 15, 49–51, 83, 138, 157; grief 136–137, 153, 157–159; guilt 39, 43, 158; happy 15, 44, 101, 127, 157; hope 76, 84, 114, 144, 158; joy 49, 68, 147–148, 162; love 22, 27–28, 30, 44, 46–47, 49, 51, 66, 90, 108, 137, 139; optimistic 15, 17, 19; overwhelmed 15, 18, 44, 59, 77, 154; passion 44, 68, 133, 167; sadness 40, 49, 138; vulnerable 38–39, 46–47, 51, 69, 83, 91, 114, 123, 125, 132, 138–139, 161

equity 47, 66–68, 72–74, 98, 126, 132–133, 135, 139, 142; injustice 36, 37, 72

Espinoza, D. 121

evaluation 3, 25, 38, 53, 74, 107, 109, 112, 115, 121, 123, 127, 166–167

expectations 16–17, 26, 30, 37–38, 44, 51, 58, 77, 81–82, 84, 86, 92, 97, 101, 110–111, 113, 142, 144–145, 147–148, 157, 165

Facebook 51

feedback 25–26, 29, 31, 50, 67, 69–71, 74, 79–83, 98, 101–102, 107, 109, 115, 122–124, 135, 143, 149, 156, 161

Feiman-Nemser, S. 164

first-year teacher 14–16, 18–19, 48, 60, 77, 80, 86, 89–91, 108, 119, 124, 128

friend/friendship 12, 15, 38, 44–46, 56, 65, 69, 76, 108, 127, 162, 166

Garcia, A. 34

Gracia, E. 106

García-Carrión, R. 98

Gay, G. 66, 68, 74

Genor, M. 121

Glass, O. 154

grade level: kindergarten 135; PK-12 23, 55, 119–121, 124, 126–127; PK-6 23; PreK-3 23

graduates 22–25, 96–98, 102, 121, 141, 144–146, 148, 150, 165

growth 53, 55, 58, 60, 66–70, 74, 80, 83, 102–103, 106, 111, 143; academic growth 71, 146; growth mindset 15, 54–57, 59–61; intellectual growth 38

Guirguis, R. V. 28, 31

170 Index

Hattie, J. 83
health 11–12, 34, 36–37, 40, 46–49, 53, 107, 110, 112, 154–155, 162
Herman, K. C. 12, 18
Heynoski, K. 53
Hobson, A. J. 90
Hong, J. 111
hooks, b. 47, 51, 66, 71

individual monthly action plan (I-MAP) 81
identity: personal 38; professional 2, 83–84, 164; student 34, 36, 38, 66–67; teacher 40, 43–44, 92, 94, 107, 110–112, 133, 167
induction: experience(s) 6, 44, 50, 69, 144–145; mentoring/mentorship 66, 72, 83, 121, 123; phase 2, 31, 49, 65, 66; practices 55, 60, 86–88, 92; process(es) 65, 68, 88–90, 92–93, 120; program(s) 3–5, 17, 19, 35, 37, 40–41, 54–55, 60, 69, 80, 84, 88–89, 96–98, 107, 109, 114, 120–122, 130–132, 136, 142, 165, 167; teachers 22–24, 26, 28–29, 31–32, 43, 46, 49, 76–84; years 5, 19, 23, 31, 40, 43, 45–51, 76–77, 79, 81, 83, 111, 164
Ingersoll, R. M. 121
intervention 57, 92, 125, 154
Institutional Review Board (IRB) 24, 36
isolation 82, 84, 86, 89–90, 125, 143, 159

justice 36–37, 39, 72, 132, 134; *see also* equity

K-12: classroom 1, 165; students 4, 36–37, 40, 146, 165; teachers 141
Keese, J. 127
Keh, A. 77
Keltchtermans, G. 98
kids 15, 27, 30, 43, 50, 108, 110, 157–158; *see also* students
Kipchoge, E. 77, 85
Klein, A. 112
Knight, J. 109
Kobabe, M. 47
Kostogriz, A. 89
Kraft, M. A. 53

leader(s) 36, 51, 82, 109, 127, 133, 135, 145, 162; school/campus 55, 92, 131–132, 137, 162; teacher 131, 145
leadership 59, 84, 133–134; grant 101, 126; program 107; school 87–89, 91–93; styles 111
learning 11–12, 22–23, 25, 29–31, 34–36, 38, 41, 43, 45, 47, 53–54, 56–57, 66–67, 69–74, 76, 78–81, 83–84, 86, 90, 93–94, 96, 98, 100–101, 107, 120, 125–127, 130, 132, 134–135, 139, 141–146, 150, 153, 158, 164; environment 11, 66–70, 73, 82, 142, 146, 149; goal(s)/target(s) 57, 77–80, 82, 101; new teacher learning community (NTLC)

119, 122–124, 126–127; professional learning 35, 54, 93, 127, 132, 134–135, 139, 141, 143; professional learning community (PLC) 98, 141–146, 149–150; social emotional learning 34, 36, 47, 123; student learning 11, 68, 77, 106, 111, 121, 126; visible learning 83
Learning Policy Institute 106
leave the profession 53, 55, 106, 111, 130, 135–136
Lepore, S. J. 154–155
literacy 34, 54, 76, 131; media literacy 78; racial literacy 39, 41
Longmuir, F. 92
Love, D. 113

März, V. 98
mathematics: as subject 23, 58, 67–68, 70, 73–74, 101, 134; teacher; *see* teacher, mathematics; teacher education; *see* teacher education, mathematics
McDonald, J. P. 98
McQueen, K. 55
mentorship 41, 50, 66–67, 69, 72–74, 76–78, 80, 83–85, 139, 141–143; mentee 41, 66, 68–70, 72, 74, 76–77, 83–84, 142–143, 146–148; mentor 3, 17, 19, 35, 37, 40–41, 46, 50, 54–55, 57–58, 60–61, 66, 68–70, 72, 74, 76–77, 79, 81, 83–84, 89, 91–93, 110, 112–113, 120–123, 127, 130, 132, 136, 139, 142–150, 164–166; mentoring 3, 37, 41, 53–55, 58, 61, 84, 89, 96, 107, 113, 119, 130–134, 138–139, 141–143, 146, 149, 165–166
Microsoft: PowerPoint 38, 99, 119; Teams 134
middle school 14, 23, 37, 125, 131; middle school students 35, 146; middle school teachers 156
mistakes 60, 71–72, 126, 149
modeling 55–57, 59–60, 69, 71–72, 74, 77–78, 98, 103, 121, 125
Mokoena, S. 55
Morrison, T. 160
motivation 84, 111, 155, 167

National Council of Teachers of English (NCTE) 50
need(s) 22, 25–29, 34–35, 40–41, 43, 53, 55, 57–59, 61, 66, 69, 71, 74, 77, 82, 86–87, 89, 91–93, 97, 99, 107–109, 120–121, 125, 130–132, 134, 136, 138, 144–145, 148–149, 155, 160, 165–167; assumed/presumed 35, 38, 40, 87, 92, 108, 144, 149; expressed 22, 35, 38, 40, 93, 97, 108, 144, 148–149, 165–166; high-need 13, 97, 141, 143, 145; self-care 11–13, 19; social-emotional 35, 41, 55, 59, 61, 126, 137, 146; student 28, 30–32, 34, 37–40, 77, 83, 86, 91, 96–97, 145, 147

NHSTs; *see* teachers, newly hired science
Noddings, N. 4, 12–13, 19, 35, 54, 66, 68, 74, 87, 92–93, 96–97, 108, 121, 132
novice teacher 22–23, 26, 28–32, 35, 40, 74, 96, 98, 101–103, 107, 110–114, 134, 154–155, 160–162
Noyce Teacher Scholarship Program 13, 17–18, 96–97, 103, 141–146, 148–149
National Writing Project (NWP) 154, 156, 161

Oklahoma State University 107
Oklahoma The Retention of Innovative Educators (THRIVE) 107
online instruction 1, 11, 23, 37, 124, 156

pain 47–48, 153, 155–158, 162
pandemic 1, 23, 34–37, 40, 47, 53, 65, 74, 76, 86, 90–92, 94, 96, 101, 106–107, 113, 120, 124, 130–131, 135, 138, 141, 143–144, 146–149, 153, 155–158, 162, 167; *see also* COVID/COVID-19
parents 12, 28, 30, 32, 38–41, 47, 79, 86, 92, 96, 101, 133, 137–138, 147, 158
partnerships 50, 68, 70, 73–74, 109, 121, 127, 130–131, 143, 165, 167
pedagogy 2, 22, 65, 67–68, 74, 90, 120, 126, 143, 146
Pennebaker, J. W. 154–155
persistence 1, 3, 101, 141, 143, 146, 157
planning for instruction 3, 14–15, 18, 25, 32, 38, 57, 69, 77–79, 82, 87, 91, 121, 146, 157; co-planning 55–57, 60–61
PLC; *see* learning community, PLC
policy 67, 89–91, 121, 135–136; policymakers 41; school policy 88
power 68–71, 73–74, 83, 158–160; *see also* equity
preservice teacher 1, 22–23, 26, 28–29, 31, 43–47, 49–51, 90–91, 102, 120–121, 124, 127, 129–130, 139, 150, 166; *see also* teacher candidate
pressure 12, 54, 57, 59, 92, 106, 136, 146
principal investigator 24–25, 98–99, 102, 131

racism 12, 36, 39, 41; *see also* equity
reflection: as data 13, 35, 43–44, 58, 77, 83, 102, 124–126, 132–134, 137–138, 154–156, 159–160; as practice 39, 44, 54–55, 67–68, 71–73, 79, 83–84, 111, 113–114, 120–121, 146, 149, 161
relationships 4, 14, 34, 46–47, 51, 57, 96, 120–123, 136, 143, 145, 167; building relationships 22, 25–29, 30–31, 46, 60, 68, 77, 97, 120, 123, 131, 133–134, 143; with mentors 54, 60–61, 65–66, 68–70, 73–74, 77–78, 83–84, 89, 91–93, 113, 131–134, 138–139, 142–143, 147, 149, 165–166; with

students 22–23, 25–32, 44, 58, 82, 97, 108, 120
resilience 17, 49, 53–57, 59–61, 85, 129, 131, 154–155
respect 25, 28–29, 39–40, 51, 66–68, 70–71, 73, 76, 82, 102–103, 108–109, 121
responsibility 3, 25–26, 39, 70–71, 92–93, 97, 113, 119, 133, 149–150, 156; teacher 2, 14, 38, 46, 49, 68, 86, 89, 96, 98
retention; *see* teacher retention
Ronfeldt, M. 55

safe: classroom environment 67–68, 72, 82; feeling 25, 49, 51, 53, 59, 83, 92, 103, 108–109, 114, 122, 132, 138–139, 146–147
school 12–19, 24–26, 29–31, 35, 37–38, 40–41, 43–46, 48–50, 54–55, 59–60, 66, 70, 72–73, 76–77, 79–80, 83–84, 86–94, 96–98, 101–103, 105–106, 108, 112–113, 119, 125–126, 130–131, 133–137, 142–146, 149–150, 153–154, 156–157, 159–160, 162, 167; high-need school 13, 97, 141, 143, 145; rural 13–15, 45, 76, 97, 121; school board 46, 49, 150; school community 88, 136, 153, 157; school context 12–13, 24, 89, 92, 144; school year 13, 44, 60, 77, 79, 126, 131, 135, 145; suburban 13, 16, 37; urban 13, 96
school principal 24–26, 28–30, 38, 48, 59, 88, 91, 122, 102, 133, 147, 153
Scott, C. 22
self-care 11–21, 35, 91, 93, 126–127, 145, 147–149, 162
self-efficacy 53, 56, 84, 107, 113–115, 123, 131
sense of belonging; *see* belonging, sense of
Shoffner, M. 35, 54, 107
Sidhu, P. 108
Sieben, N. 76, 84
Smith, T. M. 121
Smyth, J. M. 154–155
social and emotional learning (SEL) 31, 34–41, 47, 55, 59–61, 120, 123–124, 126, 131, 137, 146
social media 44, 49, 51, 112, 125, 150; GroupMe 143–145; Snapchat 72; TikTok 49
STEM 141, 166
stress 11–16, 18–19, 43, 53, 59, 77, 86, 92, 107, 112–114, 133, 146, 153–154, 157–162
student 11–12, 14–19, 22–32, 34–41, 45–51, 55–59, 65–74, 76–84, 86, 88–92, 96–97, 100–102, 106, 108, 110–113, 116, 119–121, 125–131, 133–134, 136–137, 145–148, 153–160, 164–165, 167; apathy 15, 18, 77; behavior 12, 18, 25, 31–32, 40, 57, 120, 125; choice 25–26, 28–29; engagement 30, 36, 69, 77, 101; needs 25, 28–32, 34, 40, 92, 97, 145, 147; stress 36, 38–39, 72; struggle 38, 44

172 Index

student teacher 15, 26, 24, 78–79, 130, 145
student teaching 15, 34–37, 45, 76–78, 84, 110, 131
success 12–13, 59–61, 74, 81–84, 98–103, 109, 113, 115, 119–120, 122–125, 130, 136, 147, 149–150, 165–166; Success Analysis and Reflective Questions Protocol 99–101
support 11–12, 14, 16–19, 22–23, 26–27, 29–32, 35–41, 43, 45–49, 51, 53–61, 65, 67–68, 70, 72, 74, 76–77, 79, 81–87, 89–92, 94, 96–99, 102–103, 106–115, 119–128, 130–134, 136–139, 141–150, 153–154, 156–157, 160–161, 164–167; emotional 40, 55, 59–61, 81, 147; responsive 107–108; social 12, 16
Sutcher, L. 106

Teacher: beginning; *see* beginning teacher; beliefs 17, 38, 67, 70, 73, 88, 93, 109–111, 114, 146, 167; candidate 22–24, 31, 35, 97, 144, 153; early career (ECT); *see* early career teacher; elementary 56, 156; English 34–38, 44–45, 76, 87, 90–91, 125; first-year; *see* first-year teacher; mathematics 14, 60, 125, 141–142, 146; new (NT) 119, 122–126, 128; novice; *see* novice teacher; retention 2, 53, 84, 86, 102–103, 106–107, 115, 120–122, 125–126, 128, 130, 136, 142, 167; science 11, 13–21, 23, 125, 141–142, 144–145; shortage 2, 14, 34, 53, 106, 130, 141; strengths 25, 31, 111–112, 120–121, 143; struggle 14, 18, 23, 28, 38, 54, 56, 60, 82, 108–111, 113, 138, 147, 158, 162; turnover 37, 97, 120, 130–131; veteran 53, 76–77, 82, 110, 113, 119, 124, 147, 153–154, 156, 160; voice 26, 40, 47–49, 71, 108–110, 114, 126, 137
teacher candidate; *see* teacher, candidate
teacher education 19, 22–23, 26, 29, 31–32, 35, 37, 40–41, 48, 51, 65, 70, 76, 96–97, 119–120, 127, 130, 141–145, 148–150, 164–165, 167; elementary teacher education 23–24, 30–31; secondary teacher education 36, 46, 56, 66, 76, 97, 121, 124, 150; teacher preparation 17, 23, 25, 43, 65, 103, 106, 110, 113, 130, 142, 146, 165
teacher educator 22, 31, 34, 43, 46–47, 83–84, 88, 131, 144, 146, 150, 156, 164–165
teacher leader 51, 131–139
technology 35, 51, 101, 141; Google Classroom 162; Google Earth 101; Google Forms 24, 83; Jamboard 101; Nearpod 101; Zoom 25, 38, 91, 100, 156, 158
Texas Education Supporting Thriving and Advancing Resiliency in Teaching (START) 131, 134, 136
time 12, 14–16, 18–19, 27, 30–32, 41, 43–47,

50–51, 53–61, 67–68, 77–82, 90, 92–93, 98–102, 107, 111–112, 114, 119, 121, 124–128, 133, 136–138, 147, 149, 153, 156–158, 160–162, 165–166
trauma 12, 14, 18, 35, 37, 54, 71, 137–138, 153–162
trust 39, 48, 60, 68–69, 70, 72, 74, 92–93, 96–97, 102, 108, 121, 136, 138, 143, 147, 159, 161–162; of teachers 1, 46, 89, 144, 149, 167

university 1, 3–5, 17, 23, 34, 36, 42, 44, 47, 51, 55, 66, 84, 88, 91, 103, 121, 141, 145, 149, 153–154, 165, 67; faculty 23, 34, 40, 55, 96–97, 102, 120–128, 131, 145–146, 150, 166; university-based induction 107, 149, 167
University of South Carolina 107

validation 50, 136, 139, 150
value 58, 67, 79, 84, 102, 103, 157, 165; feeling valued 28, 48, 54, 60, 70, 73, 82, 103, 109; of relationships 26, 31; of student learning 30, 45, 80; of time 56, 125
values 47, 51, 84, 88, 93, 111, 144; community values 45–46
van Nieuwerburgh, C. 109, 111, 113
Venet, A. S. 66, 68, 74
violence 12, 65, 96, 113, 157; gun violence 137, 154
Victorian Institute of Teaching (VIT) 87–89, 92
Virginia Commonwealth University 96–98, 103–104

Weaver, J. 107
Webb, A. W. 35, 54, 98
Weiss, E. 106
well-being 11, 19, 23, 31, 36, 41, 46, 47, 53, 55, 59, 66–67, 69, 71–74, 87–88, 113, 123, 125, 135, 139, 145, 149, 155
Whitney, A. 155
Wiggins, G. 79
Willis, R. 107
Wilson C. 113
Witte, S. 107
work 11–12, 14–17, 19, 23, 25–28, 31, 34, 39, 41, 43, 46–47, 50–51, 54–59, 61, 66–67, 73, 76, 78, 80–83, 86–89, 91–93, 96–101, 103, 107–108, 110–114, 120–121, 126–128, 130–132, 134–135, 137–139, 142, 144–150, 156, 158, 161–162, 166–167; boundaries 14, 17, 19; with new teachers 19, 32, 46, 103, 134–135, 144–146, 149; with preservice teachers 91, 144, 146; work-life balance 11–12, 14–16, 19, 35, 80, 113, 124
worry 37–39, 46, 50–51, 66, 110, 162

Printed in the United States
by Baker & Taylor Publisher Services